THE ANNOTATED SHAKESPEARE

Othello

William Shakespeare

Fully annotated, with an Introduction, by Burton Raffel

With an essay by Harold Bloom

THE ANNOTATED SHAKESPEARE

Yale University Press • *New Haven and London*

Designed by Rebecca Gibb.
Set in Bembo type by The Composing Room of Michigan, Inc.
Printed in the United States of America.

Library of Congress Cataloging-in-Publication Information
Shakespeare, William, 1564–1616.
Othello / William Shakespeare ; fully annotated with an introduction by
Burton Raffel ; with an essay by Harold Bloom.
p.   cm. — (The annotated Shakespeare)
Includes bibliographical references.
ISBN 978-0-300-10807-1 (paperbound)
1. Othello (Fictitious character)—Drama.   2. Venice (Italy)—Drama.
3. Jealousy—Drama.   4. Muslims—Drama.   I. Raffel, Burton.
II. Bloom, Harold.   III. Title.   IV. Series
PR2829.A2R34   2005
822.3′3—dc22
2005007312

A catalogue record for this book is available from the British Library.

10 9 8 7 6

For Stephen Pride and, of course, Shifra

CONTENTS

ABOUT THIS BOOK

Written four centuries ago, in a fairly early form of Modern English, *Othello* is a gorgeously passionate, witty, and complex text. Many of the play's social and historical underpinnings necessarily need, for the modern reader, the kinds of explanation offered in the Introduction. But what needs even more, and far more detailed, explanation are the play's very words. Here is Iago, as he so often is, complaining that he did not get the job he deserved:

> Three great ones of the city,
> In personal suit to make me his lieutenant,
> Off-capped to him, and by the faith of man,
> I know my price, I am worth no worse a place.
> But he, as loving his own pride and purposes,
> Evades them with a bumbast circumstance,
> Horribly stuffed with epithets of war,
> Nonsuits my mediators.

> (1.1.7–14)

In twenty-first-century America, "suit" tends to mean a legal action. Here, however, it means a request.

"Off-capped" is founded on the fact that everyone wore a hat and that to "doff," or remove, one's hat was a sign of respect.

"The faith of man" is not some vaguely humanistic doctrine but a simple reference to what Renaissance Europe regarded as *the* faith, Christianity.

In twenty-first-century America, again, "price" means the cost of something. Here, however, it refers to Iago's self-evaluation, his "value."

"Place" is for us almost entirely spatial, locational. We go to a "place," we live in a "place." But here it means post or position.

The construction "as loving" means "being someone who loves." Prepositions were very much more elastic, in Shakespeare's day.

In the phrase "pride and purposes," the first word remains clear to us. But we tend to hesitate at "purposes," which here means intentions.

And as "evades them" indicates, pronouns and their antecedents are also employed more loosely. "Them" refers to the "great ones of the city." Verb tenses, too, have changed: "evades" is clearly a present tense, today. But here, "evades" is in the historical present tense, which effectively means the past rather than the present.

We might be able to guess at the meaning of "bumbast," but certainty is preferable to supposition. It is indeed the ancestor of our word "bombast." But "circumstance" would be impervious to guessing, for it means circumlocution, or beating around the bush.

"Horribly stuffed" has nothing to do with warfare: it means dreadfully padded.

"Epithet" has considerably shifted, in our time, having come to mean words of insult or scorn. Here, however, "epithets" refer only to vocabulary or verbal terms.

"Nonsuits" means to rebuff or turn aside.

And "mediators" refers, not to arbitration cases, but to go-betweens.

In this very fully annotated edition, I therefore present this passage, not in the bare form quoted above, but thoroughly supported by bottom-of-the-page notes:

Three great ones[1] of the city,[2]
In personal suit[3] to make me his lieutenant,
Off-capped[4] to him, and by the faith[5] of man,
I know my price,[6] I am worth no worse a place.[7]
But he, as loving[8] his own pride and purposes,[9]
Evades[10] them with a bumbast circumstance,[11]
Horribly stuffed[12] with epithets[13] of war,
Nonsuits my mediators.[14]

1 persons
2 three GREAT ones OF the CIty
3 petition, request
4 respectfully doffing / taking off their hats
5 the faith = the true religion (Christianity)
6 value
7 post, position
8 as loving = being one who loves
9 intentions
10 evades them = avoided answering "the great ones" (historical present tense = past tense)
11 bumbast circumstance = puffed out / inflated / empty circumlocution / beating about the bush
12 horribly stuffed = exceedingly padded
13 the vocabulary, terms
14 nonsuits my mediators = turns back / rebuffs my go-betweens

The modern reader or listener of course will better understand this brief exchange in context, as the drama unfolds. But without full explanation of words that have over the years shifted in meaning, and usages that have been altered, neither the modern reader nor the modern listener is likely to be equipped for full comprehension.

I believe annotations of this sort create the necessary bridges, from Shakespeare's four-centuries-old English across to ours. Some readers, to be sure, will be able to comprehend unusual, historically different meanings without glosses. Those not familiar with the modern meaning of particular words will easily find clear, simple definitions in any modern dictionary. But most readers are not likely to understand Shakespeare's intended meaning, absent such glosses as I here offer.

My annotation practices have followed the same principles used in *The Annotated Milton,* published in 1999, and in my annotated edition of *Hamlet,* published (as the initial volume in this series) in 2003. Classroom experience has validated these editions. Classes of mixed upper-level undergraduates and graduate students have more quickly and thoroughly transcended language barriers than ever before. This allows the teacher, or a general reader without a teacher, to move more promptly and confidently to the non-linguistic matters that have made Shakespeare and Milton great and important poets.

It is the inevitable forces of linguistic change, operant in all living tongues, which have inevitably created such wide degrees of obstacles to ready comprehension—not only sharply different meanings, but subtle, partial shifts in meaning that allow us to think we understand when, alas, we do not. Speakers of related languages like Dutch and German also experience this shifting of the linguistic ground. Like early Modern English (ca. 1600) and the Modern English now current, those languages are too close for those who know only one language, and not the other, to be readily able always to recognize what they correctly understand and what they do not. When, for example, a speaker of Dutch says "Men kofer is kapot," a speaker of German will know that something belonging to the Dutchman is broken ("kapot" = "kaputt" in German, and "men" = "mein"). But without more linguistic awareness than the average person is apt to have, the German speaker will not identify "kofer" ("trunk" in Dutch) with "Körper"—a modern German word meaning "physique, build, body." The closest word to "kofer" in modern German, indeed, is "Scrankkoffer," which is too large a leap for ready comprehension. Speakers of different Romance languages (French, Spanish, Italian), and all other related but not identical tongues, all experience these difficulties, as well as the difficulty of understanding a text written in their own language five, or six, or seven hundred years earlier. Shakespeare's English is not yet so old that it requires, like many historical texts in French and German, or like Old English texts—for example, *Beowulf*—a modern translation. Much poetry evaporates in translation: language is immensely particular. The sheer *sound* of Dante in thirteenth-century Italian is profoundly worth preserving. So too is the sound of Shakespeare.

I have annotated prosody (metrics) only when it seemed truly necessary or particularly helpful. Readers should have no problem with the silent "e": whenever an "e" in Shakespeare is *not* silent, it is marked "è" (except, to be sure, in words which modern usage always syllabifies, like "tented," "excepted," "headed"). The notation used for prosody, which is also used in the explanation of Elizabethan pronunciation, follows the extremely simple form of among the original printed texts seem either marked or of un-usual interest.

In the interests of compactness and brevity, I have employed in my annotations (as consistently as I am able) a number of stylistic and typographical devices:

- The annotation of a single word does not repeat that word

- The annotation of more than one word repeats the words being annotated, which are followed by an equals sign and then by the annotation; the footnote number in the text is placed after the last of the words being annotated

- In annotations of a single word, alternative meanings are usually separated by commas; if there are distinctly different ranges of meaning, the annotations are separated by arabic numerals inside parentheses—(1), (2), and so on; in more complexly worded annotations, alternative meanings expressed by a single word are linked by a forward slash, or solidus: /

- Explanations of textual meaning are not in parentheses; comments about textual meaning are

- Except for proper nouns, the word at the beginning of all annotations is in lower case

- Uncertainties are followed by a question mark, set in parentheses: (?)

- When particularly relevant, "translations" into twenty-first-century English have been added, in parentheses

- Annotations of repeated words are *not* repeated. Explanations of the *first* instance of such common words are followed by the sign ★. Readers may easily track down the first annotation, using the brief Finding List at the back of the book. Words with entirely separate meanings are annotated *only* for meanings no longer current in Modern English.

The most important typographical device here employed is the sign ★ placed after the first (and only) annotation of words and phrases occurring more than once. There is an alphabetically arranged listing of such words and phrases in the Finding List at the back of the book. The Finding List contains no annotations but simply gives the words or phrases themselves and the numbers of the relevant act, the scene within that act, and the footnote number within that scene for the word's first occurrence.

INTRODUCTION

Over the past four hundred years, neither the text of *Othello,* nor the "true" understanding of that text, has been fully settled. We lack manuscript copies of any of Shakespeare's plays, and different printed sources frequently provide quite different readings. Given the nature of this annotated edition, however, and the fact that *Othello*'s textual issues are more or less resolvable (especially in the light of Scott McMillin's extremely helpful edition of the play's *First Quarto*), I want to deal first with interpretation and more briefly, and only thereafter, with textual issues.

The primary focus of interpretive disagreement has become the character Othello. Who and what he is meant to be—his origins, his nature—have recently been intensely disputed. Traditionally, Othello was taken to be a black African. But the fact that he is described by Shakespeare as "the Moor" has led to the contention that, knowing pretty clearly what a "Moor" was, but not being anything like so well informed as to black Africans, Shakespeare must have intended Othello to be a dark-skinned non-Negroid Muslim, a good deal more Arab than Ethiopian.

However, "as late as the 17th century," records *The Oxford En-*

glish Dictionary, under "*Moor* 1," "the Moors were commonly supposed to be mostly black or swarthy (though the existence of 'white Moors' was recognized), and hence the word was often used for 'Negro.'" Still, the play's repeated references to Othello as "black," it is argued, are no more definitive than the early-seven-teenth-century meaning of the word "black" itself. And the defi-nition under "*black* 1c" explains that, though "strictly applied to negroes and negritos, and other dark-skinned races . . . [the word is applied] often, loosely, to non-European races, little darker than many Europeans." The play's reference to Othello as "thick-lipped" has been similarly debated.

What had earlier been understood as racial and cultural differ-ences in Othello's psychology and behavior are therefore, it is contended, simply personal to Othello, like the epilepsy from which Iago (but no one else in the play) says he suffers. Accord-ingly, whether Othello is indeed black in the current meaning of the word is a matter of basic importance in understanding both the character and the play that bears his name.

Shakespeare's Knowledge of Black Africans

"I will not say," wrote A. C. Bradley a hundred years ago, "that Shakespeare imagined him [Othello] as a Negro and not as a Moor, for that might imply that he distinguished Negroes and Moors precisely as we do."[1] In fact, there were highly visible Moors in Shakespeare's London; there can be small doubt that he knew quite well what Moors looked like. He may well not have known a great deal about them, at least at firsthand; he seems un-likely to have met or had any dealings with Moorish ambassadors and other such lofty folk. Yet on the evidence, he appears to have known black Africans a good deal better. "By 1596 [ten years before the probable date of *Othello*'s composition] there were so many black people in London that Queen Elizabeth I issued an edict demanding that they leave. . . . When Shakespeare wrote *Othello* he was not . . . particularly 'confused' about racial identities. . . . [He] would have seen black people on the streets of London for most of his adult life, and so would his audience. Racial jokes and word play were well within their experience and understanding."[2]

London's black population of perhaps five or ten thousand was to some extent created by upper-class fashions. Starting with Queen Elizabeth herself, "black people were seen as fashionable accessories . . . and the use of black servants and entertainers by royalty and nobility filtered down to much less affluent households and establishments. . . . Whites 'blacked up' for roles as Africans in plays and masques."[3]

But apart from the dictates of fashion and the upper classes, and distinctly "within Shakespeare's lifetime," London had become deeply involved in "the exchange of goods and slaves between Britain, Africa and the Americas. [This] was a trade which permanently transformed the economies of all three areas." Black sailors appeared on streets and in pubs; "planters returned home with their black servants."[4] We are now aware—there having been a surge, in the past few decades, of British historical investigation into these matters, clearly caused by the massive post–World War Two in-migration of black people from British colonies—that the chronological start of this earlier, more limited, but still significantly sized in-migration began as early as 1555 (before Shakespeare's birth) and no later than 1588.[5] Shakespeare's demonstrable familiarity with the sweep of daily life in England's teeming capital city, and his fairly detailed knowledge of many trades and professions, across a wide-ranging social scale, enhances the likelihood that he may well have socialized with, and even more probably seen close up and conversed or spent time with, a good number of black Africans.

This is of course not a certainty, but only a preponderance of evidence, supporting the likelihood of Shakespeare's personal knowledge of black Africans and Othello's racial origins. To counterbalance these probabilities, there is Iago's reference to Othello as a "Barbary [Arabic] horse" (1.1.110) and also Iago's bald lie that, after leaving Cyprus, Othello and his wife will proceed, not to Venice, but to Mauritania, the Moorish "homeland" (4.2.221). The historical evidence as we now have it seems a good deal more reliable than the perpetually untruthful Iago.

Othello: Social and Psychological Factors

Black Africans lived in a wide variety of landscapes, spoke a great many different languages, yet tended to share certain basic social characteristics. "It is important to stress the traditional nature of Africa," writes the Ghanian W. E. Abraham.[6] That is, rather than transcontinental political unity, black African societies were structured around relatively fixed customs and practices, transmitted as intact as possible from generation to generation. This was not an existence formed or governed either by electoral choices or by externalized hierarchies. "We know that such societies," explains Eli Sagan, "though lacking a state, did not live in social chaos. . . . Custom and the power of custom, reinforced by the inexorable pressure of the kin, maintained order." Though inevitably affected by outside forces, and local group rivalries, this remained an essentially stable way of life. Not surprisingly, the attitude of traditional societies toward individualism in thought or action was "cool, if not downright hostile." [7] All the sacred, unsolvable matters of life were dealt with not by personal decisions but by magic.

These circumstances, in turn, fostered what Bronislaw Malinowski has called a "clear-cut division" between conditions which are known and natural and, on the other hand, "the domain of the unaccountable and adverse influences, as well as the great unearned increment of fortunate coincidences. The first conditions are coped with by knowledge and work, the second by magic."[8] As Sagan puts it, "Witchcraft, not a moralistic religion, made the world go round."[9] Accordingly, it is not that the fundamental cause-and-effect stance of modern Western societies is absent from traditional societies, but rather that it is only selectively relevant. "Magic, which is so important in the religious and moral life [of traditional cultures], is probably the most effective means of social control."[10]

Nor are these matters that have changed a great deal, over the past five hundred years. "The persistence of [traditional] culture is indicated by the similarity of twentieth-century traditions . . . and sixteenth-century reports . . . [In southeast Africa, for example,] they eat the same kind of seed cakes, wear the same dress at military dances, follow the same pattern of symbolic dancing, live by the same type of social organization, and practice the same economy that characterized their different groups when [in the early sixteenth century] the Portuguese first encountered them."[11] Traditional cultures being, by definition, group-oriented, someone born into such a social setting necessarily adheres to and depends upon the group for both social and inner psychological stability. Deprived of the group, the individual inevitably lacks many basic resources, and most especially those for dealing with adverse circumstances.

These are enormously important matters for understanding Othello. He is likely to have been born and raised in a traditional society; he also claims to have been of royal descent, and we know nothing to the contrary. Kidnapped, enslaved, he literally fought his way to ascendancy, ending as a valued, powerful general in the hired service of the Venetian state. Along the way, he became a believing and practicing Christian, and acquired much of the manners and mores of the Christian West. (It is worth nothing that, had he been a Muslim, conversion to Christianity might have been more problematical.) That is, in the process of struggling with the urgent strictures of his difficult, uprooted existence, but drawing on the deep strengths of his apparently innate physical and military abilities, Othello created both an impressive career and, within its bounds, a stable, well-functioning personality. The Othello we see in act 1 is strong, forceful, contained—an admirable, profoundly functional commanding officer.

Yet as the play plainly shows, the twin forces of traditional, custom-ruled society, and the magic which controls it, cannot help but be persistent, even if for the moment dormant. Othello's immensely successful military career thus remains a structure of narrow focus; the bright polish of success remains a relatively thin veneer. As long as he continues to follow his military path, he is secure and will likely continue to be successful. The Othello we see in act 1, however, is a man already in the early stages of being drawn past the boundaries of a purely military sphere. The soldier's world, as he so eloquently explains, is all-male, rough and perpetually isolated from the non-traditional world of sophisticated, westernized Venice—which is of course, for Shakespeare and his audience, the world of early Jacobean England and, most particularly, of swirling, cosmopolitan London.

Before the start of act 1, Othello has eloped with a young, wealthy, and white heiress, a native Venetian. He is newly married and about to take on domestic and a host of other social involvements that, in this non-traditional western world, he has never before had to face. The excitement of new and understandably rich satisfactions for a time sustains him. "O my fair warrior!" he greets Desdemona, when in the first scene of act 2 they are reunited on Cyprus. "O my soul's joy!" (lines 177, 179). Even in act 2's third scene, which would appear to involve—but does not—the strictly military matter of a drunken fight between soldiers, Othello remains solidly in control.

But the drunken fight, like a runaway wagon, has with Iago's shoulder at the wheel begun to roll the world away from Othello. When in act 3, scene 4, Othello expatiates at some length about the magical powers of his handkerchief—a treasure given him, he says, by his mother, before his abrupt and violent removal from his own culture—we need to pay extremely close attention. Desdemona no longer has the handkerchief; Othello no longer has the absolute trust he once had in both Cassio and Desdemona. The whole origin for Othello's disquisition, here, is that the mover and shaker of the play, Iago, has begun to plant his poisonous speculative suspicions. Desdemona has been unable to produce the magical handkerchief. "That is a fault," Othello says, and terribly seriously, just before the first words quoted below (3.4.52). The handwriting is on the wall. Once magic has been set into motion, Othello knows in his bones how desperately powerful and how powerfully real are the consequences. He is a genuine Christian, to be sure. But he cannot escape from the world that created him, cannot help sensing that Desdemona's unfaithfulness would destroy the very fabric of his existence. By the end of the scene—

not in the lines quoted below, but immediately thereafter—his inner collapse is not only well under way, but starkly visible. Othello becomes stentorian, pounding out his demand that his wife produce the magic handkerchief, and ends by shouting "Away!" and stalking off. This is emphatically not the Othello of act 1.

Othello　　　　　That handkerchief
　　Did an Egyptian to my mother give.
　　She was a charmer, and could almost read
　　The thoughts of people. She told her, while she kept it
　　'Twould make her amiable and subdue my father
　　Entirely to her love. But if she lost it,
　　Or made a gift of it, my father's eye
　　Should hold her loathèd, and his spirits should hunt
　　After new fancies. She, dying, gave it me,
　　And bid me, when my fate would have me wive,
　　To give it her. I did so, and take heed on't,
　　Make it a darling, like your precious eye.
　　To lose't or give't away were such perdition
　　As nothing else could match.
Desdemona　　　　　　　　　Is't possible?
Othello 'Tis true. There's magic in the web of it.
　　A sibyl, that had numbered in the world
　　The sun to course two hundred compasses,
　　In her prophetic fury sewed the work.
　　The worms were hallowed that did breed the silk,
　　And it was dyed in mummy, which the skillful
　　Conserved of maiden's hearts.
Desdemona　　　　　　　　　Indeed? Is't true?
Othello Most veritable, therefore look to't well. (3.4.53–74)

Note that, for Shakespeare and his audience, "perdition" was more than mere ruin or destruction. It evoked the ultimate threat of *final* ruin, the eternal incarceration of the human spirit in hell. In our world, "damnation" has become an imprecation and very little more. In Renaissance England, it had terrible and universally known significance. And Othello's steep descent, which I will briefly examine in a moment, is clearly hell-bound: "Blow me about in winds, roast me in sulphur," he cries (late in the play's final scene). "Wash me in steep-down gulfs of liquid fire!" The devils he invokes to "whip me" are not meant to be metaphorical.

When Othello next appears, at the start of act 4, we see him firmly ensnared in Iago's web, engaged in an elaborate discussion of the entirely imaginary "details" of Desdemona's entirely imaginary adultery with Cassio. Three dozen lines later, his unraveling is complete:

Othello Lie with her? Lie on her? We say lie on her, when they
belie her. Lie with her. That's fulsome. Handkerchief –
confessions – handkerchief! To confess, and be hanged for his
labor, first to be hanged, and then to confess. I tremble at it.
Nature would not invest herself in such shadowing passion
without some instruction. It is not words that shake me thus.
– Pish – Noses, ears, and lips. Is't possible? Confess –
handkerchief! O devil! – (4.1.35–42)

Othello then falls to the ground, in a trance. But his psychosocial dissolution is not, as Iago tells Cassio that it is, the result of epilepsy. The disease was not even so well understood, in Shakespeare's time, as it is today (and it remains at best uncertainly explainable). But Iago's bold, pseudo-diagnostic lie is preceded by a more than sufficient rebuttal, out of his own mouth: "My medicine works!" he exclaims, looking down at the unconscious, just-fallen body of Othello (4.1.44). Iago is in truth a "medicine man," though his is completely black medicine, as he himself is a witch rather than a healer.

And Othello is doomed. The slide into hell has become a rout, and Othello lacks the reserves or the strategic knowledge to deal with forces that, in the end, emerge out his own being. Acts 4 and 5 present some of the saddest, most profoundly pitiful moments of human destruction ever recorded.

Desdemona

Aristotle's definition of "tragedy" is supremely applicable to both Othello and to his wife. "The change from prosperity to adversity should not be represented as happening to a virtuous character," Aristotle explained. Nor "should the fall of a very bad man from prosperous to adverse fortune be represented."[12] In other words, no one who is consistently "virtuous" can be the central figure in a true tragedy, but neither can anyone who is utterly without virtue play such a role. Aristotle spoke of the virtuous figure's downfall being caused by "some error of human frailty"; this has come to be called the "tragic flaw." And, again, there can be no doubt that Othello, like King Oedipus and a host of tragic heroes after Oedipus, presents a striking instance of exactly that nature. Oedipus is arrogant, wrathful, rash, but has no awareness that he suffers from any of these fatal imperfections. Othello is a social simpleton, a military bull in a civilian china shop, and similarly has no idea of these crucial deficiencies. Both men are resplendent heroes, and both fall like broken statues.

But Desdemona? "Almost all children until the end of the six-teenth century were so conditioned by their upbringing . . . that they acquiesced without much objection in the matches contrived for them by their parents. . . . [Indeed,] the accepted wisdom of the age was that marriage based on personal selection, and thus inevitably influenced by such ephemeral factors as sexual attraction or romantic love, was if anything less likely to produce lasting happiness than one arranged by more prudent and more mature heads."[13] We have no idea what Shakespeare's personal views were, on this or on any other subject, but paternal control of marriage was a basic component of his time's culture.

It is not the whole story. Tudor and Stuart England clearly took a relatively flexible approach. "Gentry marriages were not all heartlessly commercial or mere dynastic arrangements. . . . The woman had the option of being more or less tractable, of offering or withholding affection, of generally signaling her inclinations. The woman's role was passive, but not entirely passive."[14] *Othello* being an English play, it is less relevant that "the power of the Italian patrician family over its daughters during the sixteenth century could be described as absolute."[15] Shakespeare's audience was not composed of modern historians, nor did they react as anything but what they were, Renaissance Englishmen. Nevertheless, "a well-born woman was always defined and identified by her relation to . . . men: daughter to her father, wife to her husband."[16] Desdemona refers to both her father and her husband as her "lord," for "according to tradition as old as the laws and customs of the Roman, Hebrew, Celtic, and Germanic peoples, by her marriage a young woman passed from the guardianship of one male to the guardianship of another."[17]

Seen through these lenses, rather than those of the twenty-first century, Desdemona is virtuous but not entirely innocent, "free from moral wrong, sin, or guilt."[18] It is her father who presents her with her first opportunity, in the play at least, for less than innocent behavior:

Othello Her father loved me, oft invited me,
   Still questioned me the story of my life,
   From year to year – the battles, sieges, fortunes,
   That I have passed. (1.3.128–31)

Proper young women, especially of prosperous descent, were secluded, kept from contact with non-familial males. Brabantio makes Othello a friend of the family, and Desdemona listens as Othello rehearses "the story of my life." Though actively concerned with "house affairs," and drawn away from Othello's enchanting tales, "These things to hear / Would Desdemona seriously incline" (1.3.145–46). There is of course nothing directly sinful about listening: it is in what follows that the girl strays. Othello notes her "greedy" ear and, taking "once a pliant hour, . . . found good means / To draw from her a prayer of earnest heart / That I would all my pilgrimage dilate, / Whereof by parcels she had something heard, / But not intentively" (1.3.151–55). Carefully following the forms of proper behavior, Othello leads her to ask for more—that is, more stories. "I did consent," he says (1.3.155).

But he is an unattached man (his precise age is unknown to us, though clearly he is older than Desdemona), and "more" of his life's story leads, as Othello plainly desires that it would, to other kinds of "more":

        I did consent,
  And often did beguile her of her tears,
  When I did speak of some distressful stroke
  That my youth suffered. My story being done,
  She gave me for my pains a world of kisses. (1.3.155–59)

This much intimacy of male and female is likely to lead to still greater intimacy, as here it does. As Othello himself describes the proceedings, from the perspectives of Shakespeare's audience such heightened intimacy clearly involves Desdemona in "forward" behavior—presumptuous, bold, immodest:

> She swore, in faith, 'twas strange, 'twas passing strange,
> 'Twas pitiful, 'twas wondrous pitiful.
> She wished she had not heard it, yet she wished
> That heaven had made her such a man. She thanked me,
> And bade me, if I had a friend that loved her,
> I should but teach him how to tell my story,
> And that would woo her. Upon this hint I spake:
> She loved me for the dangers I had passed,
> And I loved her that she did pity them.
> (1.3.160–68)

In a strictly formal sense, to be sure, Desdemona may seem to be playing not an active/improper role, here, but a passive one. But as François Hotman observed, in 1573, "If you loose the reins with women, as with an unruly nature and an untamed beast, you must expect uncontrolled actions."[19] Hotman takes the narrowest road, and Shakespeare's audience surely knew that "even the exigencies of law, of moral prescription, and of social convention, when joined to behavior modification, could not wholly stifle women's wit, wisdom, shrewishness, and wantonness."[20] "I spake," says Othello, indicating that he, not she, proposed marriage. Aside from strict formality, however, it is plainly she who has, from the first, taken the initiative.

Nor does either her "boldness" and therefore her culpability stop there. In both custom and law, a woman did not "own" herself. Before marriage, she belonged to her father. After marriage, she belonged to her husband. Desdemona's father had the "right" to award his daughter to whatever man he chose for her, and Desdemona plainly anticipated that he would exercise that right and veto her marriage to a black man. She therefore arranged matters, with to be sure Othello's participation (the play does not specifically inform us of such details), so that the marriage would be clandestine. In a word, she eloped. And having become her husband's property, as she wishes to be, she "boldly" rejects her father's claim:

Desdemona   My noble father,
   I do perceive here a divided duty.
   To you I am bound for life and education.
   My life and education both do learn me
   How to respect you. You are the lord of duty,
   I am hitherto your daughter. But here's my husband,
   And so much duty as my mother showed
   To you, preferring you before her father,
   So much I challenge that I may profess
   Due to the Moor, my lord. (1.3.180–89)

It is a noble speech, to our ears. But four hundred years ago, it surely rang differently in many men's hearts, as we see that it did for Brabantio. "God be with you," he responds heavily. "I have done" (1.3.190).

It is impossible to present Shakespeare as an advocate of virtually any clear social or religious position. But on the evidence, as I have argued elsewhere, Shakespeare is the very farthest thing from anti-woman. Indeed, his portraits of women show us, far more often, creatures of much higher intelligence and general capability than the men around them. As an individual, however, Desdemona *is* inclined to what her time considered boldness, and as a married woman seeking to influence her husband's judgment she once again displays that capacity. "I give thee warrant [guarantee]" of thy place, she declares to Cassio in act 3, scene 3:

> Assure thee,
> If I do vow a friendship, I'll perform it
> To the last article. My lord shall never rest,
> I'll watch him tame, and talk him out of patience.
> His bed shall seem a school, his board a shrift,
> I'll intermingle everything he does
> With Cassio's suit. Therefore be merry, Cassio,
> For thy solicitor shall rather die
> Than give thy cause away. (3.3.20–28)

She of course means to speak metaphorically, when she vows to "rather die" than abandon his suit for reinstatement. Yet quite as much as any causative factor, it is her "bold" persistence in arguing for Cassio that brings about her death. Human beings are of a piece, Shakespeare shows us in his plays, over and over and over. Desdemona is unrelenting in her way, as Iago is in his. Their ways are very different, as Othello's way, too, is different from either of theirs. But they are all consistently who they are, for better and for worse.

Iago

Shakespeare's plays, especially when named for their heroes, generally give those heroes primary stage exposure. In the three later plays bearing their heroes' names, all of roughly the same vintage, Hamlet is on stage approximately 66 percent of the time (the king, no hero he, is second with 37 percent); Macbeth is on stage just under 60 percent (Lady Macbeth is second, at 30 percent); and Lear is on stage roughly 48 percent of the time (Kent and

Gloucester both being just under 40 percent) However, *Othello* is structured very differently. It is Iago who has the most on-stage time, at approximately 64 percent, and Othello who comes second, with 59 percent.

There is absolutely nothing heroic about Iago. He is not noble, or generous, or kind. He has extraordinary talents—quick wits, high-order verbality, and an infallible nose for other peoples' weaknesses—but does nothing but evil. His malignity is universal; no one is spared. Morally, he measures at 0 percent on any scale. Nothing and no one, no matter their sex, age, or position, merit his respect. Fanatically self-centered, he is a boaster, a liar, and at the same time a whiner and, remarkably, both a total coward and an incompetent swordsman. Plodding Cassio, even when dead drunk, mercilessly whips Rodrigo, sword in hand, but Iago, face-à-face with Rodrigo, does not so much as scratch him. When he kills Rodrigo, it is in the dark, with the seriously wounded man lying helpless on the ground. Iago is even unable to kill his wife until the other men in the room are preoccupied with Othello, who has tried to run Iago through.

Like many sociopaths, Iago is quixotically fascinating, even at times extremely charming. Measured by the time-honored standard, "Does it hold the stage?" Iago's ever-restless driving urge to nothingness leaves him, as stage character, smelling of roses. Not only is he non-heroic, and non-moral, but he is also unpredictably irrational. No scheme is ever enough, no goal is ever the final one, since in truth there *is* no goal. A sociopath does not seek anything except the venting of his malignancy. On the verge of having successfully ruined Othello, Desdemona, and Cassio, Iago declares at the end of act 5, scene 1, "This is the night / That either makes me or fordoes me quite" (lines 128–29). Yet what success, what fortune, can he conceivably attain to? He had begun by wanting, he says, to despoil Rodrigo and displace Cassio. He has in fact long since done both, and the fact is, for him, of no significance. At the end of act 5, scene 1, he is preparing to have Desdemona killed, a murder which will have to destroy Othello. What possible gain is there for Iago, either in Desdemona's death or Othello's destruction? He cannot replace either one of them, as he has declared he wanted to do with Cassio; he cannot inherit from either of them. Indeed, without Othello as temporary governor of Cyprus, Iago will be left without any post at all and would, presumably, be obliged to return, jobless, to Venice. What has he done with Roderigo's money? We are never given so much as a hint—because, to this consummate villain, all such considerations are irrelevant. At age twenty-eight (as he says), he has nowhere to go but down, and that is the only direction he knows. Like the prototypical serial killers of our own time, he lives exclusively for the evil he does. Compared to Iago, King Kong is a romantic, Holofernes a good soldier with a tad too much testosterone, and Attila the Hun a restless rambler. Only the white whale, Moby-Dick, matches him in an inexorable drive toward destruction. And like Moby-Dick, Iago is utterly fascinating, completely compelling.

How can we resist watching this matchless spinner of wickedness weave his webs? Iago richly deserves the prime time his author (no dramatic fool, he!) has given him, as Iago will richly deserve everything that happens to him once the stage goes dark.

The Text

There are two almost exactly contemporaneous printed versions of *Othello,* a separate Quarto edition that appeared in 1622 and the collective Folio edition of 1623. The play was written some-where between 1601 and 1604 and performed many times, over the next two decades (though we do not have a full record). Shakespeare died in 1616. Half of his plays, more or less, appeared in print during his lifetime, but he seems to have played no role in those publications. There is no detectable pattern in which plays were published, before 1623, and which were not. Publication would not have been of much importance to him: neither his professional life nor his literary reputation was dependent on books, except as a source of plots.

Shakespeare's longtime theatrical associates were responsible for the 1623 Folio, which appears to have been compiled from documents long in possession of the acting company. It is not known from what resources the 1622 Quarto was printed. The Quarto is a significantly shorter version, particularly in the last two acts, and there are also a good many differences in wording.

I am fully persuaded that Scott McMillin's carefully cautious "solution" to *Othello*'s textual uncertainties is as close to a defini-tive formulation as we are likely ever to have. After an exceed-ingly close and knowledgeable examination, Professor McMillin believes that

1. The 1622 Quarto was of relatively late date;
2. The Quarto was written, in the first place, by a professional scribe ("stenographer") who had only his ears to guide him—this being, on the evidence, a fairly common practice, though we have no idea who the scribe was or who employed him;
3. The Quarto was thereafter "corrected," though we do not know when or by whom;

4. Many of the Quarto's longish cuts conform to theatrical practice and do not represent Shakespeare's text;

5. Many, even most of the verbal changes correspond to actor-originated alterations in Shakespeare's text; and

6. There may well be compositor ("printer") errors in either or both printed versions of the play, but printer error cannot be the sole or the major cause of textual differences.

I have therefore used the 1623 Folio as my "copy" text—that is, the basic source of the play. I have occasionally, in small verbal matters, chosen the Quarto text, and so indicated in a footnote. Brian Gibbons, general editor of the Cambridge series in which McMillin's Quarto edition appears, puts the editorial process into a blunt, clear perspective: "There is no avoiding edited Shakespeare . . . there is no direct access to Shakespeare's play-manuscripts—there is only print, and this implies editing," given the nature of our printed sources.[21]

Notes

1. A. C. Bradley, *Shakespearean Tragedy* (London: Macmillan 1904; reprint ed., London: St. Martin's Library, 1957), 162.

2. Gretchen Holbrook Gerzina, *Black London: Life before Emancipation* (New Brunswick, N.J.: Rutgers University Press, 1995), 3, 5; see also Eldred Jones, *Othello's Countrymen: The African in English Renaissance Drama* (London: Oxford University Press, 1965), 1–26.

3. Gerzina, *Black London,* 4.

4. Gerzina, *Black London,* 5.

5. Gerzina, *Black London,* 205nn. 2, 3, 7.

6. W. E. Abraham, *The Mind of Africa* (Chicago: University of Chicago Press, 1962), 36.

7. Eli Sagan, *At the Dawn of Tyranny: The Origins of Individualism, Political Oppression, and the State* (New York: Knopf, 1985), xvi–xvii.

8. Bronislaw Malinowski, *Magic, Science and Religion, and Other Essays,* Selected and with an Introduction by Robert Redfield (Boston: Beacon Press, 1948), 29.

9. Sagan, *Dawn of Tyranny,* xvii.

10. Harold K. Schneider, "Pakot Resistance to Change," in William R. Bascom and Melville J. Herskovits, eds., *Continuity and Change in African Cultures* (Chicago: University of Chicago Press, 1959), 158.

11. Charles Edward Fuller, "Ethnohistory in the Study of Culture Change in Southeast Africa," in Bascom and Herskovits, eds., *Continuity and Change in African Cultures,* 117.

12. Aristotle, *Poetics,* Everyman Library (New York: Dutton, 1934), 25.

13. Lawrence Stone, *The Family, Sex and Marriage in England, 1500–1800* (New York: Harper, 1977), 180–81.

14. David Cressy, *Birth, Marriage, and Death: Ritual, Religion, and the Life-Cycle in Tudor and Stuart England* (New York: Oxford University Press, 1997), 254.

15. Olwen Hufton, *The Prospect before Her: A History of Women in Western Europe, 1500–1800* (New York: Knopf, 1996), 105.

16. Bonnie S. Anderson and Judith P. Zinsser, *A History of Their Own: Women in Europe from Prehistory to the Present,* 2 vols. (New York: Harper, 1988), 1: 279.

17. Anderson and Zinsser, *History of Their Own,* 1: 400.

18. *Oxford English Dictionary, s.v.* "innocent," 1a.

19. David Englander et al., eds., *Culture and Belief in Europe, 1459–1600: An Anthology of Sources* (Oxford: Blackwell, 1990), 412.

20. Lena Cowen Orlin, "Three Ways to Be Invisible in the Renaissance: Sex, Reputation, and Stitchery," in *Renaissance Culture and the Everyday,* ed. Patricia Fumerton and Simon Hunt (Philadelphia: University of Pennsylvania Press, 1999), 199.

21. Scott McMillan, ed., *The First Quarto of Othello,* The New Cambridge Shakespeare (Cambridge: Cambridge University Press, 2001), vi.

SOME ESSENTIALS OF THE
SHAKESPEAREAN STAGE

The Stage

- There was no *scenery* (backdrops, flats, and so on).

- Compared to today's elaborate, high-tech productions, the Elizabethan stage had few *on-stage* props. These were mostly handheld: a sword or dagger, a torch or candle, a cup or flask. Larger props, such as furniture, were used sparingly.

- Costumes (some of which were upper-class castoffs, belonging to the individual actors) were elaborate. As in most premodern and very hierarchical societies, clothing was the distinctive mark of who and what a person was.

- What the actors *spoke,* accordingly, contained both the dramatic and narrative material we have come to expect in a theater (or movie house) and (1) the setting, including details of the time of day, the weather, and so on, and (2) the occasion. The *dramaturgy* is thus very different from that of our own time, requiring much more attention to verbal and gestural matters. Strict realism was neither intended nor, under the circumstances, possible.

- There was *no curtain.* Actors entered and left via doors in the back of the stage, behind which was the "tiring-room," where actors put on or changed their costumes.

- In *public theaters* (which were open-air structures), there was no *lighting;* performances could take place only in daylight hours.

- For *private* theaters, located in large halls of aristocratic houses, candlelight illumination was possible.

The Actors

- Actors worked in *professional,* for-profit companies, sometimes organized and owned by other actors, and sometimes by entrepreneurs who could afford to erect or rent the company's building. Public theaters could hold, on average, two thousand playgoers, most of whom viewed and listened while standing. Significant profits could be and were made. Private theaters were smaller, more exclusive.

- There was *no director.* A book-holder/prompter/props manager, standing in the tiring-room behind the backstage doors, worked from a text marked with entrances and exits and notations of any special effects required for that particular script. A few such books have survived. Actors had texts only of their own parts, speeches being cued to a few prior words. There were few and often no rehearsals, in our modern use of the term, though there was often some coaching of individuals. Since Shakespeare's England was largely an oral culture, actors learned their parts rapidly and retained them for years. This was *repertory* theater, repeating popular plays and introducing some new ones each season.

- *Women* were not permitted on the professional stage. Most female roles were acted by *boys;* elderly women were played by grown men.

The Audience

- London's professional theater operated in what might be called a "red-light" district, featuring brothels, restaurants, and the kind of *open-air entertainment* then most popular, like bear-baiting (in which a bear, tied to a stake, was set on by dogs).

- A theater audience, like most of the population of Shakespeare's England, was largely made up of *illiterates.* Being able to read and write, however, had nothing to do with intelligence or concern with language, narrative, and characterization. People attracted to the theater tended to be both extremely verbal and extremely volatile. Actors were sometimes attacked, when the audience was dissatisfied; quarrels and fights were relatively common. Women were regularly in attendance, though no reliable statistics exist.

- Drama did not have the cultural esteem it has in our time, and plays were not regularly printed. Shakespeare's often appeared in book form, but not with any supervision or other involvement on his part. He wrote a good deal of nondramatic poetry as well, yet so far as we know he did not authorize or supervise *any* work of his that appeared in print during his lifetime.

- Playgoers, who had paid good money to see and hear, plainly gave dramatic performances careful, detailed attention. For some closer examination of such matters, see Burton Raffel, "Who Heard the Rhymes and How: Shakespeare's Dramaturgical Signals," *Oral Tradition* 11 (October 1996): 190–221, and Raffel, "Metrical Dramaturgy in Shakespeare's Earlier Plays," *CEA Critic* 57 (Spring–Summer 1995): 51–65.

CHARACTERS (DRAMATIS PERSONAE)

Othello (the Moor)

Brabantio (Senator of Venice, Desdemona'a father)

Gratiano (Brabantio's brother, Desdemona's uncle)

Lodovico (Desdemona's cousin)[1]

Duke (of Venice)

Senators (of Venice)

Cassio (Othello's lieutenant)[2]

Iago (Othello's ancient)[3]

Roderigo (Venetian gentleman)

Montano (Governor of Cyprus, Othello's predecessor)

Sailors

Clown

Herald[4]

Desdemona (Brabantio's daughter, Othello's wife)

Emilia (Iago's wife, Desdemona's maid)

Bianca (courtesan, Cassio's mistress)

Officers, Gentlemen, Messenger, Musicians, Attendants

---

1 Gratiano's son?
2 second in command★
3 ensign, standard-bearer★
4 ceremonial message-bearer

Act I

SCENE I
Venice. A street.

ENTER RODERIGO AND IAGO

Roderigo Never[1] tell me, I take it much unkindly[2]
   That thou, Iago, who hast had my purse
   As if the strings were thine, shouldst know of this.[3]

Iago   But you will not[4] hear me. If ever I did dream[5]
   Of such a matter, abhor[6] me.

Roderigo   Thou told'st me   5
   Thou didst hold him[7] in thy hate.[8]

Iago   Despise[9] me

---

1 don't (emphatic)
2 much unkindly = with great dissatisfaction/resentment
3 Desdemona's elopement with Othello
4 will not = don't want to
5 but you WILL not HEAR me if EVer I did DREAM
6 loathe, hate
7 hold him = keep/bear Othello
8 THOU toldst ME / THOU didst HOLD him IN thy HATE
9 have contempt for, scorn

If I do not. Three great ones[10] of the city,[11]
In personal suit[12] to make me his lieutenant,
Off-capped[13] to him, and by the faith[14] of man,
10   I know my price,[15] I am worth no worse a place.[16]
But he, as loving[17] his own pride and purposes,[18]
Evades them[19] with a bumbast circumstance,[20]
Horribly stuffed[21] with epithets[22] of war,
Nonsuits my mediators.[23] For "Certes,"[24] says he,
15   "I have already chose my officer."
And what[25] was he?
Forsooth,[26] a great arithmetician,[27]
One Michael Cassio, a Florentine,
A fellow almost damned[28] in a fair wife,[29]

10 persons
11 Venice, then an independent state (IF i DO not. three GREAT ones OF the
   City)
12 petition, request★
13 respectfully doffing/taking off their hats
14 the faith = the true religion (Christianity)
15 value, worth★
16 post, position★
17 as loving = being one who loves
18 intentions★
19 evades them = avoided answering "the great ones" (historical present tense =
   past tense)
20 bumbast circumstance = puffed out/inflated/empty circumlocution/
   beating about the bush
21 horribly stuffed = exceedingly padded
22 the vocabulary/terms
23 nonsuits my mediators = turns back/rebuffs my go-betweens
24 in fact, in truth★
25 who
26 truly, indeed
27 number-juggler, bookkeeper (aRITHmeTIseeYUN)
28 doomed, cursed
29 a reference no one has ever understood, since Cassio is unmarried

That never set[30] a squadron[31] in the field,   20
Nor the division[32] of a battle[33] knows
More than a spinster,[34] unless the bookish theoric,[35]
Wherein[36] the togèd consuls[37] can propose[38]
As masterly as he. Mere prattle,[39] without practice,[40]
Is all his soldiership. But he, sir, had th'election,[41]   25
And I, of whom his[42] eyes had seen the proof[43]
At Rhodes, at Cyprus, and on other grounds,[44]
Christian and heathen, must be be-lee'd and calmed[45]
By debitor and creditor,[46] this counter-caster.[47]
He, in good time,[48] must his[49] lieutenant be,   30

---

30 that never set = who never placed/positioned
31 (1) relatively small military grouping, (2) a square military formation
32 methodical arrangement
33 army
34 more than a spinster = any more than someone of either sex (usually a
   woman) who practices the craft of spinning
35 unless the bookish theoric = except as a matter of book-learned theory
36 in which★
37 wherein the togèd consuls = in which advisers/councillors? wearing formal
   gowns/togas (TOged)
38 put forward
39 idle talk/chatter
40 experience, actual doing★
41 choice
42 of whom his = whose own
43 proven results, tests, experience★
44 soil, lands
45 be-lee'd and calmed = like a ship cut off from the wind and thereby
   detained/kept motionless
46 debitor and creditor = an account book
47 someone who casts/keeps accounts
48 in good time = if you can believe it, amazingly enough
49 Othello's

And I, God bless the mark,[50] his Moorship's[51] ancient.

Roderigo   By heaven, I rather would have been his hangman.[52]

Iago   Why, there's no remedy. 'Tis the curse of service,[53]

Preferment[54] goes by letter and affection,[55]

35   And not by old gradation,[56] where each second[57]

Stood heir to the first.[58] Now sir, be judge yourself

Whether I in any just term[59] am affined[60]

To love the Moor.

Roderigo   I would not follow[61] him, then.

Iago   O, sir, content you,[62]

40   I follow him to serve my turn upon[63] him.

We cannot all be masters, nor all masters

Cannot be truly[64] followed. You shall mark[65]

Many a duteous[66] and knee-crooking knave[67]

---

50 bless the mark = save us from the (1) event, happening, (2) fool, ninny, naive
incompetent, (3) people like him (Cassio)

51 Othello's (a saracastic pun on the then familiar usage, "bless his worship," his
"honor")

52 (Roderigo, fancying himself Othello's rival for Desdemona's hand, swears
that he would rather have killed than served Othello)

53 serving a master/employer★

54 promotion

55 letter and affection = rules and influence

56 old gradation = the former tradition of length in service and stage-by-stage
progress

57 number two in rank

58 number one in rank

59 just term = correct/honorable★ sense of the word

60 bound

61 serve

62 content you = be satisfied

63 my turn upon = my own needs/purposes on/by means of

64 loyally, faithfully★

65 note, notice, observe★

66 submissive, obedient

67 knee-crooking knave = bowing and scraping rascal★ (MAny a DOOTyus
AND knee CROOKing KNAVE)

That, doting on[68] his own obsequious bondage,[69]

Wears out his time,[70] much like his master's ass,[71]   45

For nought but provender,[72] and when he's old, cashiered.[73]

Whip me[74] such honest knaves! Others there are

Who, trimmed[75] in forms and visages[76] of duty,[77]

Keep yet their hearts attending on[78] themselves,

And throwing but[79] shows[80] of service on their lords,   50

Do well thrive[81] by them, and when they have lined their coats[82]

Do themselves homage.[83] These fellows have some soul,[84]

And such a one do I profess myself.

For, sir, it is as sure[85] as you are Roderigo,[86]

Were I the Moor, I would not be Iago.   55

In following him, I follow but myself.

Heaven is my judge, not I for[87] love and duty,

68 doting on = foolishly infatuated by

69 obsequious bondage = dutiful/submissive servitude

70 wears out his time = wastes his life

71 donkey (in British usage, "arse" = the rear end of a human being)

72 food/fodder

73 is dismissed

74 whip me = as for me, whip/flog (whipping subordinates was more or less universal)

75 prepared, skilled

76 forms and visages = patterns/methods and appearances

77 respect, deference, submission★

78 attending on = doing service to

79 throwing but = casting/tossing/delivering only★

80 appearances★

81 flourish, prosper★

82 do WELL thrive BY them and WHEN they've LINED their COATS

83 do themselves homage = declare allegiance to themselves (do THEMselves HOMage)

84 intellectual/spiritual power ("life in them")

85 certain, trustworthy★

86 for SIR it IS as SURE as YOU are roDRIgo

87 on account of

But seeming so for my peculiar end.[88]

For when my outward action doth demonstrate[89]

60   The native act and figure[90] of my heart

In complement extern,[91] 'tis not[92] long after

But I will wear my heart upon my sleeve

For daws[93] to peck at. I am not what I am.[94]

Roderigo   What a full[95] fortune does the thick lips owe,[96]

If he can carry't[97] thus!

65   *Iago*   Call up[98] her father,

Rouse him,[99] make after[100] him, poison his delight,

Proclaim him[101] in the streets. Incense her kinsmen,

And though he[102] in a fertile climate[103] dwell,

Plague[104] him with flies.[105] Though that[106] his joy be joy,

70   Yet throw such changes of vexation on't[107]

---

88 peculiar end = private/independent★ goal/purpose
89 make known, manifest (deMONstrate)★
90 native act and figure = natural/unadorned deed and attitude/bearing
91 complement extern = outward fullness/completion/totality
92 'tis not = it will not be
93 jackdaws, a type of crow
94 seem to be
95 solid, large
96 own, possess★
97 can carry't = could carry it off
98 call up = wake up
99 rouse him = stir him up
100 make after = pursue
101 proclaim him = make his name known
102 Brabantio
103 a fertile climate = an environment of abundance (he is rich and lives richly)
104 afflict, torment
105 winged insects
106 though that = even if
107 changes of vexation on't = on it variations/modulations of harassment/
      distress

As it may lose some color.[108]

Roderigo Here is her father's house, I'll call aloud.

Iago Do, with like timorous accent[109] and dire[110] yell

As when, by night and negligence, the fire[111]

Is spied in populous cities. 75

Roderigo What ho, Brabantio, Signior Brabantio, ho!

Iago Awake, what, ho, Brabantio! Thieves, thieves, thieves!

Look to your house, your daughter, and your bags![112]

Thieves, thieves!

BRABANTIO APPEARS ABOVE, AT A WINDOW

Brabantio What is the reason of this terrible summons?[113] 80

What is the matter there?

Roderigo Signior, is all your family within?

Iago Are your doors locked?

Brabantio   Why, wherefore[114] ask you

this?

Iago Zounds,[115] sir, you're robbed, for shame, put on your

gown,[116]

Your heart is burst, you have lost half your soul, 85

Even now, now, very now, an old black ram

108 tone, character, virtue
109 like timorous accent = the same fearful / dreadful voice / sound
110 horrible, dismal
111 the fire = fire
112 money bags (money meant coins; paper currency was not used)
113 terrible summons = dreadful / violent call / command
114 for what purpose / reason??
115 by God's wounds
116 (1) loose shirt-like garment, (2) senator's gown, (3) dressing gown (from
    stage direction in the Quarto, line 157)

Is tupping[117] your white[118] ewe. Arise, arise,
Awake the snorting[119] citizens with the bell,
Or else the devil will make a grandsire of you.
Arise, I say.

90   *Brabantio*   What, have you lost your wits?[120]

    Roderigo   Most reverend[121] signior, do you know my voice?

    Brabantio   Not I. What[122] are you?

    Roderigo   My name is Roderigo.

    Brabantio   The worser welcome.

I have charged[123] thee not to haunt about my doors.

95   In honest[124] plainness thou hast heard me say
My daughter is not for thee. And now, in madness,[125]
Being full of supper and distempering draughts,[126]
Upon malicious knavery[127] dost thou come
To start[128] my quiet.[129]

100 *Roderigo*   Sir, sir, sir –

    Brabantio   But thou must needs be sure
My spirit[130] and my place have in them power
To make this bitter to thee.

    Roderigo   Patience, good sir.

117 copulating with
118 innocent, virginal
119 snoring
120 minds★
121 respected
122 who
123 ordered
124 decent
125 folly
126 distempering draughts = deranging/disordering/intoxicating drinks
127 malicious knavery = wicked roguery/dishonest tricks
128 (1) attack, (2) startle
129 peace, repose?
130 disposition, attitude, character

Brabantio What tell'st thou me of robbing? This is Venice,
  My house is not a grange.[131]

Roderigo   Most grave[132] Brabantio,   105
  In simple and pure soul I come to you.

Iago   Zounds, sir, you are one of those that will not serve
  God if the devil bid you. Because we come to do you service,
  and you think we are ruffians, you'll have your daughter
  covered[133] with a Barbary[134] horse, you'll have your nephews 110
  neigh to you, you'll have coursers[135] for cousins and gennets
  for germans.[136]

Brabantio What profane wretch[137] art thou?

Iago   I am one, sir, that comes to tell you your daughter and
  the Moor are now making the beast with two backs.   115

Brabantio Thou art a villain.[138]

Iago   You are – a senator.

Brabantio This thou shalt answer.[139] I know thee, Roderigo.

Roderigo   Sir, I will answer anything. But, I beseech[140] you,
  If't be your pleasure[141] and most wise consent,
  As partly I find[142] it is, that your fair[143] daughter,   120
  At this odd-even[144] and dull watch[145] o' the night,

131 country/farm house
132 respected, worthy
133 having sexual intercourse
134 North African
135 racehorses
136 gennets for germans = Spanish horses as first cousins
137 profane wretch = ribald/blasphemous★ vile/despicable person
138 scoundrel★
139 be held responsible for★
140 entreat, beg★
141 choice, desire
142 discover, perceive★
143 beautiful (often used conventionally, politely)★
144 in-between, neither night nor morning
145 dull watch = slow/sluggish/tedious division/portion

Transported[146] with no worse nor better guard
But with a knave of common[147] hire, a gondolier,
To the gross clasps[148] of a lascivious Moor –
125   If this be known to you, and your allowance,[149]
We then have done you bold and saucy[150] wrongs.
But if you know not this, my manners[151] tell me
We have[152] your wrong[153] rebuke. Do not believe
That, from the sense[154] of all civility,[155]
130   I thus would play and trifle[156] with your reverence.
Your daughter – if you have not given her leave,
I say again – hath made a gross revolt,[157]
Tying her duty, beauty, wit,[158] and fortunes[159]
In[160] an extravagant and wheeling stranger[161]
135   Of[162] here and everywhere. Straight[163] satisfy yourself.

146 conveyed (well-born women went out of their homes only with male escorts)
147 public, general★
148 gross clasps = monstrous★ embraces
149 approval, sanction
150 bold and saucy = presumptuous/audacious/shameless★ and wanton★
151 good manners/behavior/morals
152 have been given
153 unjust, mistaken
154 from the sense = departing from ("abandoning") the proper understanding★
155 principles of good/orderly behavior
156 play and trifle = frolic/amuse myself and fool about
157 casting off of allegiance, rebellion★
158 mind, intelligence
159 (1) position, (2) prosperity, wealth, (3) possibilities, luck★
160 into, to
161 extravagant and wheeling stranger = vagrant/irregular and whirling/reeling alien/foreigner
162 who comes from/belongs
163 immediately, without delay★

If she be in her chamber, or your house,
Let loose on me the justice of the state
For thus deluding you.

Brabantio   Strike on the tinder,[164] ho!
Give me a taper,[165] call up all my people![166]
This accident[167] is not unlike my dream,   140
Belief of it oppresses[168] me already.
Light, I say, light!

EXIT BRABANTIO FROM ABOVE

Iago   (*to Roderigo*) Farewell, for I must leave you.
It seems not meet,[169] nor wholesome[170] to my place
To be produced,[171] as if I stay I shall,
Against the Moor, for I do know the state,[172]   145
However this may gall[173] him with some check,[174]
Cannot with safety cast[175] him. For he's embarked[176]
With such loud reason[177] to[178] the Cyprus wars,

164 tinderbox (containing readily lightable materials)
165 candle
166 attendants, servants, etc.
167 event, occurrence★
168 crushes, overwhelms
169 appropriate, fitting★
170 salutary, beneficial
171 brought forward as a witness
172 Venice
173 vex, harass, oppress
174 reprimand, rebuke, rebuff★
175 discard, dismiss
176 engaged
177 statements, talk (by the Venetian authorities?)
178 into ("sailed … into": a metaphor most apt, since Cyprus is an island)

Which even now stands in act,[179] that for their souls

150 Another of his fathom[180] they have none,

To lead their business.[181] In which regard,

Though I do hate him as I do hell's pains,

Yet, for necessity of present life,

I must show out[182] a flag and sign of love,

155 Which is indeed but sign.[183] That you shall surely find him,

Lead to the Sagittary[184] the raisèd search,[185]

And there will I be with him. So farewell.

EXIT IAGO

ENTER BRABANTIO AND SERVANTS WITH TORCHES

Brabantio It is too true[186] an evil. Gone she is,

And what's to come of my despisèd time

160 Is naught but bitterness. Now Roderigo,

Where didst thou see her? O unhappy[187] girl.

With the Moor, say'st thou? Who would be a father?

How didst thou know 'twas she? O, she deceives me

Past thought. What said she to you? (*to Servants*) Get more tapers.

165 Raise[188] all my kindred. (*to Roderigo*) Are they married, think you?

Roderigo Truly, I think they are.

179 stands in act = remains/continues ongoing/in process
180 ability
181 BIziNESS
182 show out = display, unfurl
183 but sign = only a pretense
184 house/inn marked by the sign of Sagittarius, a centaur (SAdgiTAree)
185 raisèd search = roused-up search for Othello and/or Desdemona
186 certain, genuine
187 ill-fated, unlucky, miserable in lot
188 rouse★

Brabantio O heaven! How got she out? O treason of the
   blood![189]

   Fathers, from hence[190] trust not your daughters' minds

   By what you see them act. Is[191] there not charms[192]

   By which the property[193] of youth and maidhood   170

   May be abused?[194] Have you not read, Roderigo,

   Of some such thing?

Roderigo   Yes, sir, I have indeed.

Brabantio (*to Servants*) Call up my brother. (*to Roderigo*) O, would
   you had had her![195]

   Some one way, some another. Do you know

   Where we may apprehend[196] her and the Moor?   175

Roderigo   I think I can discover[197] him, if you please

   To get good guard,[198] and go along with me.

Brabantio Pray you,[199] lead on. At every house I'll call,[200]

   I may command[201] at most. (*to Servants*) Get weapons, ho,

   And raise some special officers of night.[202]   180

   On, good Roderigo. I'll deserve your pains.[203]

EXEUNT

189 passions★
190 from hence = henceforward, from this time on
191 (Renaissance English syntax is often unlike that of the 21st c.)
192 spells, magic
193 character, nature
194 wronged, deceived, violated★
195 had had her = been given her in marriage
196 seize, lay hold of
197 find
198 escort, protection
199 pray you = please★
200 I'll call at every house
201 ask with authority (for armed men to join with him)
202 special officers of night = special deputy police, for nighttime emergencies
203 deserve your pains = pay/reward★ you for your troubles/efforts★

SCENE 2

Venice. Another street.

ENTER OTHELLO, IAGO, AND ATTENDANTS WITH TORCHES

Iago   Though in the trade[1] of war I have slain men,
Yet do I hold it very stuff[2] o' the conscience[3]
To do no contrived[4] murder. I lack iniquity[5]
Sometimes to do me service.[6] Nine or ten times

5   I had thought to have yerked him[7] here, under the ribs.
Othello 'Tis better as it is.

Iago   Nay, but he prated,[8]
And spoke such scurvy[9] and provoking terms
Against your honor, that with the little godliness[10] I have,[11]
I did full hard forbear[12] him. But I pray you, sir,

10   Are you fast[13] married? Be assured of this,
That the Magnifico[14] is much beloved,
And hath in his effect[15] a voice potential[16]

---

1 course ("way of life")
2 substance
3 moral sense, inner knowledge of right and wrong
4 cleverly/artfully planned (CONtrived)
5 wickedness, sinfulness
6 help, benefit
7 yerked him = struck Roderigo (with a dagger or knife)
8 chattered★
9 contemptible, shabby, discourteous
10 piety, devoutness
11 (lineation uncertain: this edition follows the Folio)
12 endure
13 firmly, securely
14 Venetian noble title (Brabantio)
15 influence, power
16 as powerful/strong (an adjective; modern usage would be "potentially")

As double as[17] the Duke's. He will divorce you,[18]
Or put upon you what[19] restraint and grievance[20]
The law, with all his[21] might to enforce[22] it on,   15
Will give him cable.[23]

Othello   Let him do his spite.[24]
My services which I have done the signiory[25]
Shall out-tongue[26] his complaints. 'Tis yet to know[27] –
Which,[28] when I know that boasting is an honor,
I shall promulgate[29] – I fetch[30] my life and being   20
From men of royal siege,[31] and my demerits[32]
May speak unbonneted[33] to as proud a fortune
As this that I have reached. For know, Iago,
But[34] that I love the gentle[35] Desdemona,
I would not my unhousèd[36] free condition[37]   25

17 as double as = twice as much as
18 divorce you = have you divorced, dissolve your marriage
19 whatever
20 restraint and grievance = limitation/constraint and oppression/hardship
21 (although "his" can mean "its," here it means his, Brabantio's)
22 strengthen, intensify
23 rope
24 insult, reproach, injury
25 signiory = Venice's governing council (in Italian, *signoria*)
26 exceed
27 yet to know = as yet unknown
28 something that
29 declare publicly
30 obtain, get
31 rank, class
32 merits
33 speak unbonneted = (?) declare respectfully
34 except
35 well-born★
36 bachelor
37 life, mode of being, state★

Put into circumscription and confine[38]

For the sea's worth. But look, what lights come yond?[39]

Iago   Those are the raisèd father and his friends.

You were best go in.

Othello   Not I. I must be found.

30   My parts,[40] my title, and my perfect[41] soul

Shall manifest[42] me rightly. Is it they?

Iago   By Janus,[43] I think no.

      ENTER CASSIO AND OFFICERS WITH TORCHES

Othello The servants of the Duke? And my lieutenant?

The goodness of the night upon you, friends!

What is the news?

35 *Cassio*   The Duke does greet[44] you, general,

And he requires[45] your haste – post-haste[46] – appearance

Even[47] on the instant.[48]

Othello   What is the matter,[49] think you?

Cassio   Something from Cyprus, as[50] I may divine.[51]

---

38 circumscription and confine = restraint/limitation and confinement

39 yonder, over there

40 qualities, character★

41 completely prepared/ready, pure

42 reveal, be evidence of, prove

43 Roman god of entrances and exits, two-faced, his heads looking in opposite directions (DJEYnis)

44 does greet = greets (do = an intensifier)

45 requests, desires

46 all possible speed

47 precisely, exactly★

48 on the instant = instantly (even ON the INstant; "even" was often pronounced EEN)

49 issue, substance

50 as far as

51 make out, guess

It is a business of some heat.[52] The galleys[53]
Have sent a dozen sequent[54] messengers   40
This very[55] night, at one another's heels.
And many of the consuls, raised and met,[56]
Are at the Duke's already. You have been hotly called for,[57]
When,[58] being not at your lodging to be found,
The Senate hath sent about[59] three several quests[60]   45
To search you out.

Othello   'Tis well I am[61] found by you.
I will but spend[62] a word here in the house,[63]
And[64] go with you.

EXIT OTHELLO

Cassio   Ancient, what makes he[65] here?
Iago   Faith,[66] he tonight hath boarded[67] a land carack.[68]
    If it prove[69] lawful prize,[70] he's made forever.   50

52 excitement, intensity
53 low, flat-built Mediterranean ship, with both oars and sails
54 following one on the other
55 exact, same
56 having met/assembled
57 hotly called for = ardently/eagerly requested/required
58 at which point
59 out (as in "out and about")
60 several quests = separate search parties
61 have been
62 speak, say
63 (where Desdemona, now his wife, is lodged)
64 and then
65 makes he = is he doing
66 truly
67 attacked
68 large ship (galleon), often employed in the rich trade with the East
69 turn out to be★
70 capture, seizure

Cassio   I do not understand.

Iago   He's married.

Cassio   To who?

ENTER OTHELLO

Iago   Marry, to – Come, captain,[71] will you go?

Othello   Have with
    you.[72]

Cassio   Here comes another troop[73] to seek for you.

Iago   It is Brabantio. General, be advised,[74]
    He comes to bad intent.

ENTER BRABANTIO, RODERIGO, AND OFFICERS
WITH TORCHES AND WEAPONS

55   *Othello*   Holla,[75] stand[76] there.

Roderigo (*to Brabantio*) Signior, it is the Moor.

Brabantio   Down with him,
    thief!

BOTH SIDES DRAW SWORDS

Iago   You, Roderigo, come sir, I am for you.[77]

Othello   Keep up[78] your bright swords, for the dew will rust
    them.

    Good signior, you shall more command with years

---

71 general (military terms were not so standardized as they are now)
72 have with you = let's go ("I will go with you")
73 party, company, group
74 warned
75 halt (exclamation)
76 stay, stop★
77 am for you = am ready to fight with you
78 keep up = put back, confine

Than with your weapons. 60

Brabantio O thou foul thief, where hast thou stowed[79] my
daughter?
Damned as thou art, thou hast enchanted her,
For I'll refer me to[80] all things of sense,[81]
If she in chains of magic were not bound
Whether a maid[82] so tender,[83] fair,[84] and happy,[85] 65
So opposite[86] to marriage that she shunned
The wealthy curlèd darlings[87] of our nation,[88]
Would[89] ever have, to incur a general mock,[90]
Run from her guardage[91] to the sooty bosom[92]
Of such a thing as thou – to fear,[93] not to delight. 70
Judge me the world,[94] if 'tis not gross in sense[95]
That thou hast practiced[96] on her with foul charms,
Abused her delicate youth with drugs or minerals[97]

79 lodged, put
80 refer me to = put my trust in
81 perception, awareness
82 unmarried/virginal young woman★
83 (1) delicate, soft, sensitive, (2) youthful, immature, (3) dearly loved
84 reputable, unstained, pure
85 fortunate, favored (having good "hap")
86 against, hostile
87 curlèd darlings = favorites with artificial curls
88 ("nation" had cultural and racial rather than political meaning; Venice was
   not a nation but a city-state)
89 whether she would
90 general mock = common/universal★ derision/contempt★
91 sheltered existence ("guardianship")
92 breast, heart★
93 a thing to be afraid of
94 judge me the world = let/may the world judge me
95 gross in sense = obvious
96 worked
97 mineral-derived drugs/poisons★

That weaken motion.[98] I'll have't disputed on[99] –
75   'Tis probable, and palpable[100] to thinking.
I therefore apprehend[101] and do attach[102] thee
For an abuser of the world, a practicer
Of arts inhibited[103] and out of warrant.[104]
Lay hold upon him. If he do resist,
Subdue him at his peril.

80 *Othello*   Hold your hands,[105]
Both you of my inclining[106] and the rest.
Were it my cue to fight, I should have known it
Without a prompter. Where will[107] you that I go
To answer this your charge?[108]

  Brabantio   To prison, till fit[109] time
85   Of law and course[110] of direct session[111]
Call thee to answer.

  Othello   What if I do obey?
How may the Duke be therewith satisfied,
Whose messengers are here about my side
Upon some present[112] business of the state,

---

98 activity of body and mind
99 disputed on = contested, challenged
100 plain, obvious
101 arrest
102 indict
103 arts inhibited = forbidden studies/learning
104 out of warrant = unlawful
105 hold your hands = desist/keep back★ your hands
106 party, following
107 wish★
108 accusation
109 proper, appropriate★
110 procedures★
111 direct session = a court in regular (not specially summoned) session
112 urgent, immediate★

To bring[113] me to him?

Officer   'Tis true, most worthy signior.   90
    The Duke's in council, and your noble self,
    I am sure, is sent for.

Brabantio   How? The Duke in council?
    In[114] this time of the night? Bring him away.[115]
    Mine's not an idle cause.[116] The Duke himself,
    Or any of my brothers of the state,   95
    Cannot but feel this wrong as[117] 'twere their own.
    For if such actions may have passage free,[118]
    Bond slaves[119] and pagans shall our statesmen be.

EXEUNT

---

113 conduct, lead, escort★
114 at
115 bring him away = escort/convey Othello on to the Duke
116 idle cause = frivolous/groundless★ legal case/suit
117 as if
118 passage free = rights ("movement") that are unrestricted★
119 bond slaves = slaves by contract rather than capture

SCENE 3
Venice. A council chamber.

DUKE AND SENATORS AT COUNCIL TABLE.
OFFICERS AND ATTENDANTS

Duke   There is no composition[1] in these news
    That gives them[2] credit.[3]
Senator 1   Indeed, they are disproportioned.[4]
    My letters say a hundred and seven galleys.[5]
Duke   And mine a hundred and forty.
Senator 2   And mine two hundred.
5   But though they jump[6] not on a just account[7] –
    As in these cases, where the aim[8] reports,
    'Tis oft with difference – yet do they all confirm
    A Turkish fleet, and bearing up[9] to Cyprus.
Duke   Nay, it is possible enough to judgment.[10]
10   I do not so secure me in[11] the error,
    But the main article[12] I do approve[13]
    In fearful[14] sense.

1 order, arrangement
2 "news" is plural
3 believability, credibility, trustworthiness
4 inconsistent
5 Turkish/enemy ships (though both sides employ galleys)
6 coincide/agree exactly★
7 just account = equal account
8 conjecture, guess
9 bearing up = keeping/sustaining a course
10 come to a conclusion/decision/deliberate opinion
11 secure me in = feel entirely safe★ about
12 chief/most important/leading portion/part/matter
13 pronounce to be good, accept★
14 in fearful sense = with a dreadful/frightening★ perception/sensation

Sailor   (*Within*) What ho, what ho, what ho!

Officer A messenger from the galleys.[15]

ENTER SAILOR

Duke   Now what's the business?

Sailor   The Turkish preparation[16] makes for Rhodes.[17]

So was I bid report here to the state   15

By Signior Angelo.[18]

Duke   (*to Senators*) How say you by[19] this change?

Senator 1   This cannot be,

By no assay of reason.[20] 'Tis a pageant[21]

To keep us in false gaze.[22] When we consider

The importancy of Cyprus to the Turk,   20

And let ourselves again but[23] understand

That, as it[24] more concerns the Turk than Rhodes,

So may he[25] with more facile question bear it,[26]

For that[27] it stands not in such warlike brace,[28]

---

15 Venetian ships
16 expedition, fleet
17 island in the Aegean Sea, W/SW of Turkey
18 first name of the interim Governor of Cyprus, Montano (?)
19 how say you by = what do you say about
20 assay of reason = process/trial★ of thought/good sense
21 trick, deception
22 false gaze = looking in the wrong direction
23 again but = further/once more/moreover just
24 Cyprus
25 the Turk
26 more facile question bear it = easier strife win/carry/conquer it (*O.E.D.*, s.v. "question," 4)
27 for that = because
28 preparation/defense

25 But altogether lacks the abilities[29]
That Rhodes is dressed in.[30] If we make thought of this,
We must not think the Turk is so unskillful
To leave that latest[31] which concerns him first,
Neglecting an attempt of ease and gain,[32]
30 To wake[33] and wage[34] a danger profitless.
Duke　　Nay, in all confidence,[35] he's[36] not for Rhodes.
Officer　　Here is more news.

ENTER MESSENGER

Messenger　The Ottomites,[37] reverend and gracious,
Steering with due[38] course toward the isle of Rhodes,
35 Have there injointed them[39] with an after[40] fleet.
Senator 1　　Ay, so I thought. How many,[41] as you guess?
Messenger　Of thirty sail.[42] And now they do re-stem[43]
Their backward course, bearing with frank[44] appearance
Their purposes toward Cyprus. Signior Montano,
40 Your trusty and most valiant servitor,

29 strengths, power
30 dressed in = equipped/provided with
31 to the last
32 advantage, profit
33 to wake = in order to exert himself (were the Turks to attack Rhodes)
34 risk
35 certainty, assurance
36 the Turk
37 Ottomans, Turks
38 straight
39 injointed them = joined, united
40 second
41 many in the second fleet
42 ships
43 re-trace (turn back and re-sail in the direction they had just come from)
44 open, undisguised

With his free[45] duty recommends[46] you thus,
And prays you to believe him.

Duke   'Tis certain, then, for Cyprus.
Marcus Luccicos,[47] is not he in town?[48]

Senator 1   He's now in Florence.   45

Duke   Write from us to him, post-post-haste despatch.[49]

Senator 1   Here comes Brabantio and the valiant Moor.

ENTER BRABANTIO, OTHELLO, IAGO, RODERIGO,
AND OFFICERS

Duke   Valiant Othello, we must straight employ you
Against the general enemy[50] Ottoman.
(*to Brabantio*) I did not see you. Welcome, gentle signior,   50
We lacked your counsel and your help tonight.

Brabantio So did I yours. Good your grace, pardon me.
Neither my place, nor aught I heard of business,
Hath raised me from my bed, nor doth the general care[51]
Take hold on me. For my particular[52] grief   55
Is of so floodgate and o'erbearing[53] nature
That it engluts[54] and swallows other sorrows,
And it is still itself.

---

45 (1) great, (2) voluntary, willing, open
46 reports, informs
47 the Greek name suggests someone of Cypriot origin, with useful on-site
  information
48 MARcos luCHIcos IS not HE in TOWN
49 speed
50 general enemy = universal enemy (for Christian Europeans)
51 concern, anxiety
52 personal, private
53 floodgate and o'erbearing = strongly streaming/torrential and verwhelming,
  overpowering
54 gulps down

Duke   Why, what's the matter?

Brabantio My daughter! O, my daughter!

Duke and Senators   Dead?

60 *Brabantio*   Ay, to me.

    She is abused, stol'n from me,[55] and corrupted

    By spells and medicines[56] bought of mountebanks.[57]

    For nature[58] so preposterously[59] to err,[60]

    Being not deficient,[61] blind, or lame of sense,

65   Sans[62] witchcraft could not.[63]

Duke   Whoe'er he be that, in this foul proceeding,

    Hath thus beguiled[64] your daughter of herself,

    And you of her,[65] the bloody book of law[66]

    You shall yourself read in the bitter letter[67]

70   After[68] your own sense, yea, though our proper[69] son

    Stood[70] in your action.[71]

Brabantio   Humbly I thank your grace.

55 stoln FROM me
56 drugs
57 itinerant quacks/charlatans
58 a character/disposition
59 irrationally, monstrously, perversely
60 go astray
61 defective
62 without (French)
63 could not = could not be, is impossible
64 cheated, deceived★
65 (fathers had legally recognized possession of unmarried daughters; after marriage, possession passed to husbands)
66 bloody book of law = bloodshed-imposing legal code/set of laws
67 read in the bitter letter = interpret/declare the hard/dire/severe words/ statutes
68 according to
69 our proper = my own (the royal "we")
70 were the accused person
71 legal proceeding

Here is the man, this Moor, whom now, it seems,
Your special mandate[72] for the state affairs[73]
Hath hither[74] brought.

Duke and Senators   We are very sorry for't.

Duke   (*to Othello*) What, in your own part,[75] can you say to
    this?   75

Brabantio   Nothing, but this is so.

Othello   Most potent,[76] grave, and reverend signiors,
My very noble and approved[77] good masters.[78]
That I have ta'en away this old man's daughter,
It is most true; true, I have married her.   80
The very head and front[79] of my offending[80]
Hath this extent,[81] no more. Rude[82] am I in my speech,
And little blessed with the soft[83] phrase of peace,
For since these arms of mine had seven years' pith,[84]
Till now some nine moons wasted,[85] they have used[86]   85
Their dearest[87] action in the tented field.[88]

72 special mandate = particular/distinct★ command/order
73 the state affairs = affairs of state
74 here★
75 in your own part = in your own interest, on your own side
76 powerful, mighty★
77 esteemed
78 chiefs, rulers ("employers")
79 head and front = summit, highest extent
80 offense, transgression
81 size
82 unsophisticated, unlearned, barbarous, rough★
83 pleasant, agreeable, smooth★
84 substance, strength
85 moons wasted = months past/unused (he has not been engaged in war for
    the past nine months)
86 performed, carried on
87 most honorable/worthy
88 tented field = battlefield (where soldiers live in tents)

And little of this great world can I speak,
More than pertains to feats of broil[89] and battle,
And therefore little shall I grace[90] my cause
90 In speaking for myself. Yet, by your gracious patience,
I will a round[91] unvarnished tale deliver[92]
Of my whole course of love, what[93] drugs, what charms,
What conjuration,[94] and what mighty magic –
For such proceeding I am charged withal[95] –
I won his daughter.

95 *Brabantio*   A maiden never bold,
Of spirit so still[96] and quiet that her motion[97]
Blushed at herself, and she, in spite of nature,
Of years,[98] of country,[99] credit, everything,
To fall in love with what she feared to look on!
100 It is[100] judgment maimed[101] and most imperfect[102]
That will confess[103] perfection[104] so could err
Against all rules of nature, and[105] must be driven

89 turmoil
90 embellish, adorn
91 full, complete
92 speak★
93 with what
94 invoking of spirits
95 likewise, moreover
96 (1) habitually silent, subdued, meek, (2) calm, unruffled
97 emotions, desires
98 the difference in years
99 race, culture★
100 it is = only a
101 deficient, crippled
102 incomplete
103 declare, concede, admit
104 completeness, finished/grown/matured excellence
105 and therefore

To find out practices of cunning[106] hell,
Why this should be. I therefore vouch[107] again,
That with some mixtures[108] powerful o'er the blood,   105
Or with some dram conjured[109] to this effect,
He wrought[110] upon her.

Duke   To vouch this is no proof,
Without more wider and more overt test[111]
Than these thin habits[112] and poor[113] likelihoods
Of modern seeming[114] do prefer[115] against him.   110

Senator 1 But, Othello, speak.
Did you by indirect and forcèd courses[116]
Subdue and poison this young maid's affections?
Or came it by request, and such fair question
As soul to soul affordeth?[117]

Othello   I do beseech you,   115
Send for the lady to[118] the Sagittary,
And let her speak of me before[119] her father.
If you do find me foul in her report,

106 skilled / clever / crafty★
107 assert, allege, bear witness★
108 compounds
109 dram conjured = draught / drink magically corrupted
110 worked, acted, operated
111 overt test = open / plain examination / evidence
112 thin habits = tenuous / flimsy / slight traits / usages
113 scanty, insufficient
114 modern seeming = ordinary / commonplace appearance
115 lay (one lays a charge against a person)
116 indirect and forcèd courses = corrupt / deceitful and imposed / unnatural
    actions / practices★
117 yields, furnishes
118 at
119 in front / the presence of

The trust, the office[120] I do hold of[121] you,

120   Not only take away, but let your sentence[122]

    Even fall upon my life.

Duke   Fetch Desdemona hither.

Othello   Ancient, conduct[123] them. You best know the place.

EXEUNT IAGO AND ATTENDANTS

    And till she come, as truly as to heaven

    I do confess the vices of my blood,[124]

125   So justly[125] to your grave ears I'll present[126]

    How I did thrive in this fair lady's love,

    And she in mine.

Duke   Say it, Othello.

Othello   Her father loved me, oft invited me,

    Still[127] questioned me the story[128] of my life,

130   From year to year – the battles, sieges, fortunes,

    That I have passed.[129]

    I ran it through, even from my boyish days

    To th'very moment that he bade me tell it.

    Wherein[130] I spake of most disastrous chances,[131]

---

120 post, employment, service, duty★

121 from

122 judgment

123 guide, lead

124 vices of my blood = moral defects/sins of my disposition/emotions
(Othello here, as elsewhere, declares himself a practicing Christian)

125 truthfully, correctly

126 describe, set forth

127 always★

128 the story = about the story/history

129 experienced, gone through

130 in telling that story

131 disastrous chances = unfortunate/ill-fated events/circumstances★

Of moving[132] accidents by flood and field,[133]   135
Of hair-breadth scapes i' the imminent[134] deadly breach,[135]
Of being taken[136] by the insolent[137] foe
And sold to slavery; of my redemption thence[138]
And portance[139] in my traveler's history,
Wherein of antres[140] vast and deserts idle,[141]   140
Rough quarries,[142] rocks, and hills whose heads touch
heaven,
It was my hint[143] to speak. Such was my process.[144]
And of the cannibals that each other eat –
The anthropophagi[145] – and men whose heads
Grew beneath their shoulders. These things to hear   145
Would Desdemona seriously incline.[146]
But still the house affairs would draw her hence.
Which ever as she could with haste dispatch,[147]
She'd come again, and with a greedy ear
Devour up my discourse. Which I observing,   150

132 affecting to feelings/mind
133 by flood and field = on water and land
134 threatening, close at hand
135 breakthrough, assault
136 captured
137 proud, arrogant, imperious
138 from that/there*
139 my behavior/conduct
140 caves, caverns
141 empty, vacant
142 rough quarries = wild/broken/uneven masses of stone
143 occasion, opportunity
144 (1) course, manner of proceeding, (2) narrative, story
145 ANthroPOfaGIY
146 seriously incline = earnestly bend/lean toward
147 settle, dispose of, finish

Took once a pliant[148] hour, and found good means[149]
To draw from her a prayer[150] of earnest[151] heart
That I would all my pilgrimage dilate,[152]
Whereof by parcels[153] she had something heard,
155 But not intentively.[154] I did consent,
And often did beguile her of[155] her tears,
When I did speak of some distressful stroke[156]
That my youth suffered. My story being done,[157]
She gave me for my pains a world of kisses.[158]
160 She swore, in faith, 'twas strange, 'twas passing[159] strange,
'Twas pitiful, 'twas wondrous pitiful.
She wished she had not heard it, yet she wished
That heaven had made her such a man. She thanked me,
And bade me, if I had a friend that loved her,
165 I should but teach him how to tell my story,
And that would woo her. Upon this hint I spake:
She loved me for the dangers I had passed,
And I loved her that she did pity[160] them.
This only is the witchcraft I have used.

148 suitable, apt
149 methods, ways★
150 request, petition
151 of earnest = made with serious/ardent
152 pilgrimage dilate = travels describe/set forth at length
153 parts, units
154 with full attention
155 beguile her of = win/draw/charm from her
156 blow, painful/injurious occurrence
157 finished★
158 light touch of the lips, as still practiced in Continental greeting (Quarto: sighs)
159 surpassingly, extremely
160 feel sorry/grieve/compassion for

Here comes the lady. Let her witness[161] it.   170

ENTER DESDEMONA, IAGO, AND ATTENDANTS

Duke   I think this tale would win my daughter too.

Good Brabantio,

Take up this mangled[162] matter at the best.[163]

Men do their broken weapons[164] rather use

Than their bare hands.

Brabantio   I pray you, hear her speak.   175

If she confess that she was half the wooer,

Destruction on my head if my bad[165] blame

Light[166] on the man. Come hither, gentle mistress.[167]

Do you perceive in all this noble company

Where most you owe obedience?[168]

Desdemona   My noble father,   180

I do perceive here a divided duty.

To you I am bound[169] for life and education.[170]

My life and education both do learn me

How to respect you. You are the lord of duty,

I am hitherto[171] your daughter. But here's my husband,   185

And so much duty as my mother showed

161 testify to
162 chopped up, confused
163 at the best = in the best way possible
164 (meaning that he remains, at least, her father?)
165 defective, faulty, incorrect
166 descend, fall
167 (before her elopement and marriage, he would have addressed he as "miss";
    mistress = the full original form of the modern abbreviation, "Mrs.")
168 oBEEDyuns
169 obliged, indebted
170 rearing, bringing up
171 until now

To you, preferring[172] you before her father,
So much I challenge[173] that I may profess
Due to the Moor, my lord.

190 *Brabantio* God be with you. I have done.
Please it[174] your grace, on to the state affairs.
I had rather to adopt a child than get[175] it.
Come hither, Moor.
I here do give thee that with all my heart

195 Which, but thou hast[176] already, with all my heart
I would keep from thee. (*to Desdemona*) For your sake,[177]
jewel,
I am glad at soul I have no other child,
For thy escape[178] would teach me tyranny,
To hang clogs[179] on them. (*to Duke*) I have done, my lord.

200 *Duke*   Let me speak like yourself, and lay a sentence[180]
Which, as a grise[181] or step, may help these lovers
Into your favor.[182]
When remedies are past, the griefs are ended
By seeing the worst, which late[183] on hopes depended.[184]

172 setting
173 assert, claim★
174 please it = may it please
175 beget, father
176 but thou hast = except that you have it
177 for your sake = because of what you have done (sake = blame, offense, guilt)
178 outrageous transgression (*O.E.D.*, s.v. "escape," 7)
179 blocks of wood hung on prisoners
180 lay a sentence = submit /present an (1) opinion, (2) maxim, aphorism
181 flight of steps, stairway
182 approving/kind regard, goodwill
183 recently
184 (1) hung, were suspended, (3) relied/were counted on

To mourn a mischief[185] that is past and gone   205
Is the next[186] way to draw new mischief on.
What cannot be preserved when fortune takes,
Patience her injury[187] a mockery makes.
The robbed that smiles[188] steals something from the thief.
He robs himself that spends[189] a bootless[190] grief.   210
Brabantio So let the Turk of Cyprus us beguile,
We lose it not so long as we can smile.
He bears the sentence well, that nothing bears
But the free comfort[191] which from thence[192] he hears.
But he bears both the sentence and the sorrow   215
That, to[193] pay grief, must of[194] poor patience borrow.
These sentences, to sugar or to gall,[195]
Being strong on both sides, are equivocal.[196]
But words are words: I never yet did hear
That the bruisèd heart was piercèd through the ears.   220
I humbly beseech you, proceed to th'affairs of state.
Duke   The Turk with a most mighty preparation makes for
Cyprus. Othello, the fortitude[197] of the place is best known

185 evil, misfortune
186 shortest, most direct
187 loss, harm
188 the robbed that smiles = he who, being robbed, smiles
189 expends, wastes words/time on
190 remediless, incurable, useless
191 free comfort = (1) noble/generous, (2) unrestricted, allowable
   encouragement/support★ (Brabantio speaks carefully tongue-in-cheek)
192 then on
193 that, to = who, in order to
194 from
195 bile, bitterness
196 ambiguous
197 strength, fortified state

to you. And though we have there a substitute[198] of most
225   allowed sufficiency,[199] yet opinion,[200] a sovereign[201] mistress
of effects,[202] throws a more safer voice[203] on you. You must
therefore be content to slubber the gloss[204] of your new
fortunes with this more stubborn and boisterous[205]
expedition.[206]

230 *Othello* The tyrant custom, most grave senators,
Hath made the flinty and steel couch[207] of war
My thrice-driven[208] bed of down. I do agnize[209]
A natural[210] and prompt alacrity[211]
I find in hardness,[212] and do undertake[213]
235   These present[214] wars against the Ottomites.
Most humbly, therefore, bending to your state,[215]
I crave[216] fit disposition[217] for my wife;

198 deputy (Montano)
199 allowed sufficiency = satisfactory competence
200 judgment, belief
201 authoritative, governing, supreme
202 results
203 judgment, vote
204 slubber the gloss = stain/smear the glow/luster
205 stubborn and boisterous = difficult/intractable and unyielding/truculent
206 warlike enterprise
207 flinty and steel couch = rugged and hard bed
208 thrice-driven = feathers that have been three times dried with a fan, and
    thus made soft enough to lie on
209 confess
210 instinctive, inherent, innate
211 prompt alacrity = ready willingness
212 rigor, difficulty
213 take on, agree to carry on
214 current ("aforesaid")
215 bending to your state = bowing to your (the Duke's) lofty status/rank/
    position
216 ask, request
217 arrangements, living conditions

Due reference of place and exhibition,[218]
With such accommodation and besort[219]
As levels[220] with her breeding.   240

Duke   Why, at her father's?

Brabantio   I will not have it so.

Othello   Nor I.

Desdemona Nor would I there reside,
To put my father in impatient[221] thoughts
By being in his eye. Most gracious Duke,   245
To my unfolding[222] lend your prosperous[223] ear,
And let me find a charter[224] in your voice
T'assist my simpleness.[225]

Duke   What would you, Desdemona?

Desdemona That I love the Moor to live[226] with him,
My downright violence[227] and storm of fortunes[228]   250
May trumpet to the world. My heart's subdued[229]
Even to the very quality[230] of my lord.
I saw Othello's visage in his mind,[231]

218 reference of place and exhibition = assignment of residence and
    maintenance/support/allowance
219 accommodation and besort = lodgings and suitable company/attendance
220 is equal/matches
221 uncomfortable, irritable
222 statement, explanation?
223 favorable
224 grant of privilege
225 innocence, guilelessness
226 to live = to the point/with the desire/purpose of living
227 downright violence = out and out/positively/thoroughly vehement/
    intense/passionate conduct
228 storm of fortunes = disturbance/tumult of events
229 conquered, overcome, overpowered
230 profession, business
231 in his mind = as he sees himself (a backhanded reference to Othello's
    blackness, which he himself is not required to see, and does not see?)

And to his honors and his valiant[232] parts

255   Did I my soul and fortunes consecrate.[233]

So that, dear lords, if I be left behind,

A moth of peace,[234] and he go to the war,

The rites[235] for which[236] I love him are bereft[237] me,

And I a heavy[238] interim shall support[239]

260   By[240] his dear absence. Let me go with him.

Othello   Let her have your voice.

Vouch with me, heaven, I therefore beg it not[241]

To please the palate[242] of my appetite,[243]

Nor to comply with heat[244] – the young affects[245]

265   In me defunct[246] – and proper[247] satisfaction,

But to be free and bounteous[248] to her mind.[249]

And heaven defend your good souls, that[250] you think

I will your serious and great business scant[251]

232 strong, brave, bold
233 dedicate, devote
234 moth of peace = fluttering insignificant / calm creature (?)
235 practices (it has been suggested that Shakespeare meant "rights": the words
    were virtual homonyms)
236 for which = because of which
237 taken from
238 gloomy, dark★
239 shall support = must endure
240 because of
241 therefore beg it not = do not ask it in order
242 liking, pleasure
243 desire, cravings
244 comply with heat = fulfill / satisfy passion / sexual excitement
245 desires, feelings
246 are extinct / dead
247 personal
248 free and bounteous = honorable / open-minded and generous
249 judgment, intention, wishes
250 if
251 diminish, neglect

For[252] she is with me. No, when light-winged toys[253]
Of feathered[254] Cupid seel[255] with wanton dullness[256]   270
My speculative and officed instruments,[257]
That my disports corrupt and taint[258] my business,
Let housewives make a skillet of[259] my helm,[260]
And all indign and base adversities[261]
Make head[262] against my estimation.[263]   275

Duke   Be[264] it as you[265] shall privately determine,
Either for her stay or going. The affair cries[266] haste,
And speed must answer[267] it.

Senator 1   You must away tonight.

Othello   With all my heart.

Duke   At nine i'the morning, here we'll[268] meet again.   280
Othello, leave some officer behind,

---

252 because
253 light-winged toys = evanescent / vaporous amorous entertainment / trifles
254 winged
255 blind, hoodwink (as a hawk with eyes stitched closed, for falconry / hunting
    training)
256 wanton dullness = undisciplined / self-indulgent sluggishness / stupidity
257 speculative and officed instruments = investigative / visual and (other)
    specially functioning organs
258 that my disports corrupt and taint my business = so that my pastimes
    pervert and tarnish / injure
259 out of, from
260 helmet
261 indign and base adversities = disgraceful / unworthy and despicable / low
    misfortunes / afflictions
262 make head = rise up, advance
263 reputation (EStiMAYseeON)
264 let it be
265 you both
266 affair cries = business / matter calls / cries out / demands
267 undertake, be responsible for
268 we = Duke and Senators

And he shall our commission[269] bring to you,
With such things else[270] of quality and respect[271]
As doth import[272] you.

Othello   So please your grace, my ancient,
285   A man he is of honesty[273] and trust.
To his conveyance[274] I assign[275] my wife,
With what else needful your good grace shall think
To be sent after me.

Duke   Let it be so.
Good night to everyone. (*to Brabantio*) And noble signior,
290   If virtue no delighted beauty[276] lack,
Your son-in-law is far more fair than black.

Senator 1   Adieu, brave[277] Moor, use[278] Desdemona well.

Brabantio   Look to her,[279] Moor, if thou hast eyes to see.
She has deceived her father, and may thee.

EXEUNT DUKE, SENATORS, OFFICERS

295   *Othello*   My life upon her faith. Honest Iago,
My Desdemona must I leave to thee
I prythee,[280] let thy wife attend[281] on her,

269 document certifying appointment and containing orders, instructions, etc.
270 things else = other★ things
271 quality and respect = rank/title★ and deference/courtesies
272 involve, relate to
273 honor, respectability, decency★
274 escorting
275 designate, consign
276 delighted beauty = delightful beauty (applicable to men as well as women)
277 worthy, excellent★
278 treat★
279 look to her = keep watch on/beware of her
280 pray thee
281 accompany, watch over, serve

And bring them after in the best advantage.[282]
Come, Desdemona, I have but an hour
Of love, of worldly matters and direction[283]   300
To spend with thee. We must obey[284] the time.[285]

EXEUNT OTHELLO AND DESDEMONA

Roderigo Iago.

Iago   What say'st thou, noble heart?[286]

Roderigo What will I do, thinkest thou?

Iago   Why, go to bed and sleep.   305

Roderigo I will incontinently[287] drown myself.

Iago   If thou dost, I shall never love thee after. Why, thou
        silly gentleman?

Roderigo It is silliness to live when to live is torment. And then
        have we a prescription[288] to die when death is our physician.   310

Iago   O villainous![289] I have looked upon the world for four
        times seven years, and since I could distinguish betwixt a ben-
        efit and an injury, I never found man that knew how to love
        himself. Ere[290] I would say I would drown myself for the love
        of a guinea-hen,[291] I would change[292] my humanity with a   315
        baboon.

282 in the best advantage = at the most favorable opportunity★ (as soon as
    possible)
283 guidance, instruction
284 submit to, comply with, act according to
285 age, era★
286 heart = familiar term of endearment (surely ironic)
287 straightway, at once
288 explicit instruction / order
289 what bad manners, how shameful / atrocious / horrible★
290 before★
291 whore
292 exchange

Roderigo   What should I do? I confess it is my shame to be so
fond,[293] but it is not in my virtue[294] to amend it.

Iago   Virtue? A fig![295] 'Tis in ourselves that we are thus or
320   thus. Our bodies are gardens, to the which our wills are
gardeners. So that if we will plant nettles or sow lettuce, set
hyssop[296] and weed up thyme, supply it with one gender[297]
of herbs or distract[298] it with many, either to have it sterile
with[299] idleness or manured with industry,[300] why, the power
325   and corrigible authority[301] of this lies in our wills. If the
balance[302] of our lives had not one scale[303] of reason to
poise[304] another[305] of sensuality, the blood and baseness of
our natures would conduct us to most preposterous
conclusions. But we have reason[306] to cool our raging
330   motions,[307] our carnal stings,[308] our unbitted[309] lusts,
whereof I take this, that you call love, to be a sect or scion.[310]

Roderigo   It cannot be.

293 infatuated, foolish, silly★
294 power
295 a fig = fiddlesticks, nonsense (contemptuous, and accompanied − as in
   Romeo and Juliet − by gestures very like today's "giving the finger")
296 set hyssop = setout/plant small bushy aromatic herb (HISSup)
297 kind
298 confuse, spoil, disorder
299 either to have it sterile with = either have it unproductive/barren from
300 manured with industry = cultivated/tilled diligently
301 corrigible authority = correctable power/right
302 (1) scale (in modern usage), (2) metaphorical balance
303 one pan of the two pans employed in a balance scale
304 balance, steady
305 another scale
306 rationality, logic, thought
307 emotions
308 irritations, pains
309 unrestrained
310 sect or scion = class or shoot/twig/descendant

Iago   It is merely a lust of the blood and a permission[311] of
the will. Come, be a man. Drown thyself? Drown cats and
blind puppies. I have professed[312] me thy friend, and I confess   335
me knit to thy deserving[313] with cables[314] of perdurable[315]
toughness. I could never better stead[316] thee than now. Put
money in thy purse,[317] follow[318] thou the wars, defeat[319] thy
favor[320] with an usurped[321] beard. I say, put money in thy
purse. It cannot be that Desdemona should long continue her   340
love to the Moor – put money in thy purse – nor he his to
her. It was a violent commencement, and thou shalt see an
answerable sequestration[322] – put but[323] money in thy purse.
These Moors are changeable in their wills.[324] Fill thy purse
with money. The food that to him now is as luscious as   345
locusts[325] shall be to him shortly as acerb[326] as the
coloquintida.[327] She must change[328] for youth. When she is

311 license, liberty
312 declared
313 knit to thy deserving = tied/knotted to your merit
314 heavy ropes
315 permanent, everlasting
316 assist, be of use/profit to
317 put money in thy purse = get cash ("make yourself liquid")
318 go forward with, accompany
319 nullify
320 face, appearance★
321 borrowed, false
322 answerable sequestration = responsive/proper/suitable separation/
     disjunction
323 put but = just put
324 desires
325 sweet fruit of the carob tree
326 sour, bitter
327 a bitter fruit (koLAkwinTEEda)
328 exchange him

sated with his body, she will find[329] the error of her choice.
She must have change,[330] she must. Therefore put money in

350 thy purse. If thou wilt needs[331] damn thyself,[332] do it a more
delicate[333] way than drowning. Make all the money thou
canst. If sanctimony[334] and a frail vow betwixt an erring[335]
barbarian and a supersubtle[336] Venetian be not too hard[337]
for my wits (and[338] all the tribe of hell),[339] thou shalt

355 enjoy[340] her. Therefore make money. A pox of[341] drowning
thyself! It is clean[342] out of the way.[343] Seek thou rather to
be hanged in compassing[344] thy joy than to be drowned and
go without her.

Roderigo   Wilt thou be fast[345] to my hopes, if I depend[346] on the
360   issue?[347]

Iago   Thou art sure of me. Go, make money: I have told thee

329 understand, discover
330 a substitution
331 necessarily
332 damn thyself: suicide was considered a grave sin
333 delightful, pleasant
334 hypocritical holiness
335 wandering, roaming★
336 over-subtle
337 difficult
338 and also for
339 (?) tribe = population; Iago pretty clearly is referring to demons, etc.; but
   why? Is this a remark to himself or to Roderigo?
340 possess, have sexual intercourse with
341 on
342 completely
343 out of the way = off the proper path,★ out of the question, mistaken ("not
   done")
344 encompassing, achieving, devising
345 firm, unshaken, steadfast
346 rely, count on
347 outcome, result★

often, and I re-tell thee again and again, I hate the Moor. My
cause is hearted;[348] thine hath no less reason. Let us be
conjunctive[349] in our revenge against him. If thou canst
cuckold him, thou dost thyself a pleasure, me a sport.[350]   365
There are many events in the womb of time which will be
delivered.[351] Traverse.[352] Go, provide thy money. We will
have more of this tomorrow. Adieu.

Roderigo Where shall we meet i' the morning?

Iago   At my lodging.   370

Roderigo I'll be with thee betimes.[353]

Iago   Go to,[354] farewell. Do you hear, Roderigo?

Roderigo What say you?

Iago   No more of drowning, do you hear?

Roderigo I am changed. I'll go sell all my land.   375

EXIT RODERIGO

Iago   Thus do I ever[355] make my fool my purse,
            For I mine own gained[356] knowledge should profane[357]
            If I would time expend[358] with such a snipe[359]
            But[360] for my sport and profit. I hate the Moor,

348 fixed/established in the heart
349 united
350 amusement, recreation, entertainment★
351 determined, resolved
352 move along, act
353 at an early hour
354 go to = go on ("oh yeah")★
355 always
356 acquired
357 violate, desecrate
358 consume
359 marsh bird (a common insult)
360 except

380   And it is thought abroad[361] that 'twixt my sheets
      He has done my office.[362] I know not if't be true,
      But I, for mere[363] suspicion in that kind,[364]
      Will do[365] as if for surety.[366] He holds me well,[367]
      The better shall my purpose work on him.

385   Cassio's a proper[368] man. Let me see now;
      To get his place, and to plume up[369] my will[370]
      In double knavery – How? How? Let's see.
      After some time, to abuse Othello's ear

390   That he[371] is too familiar with his[372] wife.
      He[373] hath a person,[374] and a smooth dispose,[375]
      To be suspected, framed[376] to make women false.[377]
      The Moor is of a free and open nature,
      That thinks men honest that but seem to be so,

395   And will as tenderly[378] be led by the nose
      As asses are.

361 widely
362 function (as a husband)
363 pure, sheer, downright★
364 in that kind = of that sort
365 act
366 certain
367 holds me well = thinks well of/esteems me
368 (1) respectable, (2) handsome★
369 adorn (with metaphorical feathers)
370 desire, inclination
371 Cassio
372 Othello's
373 Cassio
374 semblance, appearance
375 smooth dispose = pleasant/affable/plausible external manner/air
376 fashioned/made★
377 unfaithful, deceptive, deceiving
378 gently, softly

I have't. It is engendered.[379] Hell and night
Must bring this monstrous birth to the world's light.

EXIT

<hr/>

379 begotten, generated

Act 2

SCENE I
Cyprus[1]

ENTER MONTANO AND TWO GENTLEMEN

Montano What from the cape[2] can you discern at sea?

Gentleman 1 Nothing at all. It is a high-wrought flood.[3]

I cannot, 'twixt the heaven and the main,[4]

Descry[5] a sail.

5 *Montano* Methinks the wind hath spoke aloud at[6] land,

A fuller[7] blast ne'er shook our battlements.[8]

1 (editorial conjectures have Gentleman 1 placed (1) above, (2) to the side, or (3) to the back. But not only do Montano's first words make it uncertain whether Gentleman 1 is at the moment seeing or reporting what he has previously seen, but in line 36 Montano suggests that they now go "to the seaside.")
2 projecting headland / promontory
3 high-wrought flood = (1) very agitated sea, (2) sea casting up very high waves
4 mainland
5 get sight of, perceive, detect
6 spoke aloud at = sounded / reverberated loudly on
7 stronger, larger
8 fortifications built on top of defensive walls

If it hath ruffianed so[9] upon the sea,
What ribs of oak,[10] when mountains melt[11] on them,
Can hold the mortise?[12] What shall we hear of this?
Gentleman 2 A segregation[13] of the Turkish fleet.   10
For, do but[14] stand upon the foaming[15] shore,
The chidden billow[16] seems to pelt[17] the clouds,
The wind-shaked surge,[18] with high and monstrous main,[19]
Seems to cast water on the burning Bear,[20]
And quench the guards[21] of th'ever-fixèd pole.   15
I never did like molestation view[22]
On the enchafèd[23] flood.
Montano   If that[24] the Turkish fleet
Be not ensheltered and embayed,[25] they are drowned.
It is impossible to bear it out.[26]

---

9 ruffianed so = blustered/raged so violently
10 ribs of oak = curved oaken frame timbers of a ship's hull
11 mountains melt = mountainlike waves of water break (as clouds melt into rain)
12 joined beams
13 a segregation = what we shall hear is a breakup/dispersion
14 for, do but = because, just
15 covered with foam (modern usage: "foamy")
16 chidden billow = blast-driven swelling waves
17 strike
18 waves, water
19 power, force
20 star constellation Ursa Minor ("Little Bear"): starlight as metaphorical "fire"
21 stars, though just which stars is unclear
22 like molestation view [adjective, noun, verb] = such troubled/agitated waves to see ("seeing such agitated waves")
23 furious
24 if that = if it turns out that
25 ensheltered and embayed = protected/screened and enclosed in a bay or other recess
26 bear it out = sustain/endure

ENTER GENTLEMAN 3

20 *Gentleman 3* News, lads.[27] Our wars are done.

The desperate[28] tempest hath so banged[29] the Turks

That their designment[30] halts. A noble[31] ship of Venice

Hath seen a grievous wrack and sufferance[32]

On most[33] part of their fleet.

Montano   How![34] Is this true?

25 *Gentleman 3* The ship is here put in, a Veronessa.[35]

Michael Cassio,

Lieutenant to the warlike Moor, Othello,

Is[36] come on shore. The Moor himself at sea,[37]

And is in full commission here[38] for Cyprus.

30 *Montano*   I am glad on't.[39] 'Tis[40] a worthy governor.

Gentleman 3 But this same Cassio, though he speak of comfort[41]

Touching[42] the Turkish loss, yet he looks sadly,[43]

And prays the Moor be safe, for they were parted

With foul and violent tempest.

27 spirited men*

28 extreme, hopelessly bad / awful, highly dangerous

29 violently beaten, knocked about

30 undertaking, enterprise

31 large

32 wrack and sufferance = disaster / destruction / ruin and damage

33 the largest / greatest

34 (exclamation)

35 a vessel from Verona

36 has

37 at sea = is at sea

38 is in full commission here = will be here in complete command / authority

39 of it

40 it / he is

41 of comfort = comfortingly

42 about

43 grave, sober

Montano   Pray heavens he be.

   For I have served him, and the man commands   35

   Like a full[44] soldier. Let's to the seaside, ho!

   As well to see the vessel that's come in

   As to throw out[45] our eyes for brave Othello,[46]

   Even till[47] we make[48] the main and the aerial blue

   An indistinct regard.[49]

Gentleman 3   Come, let's do so.   40

   For every[50] minute is expectancy[51]

   Of more arrivancy.[52]

ENTER CASSIO

Cassio   Thanks, you the valiant of this warlike isle,[53]

   That so approve[54] the Moor. O let the heavens

   Give him defense against the elements,   45

   For I have lost[55] him on a dangerous sea.

Montano   Is he well shipped?

Cassio   His bark[56] is stoutly timbered,[57] and his pilot[58]

---

44 solid, satisfying, complete

45 throw out = look outward (to sea)

46 as TO throw OUT our EYES for BRAVE oTHELlo (n.b. as scanned, for
   prosodic purposes, but not as spoken)

47 as far as (ee'n TILL)

48 reach the point, produce / create a visual prospect in which

49 indistinct regard = indistinguishable view / prospect / sight

50 at any

51 is expectancy = there is the expectation

52 arrival

53 thanks YOU the VALyint OF this WARlike ISLE

54 commend

55 been separated from

56 comparatively small ship

57 stoutly timbered = strongly / solidly★ constructed

58 helmsman, steersman, guide

Of very expert and approved allowance,[59]

50   Therefore my hopes, not surfeited to death,[60]

Stand in bold cure.[61]

Voices within   A sail, a sail, a sail!

ENTER GENTLEMAN 4

Cassio   What noise?[62]

Gentleman 4 The town is empty.[63] On the brow o'[64] the sea

Stand ranks[65] of people, and they cry, "A sail!"

55   *Cassio*   My hopes do shape him[66] for the governor.[67]

CANNON WITHIN

Gentleman 2 They[68] do discharge their shot of courtesy.[69]

Our friends at least.[70]

Cassio   I pray you, sir, go forth,

And give us truth who 'tis that is arrived.

Gentleman 2 I shall.

---

59 expert and approved allowance = experienced/skillful and proven/tested/esteemed reputation

60 not surfeited to death = so long as they are not pushed too hard ("fed to the point of killing them")

61 stand in bold cure = remain in fearless anxiety ("confident but concerned")

62 what is that loud outcry/clamor/shouting

63 vacated

64 brow o' = hill/cliff overlooking

65 rows/lines

66 shape him = picture it (the approaching ship)

67 Othello

68 (1) Cyprus cannon, in welcome, or more probably (2) the arriving ship, as a signal of peaceful intent

69 shot of courtesy: cannon (often a specified number) were fired as a welcoming salute

70 (not that is the Turks, or any other enemy)

Montano   But good lieutenant, is your general wived?[71]   60

Cassio   Most fortunately. He hath achieved[72] a maid

That paragons[73] description and wild fame,[74]

One that excels[75] the quirks of blazoning[76] pens,

And in th'essential vesture of creation[77]

Does tire the ingeniver.[78]

ENTER GENTLEMAN 2

                    How now? Who has put in?   65

Gentleman 2 'Tis one Iago, ancient to the general.

Cassio   Ha's[79] had most favorable and happy speed.[80]

Tempests themselves,[81] high seas, and howling winds,

The guttered[82] rocks, and congregated[83] sands,

Traitors ensteeped[84] to clog[85] the guiltless keel,[86]   70

---

71 married

72 won

73 surpasses

74 wild fame = uncontrolled/extravagant public report/celebrity

75 is superior to, outdoes

76 quirks of blazoning = quibbles/tricks of portraying/descriptive

77 essential vesture of creation = inherent/intrinsic garb/raiment/clothing of
the imagination/wit/intelligence

78 tire the ingeniver = exhausts/wearies/fatigues the contriver (verbal
"engineer": Cassio himself)

79 ha's = he has

80 favorable and happy speed = agreeable/pleasing and lucky (1) good fortune,
or (2) rapidity

81 tempests themselves = even tempests

82 grooved, worn away

83 clustered, massed

84 stationed underwater

85 obstruct, hamper

86 ship's bottom

As having sense[87] of beauty, do omit[88]
Their mortal[89] natures, letting go safely by
The divine Desdemona.[90]

Montano   What is she?[91]

Cassio   She that I spake of, our great captain's captain,[92]

75   Left in the conduct of the bold Iago,
Whose footing[93] here anticipates our thoughts
A se'night's[94] speed. Great Jove, Othello guard,[95]
And swell his sail with thine own powerful breath,
That he may bless this bay with his tall ship,

80   Make love's quick pants[96] in Desdemona's arms,
Give renewed[97] fire to our extincted[98] spirits,
And bring all Cyprus comfort![99]

> ENTER DESDEMONA, EMILIA, IAGO, RODERIGO,
> AND ATTENDANTS

O, behold,

The riches of the ship is come on shore.
Ye men of Cyprus, let her have your knees.

---

87 as having sense = as if they (tempests, etc.) had a perception
88 neglect, fail to use
89 deadly, fatal
90 prosody requires either DIvine or desDEYmoNA; the latter is much more
   likely: Renaissance English shifted accents more often and more readily than
   does 21st-c. English
91 Montano has not yet heard her name
92 leader (highly rhetorical, as is Cassio himself)
93 setting foot on land
94 se'night's = seven night's ("a week")
95 Othello guard = guard Othello
96 love's quick pants = the short, rapid breathing of lovemaking
97 REnewed
98 extinguished
99 (a half-line from the Quarto, not in the Folio)

Cassio and the others kneel

Hall to thee, lady, and the grace of heaven,   85
Before, behind thee, and on every hand[100]
Enwheel[101] thee round!
Desdemona   I thank you, valiant[102] Cassio.
What tidings can you tell me of my lord?
Cassio   He is not yet arrived, nor know I aught
But that he's well, and will be shortly here.   90
Desdemona   O, but I fear – How lost you company?[103]
Cassio   The great contention[104] of the sea and skies
Parted our fellowship.[105] But, hark![106] A sail.
Voices within   A sail, a sail!

Sound of cannons within

Gentleman 2 They give their greeting to the citadel.[107]
This likewise is a friend.
Cassio   (*to Gentleman 2*) See for[108] the news.   95

exit Gentleman 2

(*to Iago*) Good ancient, you are welcome. (*to Emilia*) Welcome,
mistress.
Let it not gall[109] your patience, good Iago,

100 on every hand = from every quarter, on all sides
101 encircle, surround
102 stalwart, brave, bold (a conventional/polite usage)
103 companionship (sailing together)
104 strife, quarrel
105 parted our fellowship = divided/broke our partnership/company
106 a cry of excitement
107 fortress commanding the city/port★
108 see for = look for, try to find
109 chafe, vex, harass

That I extend[110] my manners.[111] 'Tis my breeding[112]
That gives[113] me this [114] show of courtesy.

CASSIO KISSES EMILIA

100 *Iago*   Sir, would[115] she give you so[116] much of her lips
      As of her tongue she oft bestows[117] on me,
      You'd have enough.

Desdemona   Alas, she has no speech.[118]

Iago   In faith, too much.
      I find it still when I have list[119] to sleep.

105   Marry, before your ladyship, I grant
      She puts[120] her tongue a little in her heart,
      And chides[121] with thinking.

Emilia   You have little cause[122] to say so.

Iago   Come on, come on.[123] You[124] are pictures[125] out of
      doors,
      Bells[126] in your parlors,[127] wild cats[128] in your kitchens,

110 stretch out, widen, enlarge
111 polite behavior
112 parentage, rearing, training
113 grants, bestows on
114 audacious, presumptuous
115 if she would
116 as
117 confers★
118 has no speech = can't/won't reply
119 desire, wish
120 sets, places
121 scolds, complains★
122 reason, motive★
123 come on: an expression of challenge/defiance
124 you women ("you're")
125 images/symbols (unreal representations)
126 (?) chattering noisemakers
127 private/domestic rooms
128 wild cats = savage, ill-tempered

Saints in your injuries,[129] devils being offended,   110
Players[130] in your housewifery, and housewives[131] in your
beds.

Desdemona O, fie upon thee,[132] slanderer!

Iago   Nay, it is true, or else[133] I am a Turk.[134]
You rise to play,[135] and go to bed to work.

Emilia   You shall not write my praise.

Iago   No, let me not.   115

Desdemona What wouldst thou write of me, if thou shouldst
praise me?

Iago   O gentle lady, do not put[136] me to't,
For I am nothing if not critical.[137]

Desdemona Come on, assay.[138] – There's one[139] gone to the
harbor?

Iago   Ay, madam.   120

Desdemona (aside) I am not merry,[140] but I do beguile[141]
The thing I am, by seeming otherwise.
(to Iago) Come, how wouldst thou praise me?

Iago   I am about it,[142] but indeed my invention[143]

---

129 in your injuries = when you are insulted/offended/injured
130 actors
131 hussies (women of low/improper behavior)
132 fie upon thee = for shame
133 otherwise
134 (1) cruel/tyrannical barbarian, (2) bad-tempered/unmanageable man
135 perform, frolic/fool about
136 urge, push, propose, suggest★
137 censorious, fault-finding
138 try
139 someone
140 cheerful
141 divert attention from
142 about it = busying myself/trying
143 inventiveness, powers of mental creation, imagination★

125   Comes from my pate[144] as birdlime[145] does from frize,[146]

        It plucks out brains and all. But my Muse labors,[147]

        And thus she is delivered:

        "If she be fair and wise, fairness and wit,

        The one's for use,[148] the other[149] useth it."

130 *Desdemona* Well praised. How if she be black[150] and witty?

    Iago   "If she be black, and thereto have a wit,

        She'll find a white[151] that shall her blackness fit."

    Desdemona Worse and worse.

    Emilia   How[152] if fair and foolish?

    Iago   "She never yet was foolish that was fair,

135   For even her folly helped her to[153] an heir."

    Desdemona These are old fond paradoxes to make fools laugh i'

        the alehouse.[154] What miserable praise hast thou for her that's

        foul and foolish?

    Iago   "There's none so foul and foolish thereunto,

140   But does foul pranks[155] which fair and wise ones do."

    Desdemona O heavy ignorance. Thou praisest the worst best. But

        what praise couldst thou bestow on[156] a deserving woman

---

144 head

145 birdlime = sticky plant-derived substance, spread on twigs/branches to snare birds

146 does from frize = comes/can be taken off coarse woolen cloth

147 is in labor/childbirth (the nine Muses were female)

148 wit, intelligence

149 beauty

150 foul, unattractive (foul: the opposite of fair)

151 a pun on "wight," meaning "person"?

152 what

153 to capture/marry a man who will inherit a fortune

154 pub ("bar," "saloon")

155 infamous/wicked tricks

156 bestow on = apply to

indeed?[157] One that, in the authority[158] of her merit, did
justly put on[159] the vouch of very malice[160] itself?

Iago   "She that was ever fair and never proud,   145
        Had tongue at will and yet was never loud.
        Never lacked gold and yet went never gay,[161]
        Fled from her wish, and yet said, 'Now I may.'
        She that, being angered, her revenge being nigh,
        Bade her wrong[162] stay[163] and her displeasure fly.[164]   150
        She that in wisdom never was so frail[165]
        To change the cod's head for the salmon's tail.[166]
        She that could think and ne'er disclose her mind,
        See suitors[167] following and not look behind[168]
        She was a wight,[169] if ever such wight were – "   155

Desdemona To do what?

Iago   To suckle fools[170] and chronicle small beer.[171]

Desdemona O most lame and impotent[172] conclusion! Do not

---

157 a deserving woman indeed = a woman indeed deserving
158 power
159 justly put on = correctly/rightfully/with good reason urge/encourage/
    entrust herself
160 vouch of very malice = declarations/statements of true/real wickedness★
161 too free in her conduct
162 (noun)
163 remain as it was
164 fly off/away
165 weak, easily overcome
166 cod's head for the salmon's tail = the ugly, edible part of a common fish for
    the beautiful, inedible part of an expensive fish
167 wooers
168 back
169 creature
170 babies were often referred to as "fools"
171 chronicle small beer = keep track/a record of trifles/trivial matters (i.e., be
    in charge of household affairs)
172 lame and impotent = unsatisfactory/defective and ineffectual/powerless/
    decrepit

learn of[173] him, Emilia, though he be thy husband. How say
160   you, Cassio? Is he not a most profane and liberal[174]
       counselor?

   Cassio He speaks home,[175] madam. You may relish[176] him
       more in the soldier than in the scholar.

   Iago   (aside) He takes her by the palm. Ay, well said, whisper.
165   With as little a web as this, will I ensnare as great a fly[177] as
       Cassio. Ay, smile upon her, do. I will gyve[178] thee in thine
       own courtship. You say true, 'tis so, indeed. If such tricks[179] as
       these strip[180] you out of your lieutenantry, it had been better
       you had not kissed your three fingers so oft, which now again
170   you are most apt[181] to play the sir in. Very good, well kissed,
       an excellent courtesy.[182] 'Tis so, indeed. Yet again, your
       fingers to your lips? Would they were clyster pipes[183] for
       your sake![184]

TRUMPET WITHIN

   (to the others) The Moor. I know his trumpet.[185]

   Cassio   'Tis truly so.

---

173 from
174 licentious, unrestrained by decorum (can also mean bountiful, generous, not
    its meaning here)★
175 to the heart of the matter
176 take pleasure, enjoy
177 great a fly = large and insignificant creature (?)
178 fetter, shackle
179 stratagems, shams, semblances★
180 deprive, divest, remove
181 ready, likely, disposed★
182 polite elegance
183 clyster pipes = enema tubes/syringes
184 for your sake = on account of your offenses (?)
185 trumpeter

Desdemona	Let's meet[186] him, and receive[187] him.	175
Cassio	Lo, where[188] he comes.	

ENTER OTHELLO AND ATTENDANTS

Othello   O my fair warrior.

Desdemona   My dear Othello.

Othello   It gives me wonder great as my content

To see you here before me. O my soul's joy.

If after every tempest come such calms,   180

May the winds blow till they have wakened[189] death,

And let the laboring bark[190] climb hills of seas

Olympus-high,[191] and duck[192] again as low

As hell's[193] from heaven. If it were now[194] to die,

'Twere now to be most happy, for I fear   185

My soul hath her content so absolute[195]

That not another comfort like to this

Succeeds[196] in unknown fate.

Desdemona   The heavens forbid

But that[197] our loves and comforts should increase

Even as our days do grow.

---

186 go to meet
187 greet, welcome★
188 there
189 stirred into action, aroused
190 laboring bark = pitching/rolling/struggling ship
191 Olympus-high = as high as Mt. Olympus, at the summit of which lived the
    Greek gods
192 plunge
193 hell is
194 if it were now = if this was the time
195 perfect, consummate★
196 follows, comes after
197 but that = anything but/except that

190 *Othello*   Amen to that, sweet powers.[198]

I cannot speak enough of this content,

It stops[199] me here.[200] It is too much of joy.

And this,[201] and this,[202] the greatest discords be

HE KISSES HER

That e'er our hearts shall make.

Iago   (*aside*) O, you are well

tuned[203] now!

195 But I'll set down[204] the pegs[205] that make this music,

As honest as I am.

Othello   Come, let us to the castle.[206]

(*greeting Cypriots*) News, friends, our wars are done, the Turks
are drowned.

How does my old acquaintance[207] of this isle?

(*to Desdemona*) Honey, you shall be well desired[208] in Cyprus,

200 I have found great love amongst them. O my sweet,

I prattle out of fashion,[209] and I dote

In[210] mine own comforts. I prithee, good Iago,

198 the "heavens"
199 closes, plugs up
200 his heart
201 may this
202 (1) two separate references, one to his heart, one as he reaches down to kiss
    her, or (2) repetition as emphasis, and both references being to kissing
203 well tuned = you're singing the right song, you've got the correct melody
204 slacken
205 tuning pins (on which the strings of a musical instrument are wound)
206 come LETS to the CASTle
207 does my old acquaintance = are my old friends/acquaintances
208 well desired = in demand, popular
209 out of fashion = impolitely, contrary to customary standards/rules
210 dote in = am infatuated by

Go to the bay and disembark my coffers.[211]
Bring thou the master[212] to the citadel.
He is a good one, and his worthiness   205
Does challenge much respect. Come, Desdemona,
Once more well met at Cyprus.

    EXEUNT OTHELLO, DESDEMONA, AND ATTENDANTS

Iago   (*to Roderigo*) Do thou meet me presently at the harbor.
Come hither. If thou be'st[213] valiant – as they say base men
being in love have then a nobility in their natures more than   210
is native to them – list[214] me. The lieutenant tonight
watches[215] on the court of guard.[216] First, I must tell thee
this. Desdemona is directly[217] in love with him.

Roderigo With him? Why, 'tis not possible.

Iago   Lay thy finger thus (*across his lips*), and let thy soul be   215
instructed. Mark me with what violence[218] she first loved the
Moor, but for bragging, and telling her fantastical lies. And
will she love him still for prating? Let not thy discreet[219]
heart think it. Her eye[220] must be fed. And what delight shall
she have to look on[221] the devil?[222] When the blood is made   220

---

211 disembark my coffers = bring ashore my boxes/chests ("luggage")
212 pilot or captain
213 be'st = are (second-person singular of "be")
214 listen to
215 is to be a guard/watchman
216 court of guard = body of military men posted on guard (corps de garde)?
217 absolutely, entirely
218 extreme/excessive ardor/passion
219 sage, prudent
220 eyes?
221 at
222 wretched/ugly fellow (Othello)

dull with the act of sport,[223] there should[224] be a game[225] to
inflame it and to give satiety a fresh appetite. Loveliness in
favor, sympathy in years, manners, and beauties, all which the
Moor is defective in. Now, for want[226] of these required
225   conveniences,[227] her delicate tenderness[228] will find itself
abused, begin to heave the gorge,[229] disrelish[230] and abhor
the Moor. Very nature[231] will instruct her in it, and compel
her to some second choice. Now sir, this granted – as it is a
most pregnant and unforced position[232] – who stands so
230   eminent[233] in the degree[234] of this fortune as Cassio does?
A knave very voluble,[235] no further conscionable[236] than
in putting on the mere form of civil[237] and humane[238]
seeming, for the better compass of his salt[239] and most
hidden loose affection?[240] Why, none, why, none. A slipper

223 dull with the act of sport = sluggish/slow by amorous dalliance/sexual
      intercourse
224 must
225 amusement, fun★
226 lack★
227 suitabilities, comforts, advantages
228 delicate tenderness = voluptuous/self-indulgent weakness/fragility/
      womanishness
229 heave the gorge = vomit (gorge = throat)
230 dislike
231 very nature = sheer nature, nature itself
232 pregnant and unforced position = weighty/compelling and natural
      proposition/assertion
233 prominent, high, conspicuous
234 process (the steps/stages up or down), standing, rank★
235 (1) glib, ready of speech, (2) volatile, inconstant
236 scrupulous, conscientious
237 form of civil = fashion of civilized/orderly/refined
238 kindly, courteous, compassionate
239 pungent, excessive
240 loose affection = unattached/ roving lust/passion

and subtle[241] knave, a finder out of occasions,[242] that has an   235
eye can stamp[243] and counterfeit advantages,[244] though true
advantage never present itself. A devilish knave. Besides, the
knave is handsome, young, and hath all those requisites in him
that folly and green[245] minds look after.[246] A pestilent
complete knave, and the woman hath found him already.   240

Roderigo I cannot believe that in her, she is full of most blessed
condition.[247]

Iago   Blest fig's end.[248] The wine she drinks is made of
grapes. If she had been blessed, she would never have loved
the Moor. Blessed pudding.[249] Didst thou not see her   245
paddle[250] with the palm of his hand? Didst not mark that?

Roderigo Yes, that I did. But that was but courtesy.

Iago   Lechery, by this hand.[251] An index[252] and obscure[253]
prologue to the history[254] of lust and foul thoughts. They
met so near[255] with their lips that their breaths embraced   250
together. Villainous[256] thoughts, Roderigo. When these

---

241 slipper and subtle = slippery and elusive / clever / crafty / sly
242 opportunities
243 can stamp = which can fabricate
244 opportunities
245 unripe, immature
246 look after = pursue
247 state of being
248 see act 1, scene 3, note 295
249 (1) pudding, (2) animal guts / intestines
250 play fondly
251 by this hand: an oath (compare "by my foot," "by my head," "by my nose,"
    etc.)
252 table of contents
253 dark, elusive
254 narrative, tale, story
255 close
256 wicked, depraved

mutualities[257] so marshal[258] the way, hard at hand[259] comes the master[260] and main exercise,[261] th'incorporate[262] conclusion. Pish! But, sir, be you ruled[263] by me. I have

255 brought you from Venice. Watch you tonight. For[264] the command,[265] I'll lay't upon you.[266] Cassio knows you not. I'll not be far from you. Do you find some occasion to anger Cassio, either by speaking too loud, or tainting[267] his discipline,[268] or from what other course you please, which

260 the time shall more favorably minister.[269]

Roderigo Well.

Iago　Sir, he is rash, and very sudden in choler,[270] and haply[271] may strike at you. Provoke him, that he may, for even out of that will I cause these of Cyprus to mutiny, whose

265 qualification[272] shall[273] come into no true taste[274] again but by the displanting[275] of Cassio. So shall you have a shorter journey to your desires, by the means I shall then have to

257 intimacies
258 arrange, guide, point out
259 hard at hand = close behind
260 governing
261 practice, exertion
262 united in one body
263 guided, governed
264 as for
265 commend [noun] = telling you what you're to do
266 lay't upon = give it to
267 insulting
268 military skill
269 supply
270 anger, irascibility
271 perhaps, maybe
272 character, nature
273 must thereafter
274 liking
275 supplanting, replacing

prefer[276] them. And the impediment most profitably[277]
removed, without the which there were no expectation of
our prosperity.[278]   270

Roderigo I will do this, if I can bring[279] it to any opportunity.[280]

Iago   I warrant[281] thee. Meet me by and by[282] at the citadel.
   I must fetch his[283] necessaries ashore. Farewell.

Roderigo Adieu.

EXIT RODERIGO

Iago   That Cassio loves her, I do well believe't.   275
   That she loves him, 'tis apt,[284] and of great credit.
   The Moor, howbeit that[285] I endure him not,[286]
   Is of a constant, loving, noble nature,
   And I dare think he'll prove to Desdemona
   A most dear[287] husband. Now, I do love her too,   280
   Not out of absolute lust – though peradventure[288]
   I stand accountant[289] for as great a sin[290] –
   But partly led to diet[291] my revenge,

276 advance, promote
277 advantageously, beneficially
278 success
279 lead, conduct
280 timeliness, seasonableness
281 guarantee, promise
282 immediately, at once★
283 Othello's
284 appropriate
285 howbeit that = although
286 endure him not = cannot stand him
287 worthy, loving (is there a pun on "dear" as "costly"?)
288 perchance, perhaps
289 responsible
290 (the revenge he immediately proceeds to speak of?)
291 feed

For that I do suspect the lusty[292] Moor

285   Hath leaped into my seat.[293] The thought whereof

Doth, like a poisonous mineral, gnaw my inwards,[294]

And nothing can or shall content my soul

Till I am evened with him, wife for wife,

Or, failing so, yet that I put the Moor

290   At least into a jealousy so strong

That judgment[295] cannot cure.[296] Which thing to do,

If this poor trash[297] of Venice, whom I trace[298]

For his quick hunting,[299] stand[300] the putting on,[301]

I'll have our Michael Cassio on the hip,[302]

295   Abuse him to the Moor in the rank garb[303]

(For I fear Cassio with[304] my night-cap[305] too),

Make the Moor thank me, love me, and reward me

For making him egregiously[306] an ass

And practicing[307] upon his peace and quiet

292 lustful, libidinous
293 place (as a husband)
294 guts ("insides")
295 discernment, critical thinking, reason
296 cure it
297 worthless/disreputable person
298 pursue
299 for his quick hunting = in order to rapidly catch/fleece him
300 will/can endure
301 putting on = driving, incitement
302 on the hip = at a disadvantage (as in wrestling)
303 rank garb = lustful/licentious* style/manner/fashion
304 might be wearing
305 men and women slept with their heads covered, for warmth
306 remarkably, grossly
307 plotting, scheming, conspiring

Even to madness. 'Tis[308] here, but yet confused.[309]   300
Knavery's plain[310] face is never seen till used.[311]

EXIT

308 the idea/plan is
309 not as yet in order/fully clear
310 open, direct, bare
311 employed

SCENE 2

A street

Herald It is Othello's pleasure, our noble and valiant general, that
    upon certain[1] tidings now arrived, importing[2] the mere
    perdition[3] of the Turkish fleet, every man put[4] himself into
    triumph,[5] some to dance, some to make bonfires, each man
5   to what[6] sport and revels[7] his addiction[8] leads him. For
    besides these beneficial [9] news, it[10] is the celebration of his
    nuptial. So much[11] was[12] his pleasure should be proclaimed.
    All offices[13] are open, and there is full liberty[14] of feasting
    from this present hour of five till the bell have told eleven.
10 Heaven bless the isle of Cyprus and our noble general
    Othello!

EXEUNT

1 reliable, precise
2 signifying, meaning★
3 destruction, ruin★
4 is to put
5 joyful celebration, public festivity
6 whatever
7 noisy mirth/merry making
8 inclination, leaning
9 advantageous
10 this
11 so much = thus
12 was it
13 kitchens, stores of food
14 unhindered authorization/opportunity/permission ("license")

SCENE 3

The Citadel, Cyprus

ENTER OTHELLO, DESDEMONA, CASSIO, AND ATTENDANTS

Othello Good Michael, look you to the guard tonight.
  Let's teach ourselves that honorable stop,[1]
  Not to outsport discretion.[2]

Cassio Iago hath direction[3] what to do.
  But notwithstanding, with my personal[4] eye   5
  Will I look to't.

Othello   Iago is most honest.
  Michael, good night. Tomorrow with your earliest,[5]
  Let me have speech with you. (*to Desdemona*) Come, my dear
  love.
  The purchase[6] made, the fruits[7] are to ensue:
  That profit's[8] yet to come 'tween me and you.   10
  (*to Cassio*) Goodnight.

EXEUNT OTHELLO, DESDEMONA, AND ATTENDANTS

ENTER IAGO

Cassio Welcome, Iago. We must to the watch.[9]

---

1 check, restraint, holding back
2 outsport discretion = indulge / amuse ourselves beyond reasonable / rational
  limits
3 instructions / guidance★
4 own
5 with your earliest = as early as you can make it
6 acquisition, capture, bargain
7 revenue, consequences, enjoyment
8 profit's = benefit / gain is
9 guard duty

Iago Not this hour,[10] lieutenant, 'tis not yet ten o' th' clock.
Our general cast[11] us thus early for the love of his
15 Desdemona, who let us not therefore blame. He hath not yet
made wanton[12] the night with her. And she is sport for Jove.

Cassio She's a most exquisite[13] lady.

Iago And, I'll warrant her, full of game.

Cassio Indeed, she is a most fresh[14] and delicate creature.

20 *Iago* What an eye[15] she has! Methinks it sounds a parley to[16]
provocation.[17]

Cassio An inviting[18] eye. And yet methinks right modest.[19]

Iago And when she speaks, is it not an alarm[20] to love?

Cassio She is, indeed, perfection.

25 *Iago* Well. Happiness to their sheets.[21] Come, lieutenant, I
have a stoup[22] of wine, and here without[23] are a brace[24] of
Cyprus gallants[25] that would fain[26] have a measure[27] to the
health of black Othello.

10 not this hour = not yet
11 shed, sent, got rid of
12 amorously sexual★
13 excellent, beautiful
14 invigorating, untainted, not faded/worn★
15 an eye = a look
16 sounds a parley to = gives a call/summons to a conference/discussion
   leading to
17 incitement, stimulus
18 alluring, tempting, attractive
19 right modest = altogether/completely decorous, proper
20 call to arms, signal
21 sexual activity in bed
22 jar (alcohol was not bottled)
23 outside★
24 pair
25 Cyprus gallants = local fashionable/polished gentlemen
26 be pleased/glad to★
27 tankard ("quantity," "some")

Cassio Not tonight, good Iago. I have very poor and unhappy[28]
    brains for drinking. I could well wish courtesy[29] would   30
    invent some other custom of entertainment.

Iago O, they[30] are our friends. But one cup. I'll drink for you.

Cassio I have drunk but one cup tonight, and that was craftily
    qualified[31] too. And behold, what innovation[32] it makes
    here.[33] I am unfortunate in the infirmity,[34] and dare not   35
    task[35] my weakness with any more.

Iago What, man, 'tis a night of revels. The gallants desire it.

Cassio Where are they?

Iago Here at the door. I pray you, call them in.

Cassio I'll do't, but it dislikes me.[36]   40

EXIT CASSIO

Iago If I can fasten but one cup upon him,[37]
    With that which he hath drunk tonight already
    He'll be as full of quarrel and offense
    As my young mistress'[38] dog. Now, my sick[39] fool Roderigo,
    Whom love hath turned almost the wrong side out,   45

---

28 poor and unhappy = deficient/feeble and unfortunate/miserable/
    wretched
29 polite cultivated society
30 these Cypriots? all Cypriots?
31 skillfully/cleverly restricted/restrained/measured out
32 alteration, change
33 in me
34 limitation, weakness
35 strain, stress
36 it dislikes me = it displeases/annoys/offends me
37 fasten ... upon him = induce him to accept
38 Desdemona (wife of his master)
39 deeply affected by longing ("lovesick")

To[40] Desdemona hath tonight caroused[41]
Potations pottle-deep,[42] and he's to watch.[43]
Three lads of Cyprus, noble swelling[44] spirits,
That hold their honors in a wary distance,[45]
50   The very elements[46] of this warlike isle,
Have I tonight flustered[47] with flowing cups,
And they watch[48] too. Now, 'mongst this flock[49] of drunkards,
Am I to put[50] our Cassio in some action[51]
That may offend[52] the isle.

    ENTER CASSIO, WITH MONTANO AND GENTLEMEN

55   But here they come.
If consequence[53] do but approve my dream,[54]
My boat sails freely, both with wind and stream.
Cassio 'Fore[55] heaven, they have given me a rouse[56] already.

40 in pledge / as toasts to
41 drunk freely / repeatedly, swilled
42 potations pottle-deep = drinks / draughts measuring two quarts (one pottle) down to the bottom
43 he's to watch = he is assigned to guard duty
44 proud, haughty, pretentiously pompous
45 in a wary distance = at a careful / cautious fixed interval ("aloofness")
46 basic substances
47 made half-tipsy
48 are on guard duty
49 band, company
50 am I to put = I am going / planning to push / propel / drive
51 in some action = into some deed
52 transgress / sin against, anger★
53 the results
54 approve my dream = confirm / make good my fancies / vision
55 by ("before")
56 full draught / bumper

Montano Good faith, a little one. Not past[57] a pint, as I am a
  soldier.

Iago   Some wine, ho!   60

HE SINGS

  And let me the cannakin[58] clink, clink,
  And let me the cannakin clink.
    A soldier's a man,
    O, man's life's but a span,
  Why then let a soldier drink.   65

  (*calls to servants*) Some wine, boys!

Cassio 'Fore God, an excellent song.

Iago   I learned it in England, where indeed they are most
  potent[59] in potting.[60] Your Dane, your German, and your
  swag-bellied[61] Hollander – Drink, ho! – are nothing to your   70
  English.

Cassio Is your Englishman so exquisite[62] in his drinking?

Iago   Why, he drinks you – with facility[63] – your Dane dead
  drunk. He sweats not to overthrow[64] your Almain.[65] He
  gives your Hollander a vomit[66] ere the next pottle can be   75
  filled.

57 more than
58 small can / drinking vessel
59 mighty
60 drinking
61 pendulous-paunched ("beer-bellied")
62 excellent, cultivated
63 with facility = easily
64 sweats not to overthrow = does not work/labor to defeat/demolish/ruin
65 German
66 gives ... a vomit = makes ... vomit

Cassio   To the health of our general!

Montano I am for it, lieutenant. And I'll do you justice.[67]

Iago   O sweet England!

IAGO SINGS

80   King Stephen was and-a[68] worthy peer,[69]

His breeches cost him but a crown,[70]

He held them sixpence all too dear,[71]

With that he called the tailor lown.[72]

He[73] was a wight of high renown,[74]

85   And thou[75] art but of low degree.[76]

'Tis pride that pulls the country down,

Then take[77] thine auld[78] cloak about thee.

(*to servants*) Some wine, ho!

Cassio   Why, this is a more exquisite song than the other.

90 *Iago*   Will[79] you hear it again?

Cassio   No. For I hold him to be unworthy of his place that does those things. Well, God's above all, and there be souls must be saved, and there be souls must not be saved.

Iago   It's true, good lieutenant.

67 do you justice = drink it down just as you do
68 and-a = balladic rhetorical and metrical device
69 nobleman
70 gold coin (worth 5 shillings; 1 shilling = 12 pence)
71 all too dear = too expensive
72 a rogue / rascal
73 King Stephen
74 fame, distinction
75 the tailor
76 social position / rank
77 then take = so wrap
78 old
79 do you wish to

Cassio　　For mine own part, no offense to the general, nor any　95
　　　　　man of quality, I hope to be saved.

Iago　　　And so do I too, lieutenant.

Cassio　　Ay, but, by your leave, not before me. The lieutenant
　　　　　is to be saved before the ancient. Let's have no more of this.
　　　　　Let's to our affairs. Forgive us our sins. Gentlemen, let's look　100
　　　　　to our business. Do not think, gentlemen, I am drunk. This is
　　　　　my ancient, this is my right hand, and this is my left. I am not
　　　　　drunk now. I can stand well enough, and I speak well enough.

Gentlemen　Excellent well.

Cassio　　Why, very well then. You must not think, then, that I　105
　　　　　am drunk.

EXIT CASSIO

Montano　To the platform,[80] masters. Come, let's set[81] the
　　　　　watch.

Iago　　　You see this fellow that is[82] gone before,
　　　　　He is a soldier fit to stand by Caesar
　　　　　And give direction. And do but see his vice.　　　110
　　　　　'Tis to his virtue a just equinox,[83]
　　　　　The one as long as the other. 'Tis pity of[84] him.
　　　　　I fear the trust Othello puts him in,
　　　　　On some odd[85] time of his infirmity
　　　　　Will shake[86] this island.

80 level place for cannon
81 station (verb)
82 has
83 just equinox = equal balance (of the length of day and of night, as the sun
　　crosses the equator)
84 concerning, about
85 singular, unusual
86 agitate ("destabilize")

115 *Montano*   But is he often thus?

Iago   'Tis evermore[87] his prologue to his sleep.

He'll watch the horologe[88] a double set[89]

If drink rock not his cradle.

Montano   It were well

The general were put in mind[90] of it.

120   Perhaps he sees it not, or his good nature

Prizes[91] the virtue that appears in Cassio,

And looks not on[92] his evils. Is not this true?

ENTER RODERIGO

Iago   (*aside*) How now, Roderigo?

I pray you after the lieutenant, go.

EXIT RODERIGO

125 *Montano* And 'tis great pity that the noble Moor

Should hazard[93] such a place as his own second

With one of an ingraft[94] infirmity:

It were an honest action to say

So to the Moor.

Iago   Not I, for[95] this fair island.

130   I do love Cassio well, and would do much

---

87 always
88 clock (HOARaLOWDGE)
89 a double set = two passages from 1 to 12, or 24 hours (i.e., be unable to fall asleep)
90 put in mind = made aware
91 values, esteems★
92 at
93 risk
94 fixed, attached
95 not even for

CRY WITHIN, "HELP, HELP"

To cure him of this evil. But, hark,[96] what noise?

ENTER CASSIO, PURSUING RODERIGO

Cassio	You rogue! You rascal!
Montano	What's the matter, lieutenant?
Cassio	A knave teach me my duty? I'll beat the knave into a
	twiggen[97] bottle.
Roderigo	Beat me?
Cassio	Dost thou prate, rogue?

135

STRIKES RODERIGO

Montano	Nay, good lieutenant. I pray you, sir, hold your hand.
Cassio	Let me go, sir, or I'll knock you o'er the mazard.[98]
Montano	Come, come, you're drunk.
Cassio	Drunk?

140

THEY FIGHT

Iago   (*aside to Rodrigo*) Away, I say, go out and cry[99] a mutiny.

EXIT RODERIGO

Nay, good lieutenant – Alas, gentlemen[100] –
Help, ho! – lieutenant – sir – Montano – sir –
Help, masters! Here's a goodly[101] watch indeed.

96 hear, listen★
97 wickerwork
98 head ("bowl, cup")
99 shout, exclaim, proclaim
100 Cassio and Montano
101 splendid, admirable, proper

BELL RINGS

145 Who's that which rings the bell? Diablo,[102] ho!
The town will rise.[103] Fie, fie, lieutenant,
You'll be ashamed forever.

ENTER OTHELLO AND ATTENDANTS

Othello   What is the matter here?

Montano   Zounds, I bleed still,
I am hurt to th'death. He dies![104]

MONTANO LUNGES AT CASSIO

Othello   Hold, for your lives!

150 *Iago*   Hold, ho – lieutenant – sir – Montano – gentlemen –
Have you forgot all place[105] of[106] sense and duty?
Hold! The general speaks to you. Hold, for shame!

Othello   Why, how now, ho? From whence ariseth this?
Are we turned Turks, and to ourselves do that

155 Which heaven hath forbid the Ottomites?[107]
For Christian shame, put by[108] this barbarous brawl.[109]
He that stirs next, to carve for[110] his own rage,
Holds his soul light.[111] He dies upon his motion.[112]

---

102 the Devil
103 take up arms, rebel
104 he dies = he must / will die
105 location, where you are (*O.E.D.,* s.v. "place," 5c, cites a 1704 lexicon: "Place in Fortification usually signifies the Body of a Fortress")
106 with respect to
107 Islamic law forbid Moslem soldiers to tight with one another
108 to the side
109 squabble, quarrel
110 carve for = cut / slash because of
111 holds his soul light = considers his life of little importance
112 dies upon his motion = will die the moment he moves

Silence that dreadful[113] bell, it frights the isle
From her propriety.[114] What is the matter, masters?   160
Honest Iago, that looks dead[115] with grieving,
Speak. Who began this? On thy love,[116] I charge thee.

Iago   I do not know. Friends all,[117] but now,[118] even[119] now,
In quarter,[120] and in terms[121] like bride and groom
Devesting them[122] for bed. And then, but now –   165
As if some planet[123] had unwitted[124] men –
Swords out, and tilting[125] one at other's breasts
In opposition[126] bloody. I cannot speak[127]
Any beginning to this peevish odds,[128]
And would,[129] in action glorious,[130] I had lost   170
Those legs that brought me to a part of it![131]

Othello   How comes it, Michael, you are thus forgot?[132]

Cassio   I pray you, pardon me, I cannot speak.

113 inspiring dread/fear
114 her propriety = its proper state/condition
115 benumbed, insensible
116 devotion, regard
117 friends all = everyone was friendly, all were good friends
118 but now = until now
119 precisely, exactly
120 in quarter = in this guard period
121 in terms = in (1) mutual relations, (2) words
122 undressing themselves
123 astronomical influence
124 deprived of their brains/wits
125 thrusting, striking
126 antagonism, hostility, combat
127 state
128 peevish odds = foolish/senseless/mad/perverse strife/disturbance (a noun
    in the singular)
129 I wish, I had rather
130 action glorious = fighting which was full of glory
131 to a part of it = to be involved ("a party") in it
132 lost yourself/sight of your duty/position

Othello   Worthy Montano, you were wont to be civil.[133]

175   The gravity and stillness[134] of your youth

The world hath noted, and your name is great

In mouths of wisest censure.[135] What's the matter

That you unlace[136] your reputation thus,

And spend[137] your rich opinion[138] for the name

180   Of a night-brawler? Give me answer to it.

Montano   Worthy Othello, I am hurt to[139] danger.

Your officer, Iago, can inform you –

While I spare speech, which something[140] now offends[141] me –

Of all that I do know, nor know I aught

185   By me that's said or done amiss[142] this night,

Unless self-charity[143] be sometimes a vice,

And to defend ourselves it be a sin

When violence assails[144] us.

Othello   Now, by heaven,

My blood begins my safer guides[145] to rule,[146]

190   And passion, having my best judgment collied,[147]

133 wont to be civil = in the habit★ of being polite
134 gravity and stillness = sobriety and calm/tranquillity
135 opinion, judgment
136 destroy, undo
137 give away, exhaust, consume, destroy
138 reputation
139 almost to, to the point of
140 to a degree (in British usage, "rather")
141 hurts, pains
142 wrongly, out of order
143 charity = love
144 attacks, assaults
145 safer guides = more cautious guidance/sense of direction/control
146 control, dominate
147 darkened

Assays to lead the way. If I once stir,[148]
Or do but lift this arm, the best[149] of you
Shall sink[150] in my rebuke.[151] Give me to know
How this foul rout[152] began. Who set it on,[153]
And he that is approved[154] in this offense,   195
Though he had twinned[155] with me, both at a[156] birth,
Shall lose[157] me. What, in a town of war
Yet wild,[158] the people's hearts brimful of fear,
To manage[159] private and domestic[160] quarrel,
In night, and on the court and guard of safety?[161]   200
'Tis monstrous.[162] Iago, who began't?

Montano (to Iago) If partially affined, or leagued in office,[163]

Thou dost deliver more or less than truth,

Thou art no soldier.

Iago   Touch[164] me not so near.[165]

I had rather have this tongue cut from my mouth   205

148 act, take action
149 best swordsmen / fighters
150 go under / to hell, be swallowed, perish
151 reprimand (often, then, given by blows)
152 riot, disturbance, uproar
153 set it on = instigated / incited / set in motion / started it
154 proved, convicted
155 been born as one of a pair of twins
156 at a = at one and the same
157 be separated from, deprived of
158 unruly, turbulent, highly excited
159 carry on, conduct
160 internal
161 protection
162 absurd, outrageously wrong, atrocious
163 partially affined, or leagued in office = unfairly / in any biased way related /
    connected, or joined in duty / service
164 strike, beat at, affect★
165 deeply

Than it should do offense[166] to Michael Cassio.
Yet I persuade myself, to speak the truth
Shall nothing wrong him. Thus it is, general.
Montano and myself being in speech,
210   There comes a fellow crying out for help,
And Cassio following him with determined[167] sword,
To execute upon[168] him. Sir, this gentleman
Steps in to[169] Cassio and entreats his pause.
Myself the crying[170] fellow did pursue,
215   Lest by his clamor[171] – as it so fell out[172] –
The town might fall in[173] fright. He, swift of foot,
Outran my purpose, and I returned the rather[174]
For that I heard the clink and fall[175] of swords,
And Cassio high in oath.[176] Which till tonight
220   I ne'er might say before. When I came back,
For this was brief, I found them[177] close together
At blow and thrust, even as again they were
When you yourself did part them.
More of this matter cannot I report,
225   But men are men. The best sometimes forget.
Though Cassio did some little wrong to him,[178]

166 harm, injury
167 unwavering
168 execute upon = (1) use / wield it on, (2) kill
169 steps in to = comes forward to, intervenes with
170 roaring, shouting
171 noisy utterance
172 fell out = happened, came to pass
173 fall in = yield to
174 the rather = all the more quickly
175 clink and fall = sharp ringing sounds and downward strokes
176 high in oath = forcefully / strongly / loudly swearing
177 Montano and Cassio
178 Montano

As men in rage strike those that wish them best,
Yet surely Cassio, I believe, received
From him that fled some strange indignity,[179]
Which patience could not pass.[180]

Othello   I know, Iago,   230
Thy honesty and love doth mince[181] this matter,
Making it light[182] to Cassio. Cassio, I love thee,
But never more be officer of mine.

ENTER DESDEMONA, ATTENDED

Look, if my gentle love be not raised up.
(*to Cassio*) I'll make thee an example.[183]   235
Desdemona What is the matter, dear?
Othello   All's well now, sweeting.[184]
Come away to bed. (*to Montano*) Sir, for your hurts,
Myself will be[185] your surgeon.[186] Lead him off.

EXIT MONTANO, ATTENDED

Iago, look with care about the town,
And silence those whom this vile[187] brawl distracted.[188]   240
Come, Desdemona, 'tis the soldier's life,

---

179 strange indignity = uncommon/exceptional/extreme dishonor/disgrace
180 accept, allow, tolerate
181 diminish, lessen, minimize
182 of reduced weight/importance
183 warning★
184 sweetheart, darling
185 myself will be = for my part ("on my side/as for me"), I wish to be
    responsible for
186 medical man, doctor★
187 disgusting, depraved
188 carried away/into disorder

To have their balmy[189] slumbers waked with strife.

EXEUNT ALL BUT IAGO AND CASSIO

Iago What, are you hurt, lieutenant?

Cassio Ay, past all surgery.[190]

245 *Iago* Marry, heaven forbid!

Cassio Reputation, reputation, reputation! O, I have lost my reputation. I have lost the immortal part of myself, and what remains is bestial.[191] My reputation, Iago, my reputation.

Iago As I am an honest man, I thought you[192] had received
250 some bodily wound. There is more sense[193] in that than in reputation. Reputation is an idle and most false imposition,[194] oft got without merit and lost without deserving. You have lost no reputation at all, unless you repute[195] yourself such a loser. What, man! There are ways to
255 recover[196] the general again. You are but now cast[197] in his mood,[198] a punishment more in policy[199] than in malice,[200] even so as one would beat his offenseless dog to affright[201] an imperious[202] lion. Sue[203] to him again, and he is yours.

---

189 delightful, soothing
190 medical treatment
191 mere animal
192 you were saying that you
193 (1) capacity for sensation, (2) common sense, intelligence
194 ascription, bestowal, placing on
195 consider, think, reckon
196 regain, win back
197 discarded, cashiered, thrown off⋆
198 anger, temper
199 a stratagem
200 ill-will
201 frighten, intimidate
202 overbearing (?), majestic (?)
203 appeal, petition (verb)

Cassio I will rather[204] sue to be despised than to deceive[205] so
   good a commander with so slight,[206] so drunken, and so   260
   indiscreet[207] an officer. Drunk? And speak parrot?[208] And
   squabble? Swagger?[209] Swear? And discourse fustian[210] with
   one's own shadow?[211] O thou invisible spirit of wine, if thou
   hast no name to be known by, let us call thee devil.

Iago What was he that you followed with your sword? What   265
   had he done to you?

Cassio I know not.

Iago Is't possible?

Cassio I remember a mass[212] of things, but nothing distinctly. A
   quarrel, but nothing[213] wherefore. O God, that men should   270
   put an enemy in their mouths to steal away their brains? That
   we should, with joy, pleasance, revel, and applause, transform
   ourselves into beasts.

Iago Why, but you are now well enough. How came you thus
   recovered?   275

Cassio It hath pleased the devil drunkenness to give place to the
   devil wrath. One unperfectness shows me another, to make
   me frankly[214] despise myself.

Iago Come, you are too severe a moraler.[215] As the time, the

204 will rather = would prefer to
205 betray
206 feeble, foolish, worthless, insignificant
207 lacking judgment, imprudent
208 senselessly
209 bluster, act superior
210 gibberish, rant, bombast
211 someone/something completely fleeting/ephemeral/delusive
212 amorphous lump, a quantity
213 nothing about
214 unreservedly, unconditionally
215 moralizer

280   place, and the condition of this country stands, I could
heartily wish this had not befallen.[216] But since it is as it is,
mend it for your own good.

    Cassio I will ask[217] him for my place again, he shall tell me I am
a drunkard. Had I as many mouths as Hydra,[218] such an
285   answer would stop[219] them all. To be now[220] a sensible man,
by and by a fool, and presently a beast. O strange! Every
inordinate[221] cup is unblessed, and the ingredient[222] is a
devil.

    Iago   Come, come. Good wine is a good familiar[223] creature, if
290   it be well used. Exclaim no more against it. And, good
lieutenant, I think you think I love you.

    Cassio I have well approved it, sir. I drunk?

    Iago   You, or any man living, may be drunk at a time,[224] man.
I'll tell you what you shall[225] do. Our general's wife is now
295   the general. I may say so, in this respect,[226] for that he hath
devoted and given up himself to the contemplation,[227]
mark,[228] and denotement[229] of her parts and graces. Confess

216 happened, occurred
217 if I ask
218 mythological many-headed snake, whose heads grew back as fast as they
    were cut off
219 plug, close up
220 first
221 immoderate, intemperate
222 substance that enters into it
223 (1) friendly, tame, congenial (2) ordinary, everyday
224 a time = some time
225 must
226 connection
227 beholding/thinking about
228 attention, notice
229 indications, appearances★

yourself freely to her. Importune[230] her help to put you in
your place again. She is of so free,[231] so kind, so apt, so blessed
a disposition, she holds it a vice in her goodness not to do   300
more than she is requested. This broken joint[232] between you
and her husband entreat her to splinter.[233] And, my fortunes
against any lay[234] worth naming, this crack of[235] your love
shall grow stronger than it was before.

Cassio You advise me well.   305

Iago I protest,[236] in the sincerity of love and honest kindness.

Cassio I think it freely.[237] And betimes in the morning I will
beseech the virtuous Desdemona to undertake[238] for me. I
am desperate of[239] my fortunes if they[240] check[241] me here.

Iago You are in the right. Goodnight, lieutenant, I must to the   310
watch.

Cassio Good night, honest Iago.

EXIT CASSIO

Iago And what's he, then, that says I play the villain?
When this advice is free[242] I give, and honest,

---

230 solicit, ask for, urge, press★
231 generous
232 connection
233 fix with a splint
234 wager, bet
235 in
236 affirm / declare it★
237 unreservedly, readily
238 commit herself, enter upon this
239 desperate of = in despair about
240 his fortunes
241 stop, retard
242 (1) honorable, generous, (2) unrestricted, unforced, plain-spoken

315   Probal[243] to thinking, and indeed the course

       To win the Moor again? For 'tis most easy

       The inclining[244] Desdemona to subdue[245]

       In any honest suit.[246] She's framed as fruitful[247]

       As the free elements.[248] And then for her

       To win the Moor – were't[249] to renounce his baptism,

320   All seals[250] and symbols of redeemèd sin –

       His soul is so enfettered to her love

       That she may make, unmake, do what she list,

       Even as her appetite[251] shall play the god

       With his weak function.[252] How am I then a villain,

325   To counsel Cassio to this parallel[253] course,

       Directly to his good? Divinity of hell!

       When devils will[254] the blackest sins put on

       They do suggest[255] at first with heavenly shows,

       As I do now. For whiles this honest fool[256]

330   Plies[257] Desdemona to repair[258] his fortune,

       And she for him pleads strongly to the Moor,

243 reasonable
244 well-disposed, willing
245 get the better of, persuade
246 petition (noun)
247 generous
248 free elements = abundant basic matter (earth, water, air, fire)
249 even if it were / meant
250 authenticating tokens / signs
251 desire, inclination
252 moral / intellectual powers
253 in appearance, having the same direction as good advice would advise
254 want to
255 propose, put forward, insinuate
256 Cassio
257 works hard at ("leans on")
258 recover

I'll pour this pestilence[259] into his ear
That she repeals[260] him for her body's lust.
And by how much she strives to do him[261] good,   335
She shall undo her credit with the Moor.
So will I turn her virtue into pitch,[262]
And out of her own goodness make the net
That shall enmesh them all.

ENTER RODERIGO

How now, Roderigo!

Roderigo I do follow here in the chase, not like a hound that   340
  hunts, but one that fills up the cry.[263] My money is almost
  spent, I have been tonight exceedingly well cudgeled, and I
  think the issue will be, I shall have so much experience for
  my pains. And so, with no money at all and a little more wit,
  return again to Venice.   345

Iago   How poor are they that have not patience!
  What wound did ever heal but by degrees?
  Thou know'st we work by wit, and not by witchcraft,
  And wit depends on dilatory[264] time.
  Does't not go well? Cassio hath beaten thee,   350
  And thou by that small hurt hast cashiered Cassio.
  Though other things grow fair against[265] the sun,
  Yet fruits that blossom first, will first be ripe.

259 mischief
260 (1) calls upon him, (2) urges the withdrawal of his cashiering of Cassio
261 Cassio
262 black tar
263 baying and barking of the hunting pack
264 slow, delaying
265 in the light of, when exposed to

Content thyself awhile. In troth,[266] 'tis morning,
Pleasure, and action, make the hours seem short.
355　Retire thee,[267] go where thou art billeted.[268]
Away, I say, thou shalt know more hereafter.
Nay, get thee gone.

EXIT RODERIGO

　　　　　Two things are to be done.
My wife must move[269] for Cassio to her mistress.
I'll set her on,
360　Myself a while[270] to draw the Moor apart,[271]
And bring him jump when he may Cassio find
Soliciting his wife. Ay, that's the way.
Dull not device[272] by coldness[273] and delay.

EXIT

266 (exclamatory remark: troth = truth)
267 retire thee = withdraw★
268 quartered
269 speak, urge
270 at the same time ("the while": while = a block / bit of time)
271 to the side, away★
272 dull not device = let the plan not be held back / blunted
273 apathy, indifference

Act 3

&

SCENE 1

A street

ENTER CASSIO AND MUSICIANS

Cassio   Masters, play here, I will content[1] your pains,
    Something that's brief, and bid[2] "good morrow, general."[3]

MUSIC

ENTER CLOWN

Clown   Why, masters, have your instruments been in
    Naples,[4] that they speak[5] i' the nose thus?

Musician 1 How, sir? how?   5

1 compensate, remunerate ("satisfy")
2 will offer/present
3 (Furness, ed., *Othello: A New Variorum Edition,* 154n, cites Brand, *Popular Antiquities* (1873): "The custom of awaking a couple the morning after the marriage with a concert of music, is old standing")
4 (Italy was then – and for almost 300 years more – much divided, politically and linguistically; northern Italian like that of Naples is still stigmatized: compare *napoletanismo,* "Neapolitan way of talking," and *napoletanamenta,* "in the style of Naples")
5 speak = (1) talk, (2) emit musical sound

Clown   Are these, I pray you, wind instruments?

Musician 1 Ay, marry, are they, sir.

Clown   O, thereby hangs a tale.

Musician 1 Whereby hangs a tale, sir?

10 *Clown*   Marry, sir, by many a wind[6] instrument that I know.
             But masters, here's money for you. And the general so likes
             your music, that he desires you, for love's sake, to make no
             more noise with it.

Musician 1 Well, sir, we will not.

15 *Clown*   If you have any music that may not be heard, to't
             again.[7] But, as they say, to hear music the general does not
             greatly care.

Musician 1 We have none such, sir.

Clown   Then put up your pipes in your bag, for I'll away.[8]
20   Go, vanish into air, away!

EXEUNT MUSICIANS

Cassio   Dost thou hear, mine honest friend?

Clown   No, I hear not your honest friend. I hear you.

Cassio   Pr'ythee, keep up[9] thy quillets.[10] There's a poor[11]
             piece of gold for thee. If the gentlewoman that attends the
25   general's wife be stirring, tell her there's one Cassio entreats
             her a little favor of speech. Wilt thou do this?

Clown   She is stirring, sir. If she will stir hither I shall seem[12]

---

6 farting ("tail")
7 to't again = go to it/play again
8 (meaning uncertain)
9 keep up = stop
10 verbally based jokes
11 small, inadequate
12 deign

96

to notify unto her.

Cassio Do, good my friend.[13]

EXIT CLOWN

ENTER IAGO

In happy time,[14] Iago.

Iago   You have not been a-bed, then?   30

Cassio Why no. The day had broke before we parted.

I have made bold, Iago, to send[15] in to your wife.

My suit to her is that she will to virtuous

Desdemona procure[16] me some access.

Iago   I'll send her to you presently.   35

And I'll devise[17] a mean[18] to draw the Moor

Out of the way, that your converse and business

May be more free.

Cassio I humbly thank you for't.

EXIT IAGO

I never knew

A Florentine[19] more kind and honest.   40

ENTER EMILIA

Emilia Good morrow,[20] good lieutenant. I am sorry

13 (line from the Quarto)
14 in happy time = well met
15 send a message
16 if her name is here pronounced desDEYmona, proCURE; if pronounced
   DEZdeMOna, then PROcure
17 arrange, invent
18 means (French *moyen*)
19 even someone from my own city (Cassio is a Florentine)
20 morning, day

For your displeasure.[21] But all will sure be well.
The general and his wife are talking of it,
And she speaks for you stoutly. The Moor replies
45 That he you hurt is of great fame[22] in Cyprus
And great affinity,[23] and that in wholesome[24] wisdom
He might not but refuse you.[25] But he protests he loves you
And needs no other suitor[26] but his likings
To bring[27] you in again.

Cassio   Yet I beseech you,
50 If you think fit, or that it may be done,
Give me advantage of some brief discourse
With Desdemona alone.

Emilia   Pray you, come in.
I will bestow[28] you where you shall have time
To speak your bosom freely.

Cassio   I am much bound[29] to you.

EXEUNT

21 trouble, sorrow
22 reputation, honor
23 relationship, kinship ("connections")
24 sound
25 might not but refuse you = had no choice except to reject
26 petitioner, suppliant
27 fetch
28 place, bring, locate
29 obliged

SCENE 2

The Citadel

ENTER OTHELLO, IAGO, AND GENTLEMEN

Othello	These letters give, Iago, to the pilot,[1]
	And by[2] him do my duties[3] to the Senate.
	That done,[4] I will be walking on the works.[5]
	Repair there to me.
Iago	Well,[6] my good lord, I'll do't.
Othello	This fortification, gentlemen, shall we see't?
Gentlemen	We'll wait upon[7] your lordship.

5

EXEUNT

1 (of the ship returning to Venice, on which his guests have arrived in Cyprus)
2 through, by means of
3 do my duties = express my respect / homage / deference
4 after you have done that
5 the works = the Citadel's fortifications
6 very well
7 wait upon = defer to, follow

SCENE 3

The Citadel

ENTER DESDEMONA, CASSIO, AND EMILIA

Desdemona Be thou assured, good Cassio, I will do
    All my abilities[1] in thy behalf.

Emilia   Good madam, do. I warrant it grieves my husband
    As if the cause[2] were his.

5   *Desdemona* O, that's an honest fellow. Do not doubt, Cassio,
    But I will have my lord and you again
    As friendly[3] as you were.

Cassio   Bounteous[4] madam,
    Whatever shall become of Michael Cassio,
    He's never anything but your true servant.

10 *Desdemona* I know't. I thank you. You do love my lord,
    You have known him long, and be you well assured
    He shall in strangeness[5] stand no farther off
    Than in[6] a politic[7] distance.

Cassio   Ay, but, lady,
    That policy may either last so long,

15   Or feed upon such nice and waterish[8] diet,
    Or breed[9] itself so out of circumstance,[10]

1 my abilities = of which I am capable
2 affair, business★
3 amicable
4 kind, generous
5 aloofness, coolness
6 than in = than
7 prudent, wise
8 nice and waterish = delicate★ and watery / dilute
9 develop
10 context, environment

That, I being absent, and my place supplied,[11]
My general will forget my love and service.

Desdemona Do not doubt[12] that. Before Emilia here
I give thee warrant of thy place. Assure thee,   20
If I do vow[13] a friendship, I'll perform it
To the last article.[14] My lord shall never rest,
I'll watch[15] him tame, and talk[16] him out of[17] patience.
His bed shall seem a school, his board a shrift,[18]
I'll intermingle everything he does   25
With Cassio's suit. Therefore be merry, Cassio,
For thy solicitor shall rather die
Than give thy cause away.[19]

Emilia   Madam, here comes my lord.

Cassio   Madam, I'll take my leave.   30

Desdemona Why, stay, and hear me speak.

Cassio   Madam, not now. I am very ill at ease,
Unfit for mine own purposes.

Desdemona Well, do your discretion.[20]

EXIT CASSIO

11 filled up
12 fear
13 declare, affirm, assert
14 detailed item/part
15 guard, be vigilant/alert, keep awake (as one keeps a hawk from sleeping, in
    taming it)
16 talk to
17 out of = beyond, past
18 board a shrift = eating/food a penance
19 give … away = concede, sacrifice
20 your discretion = as you think best

ENTER OTHELLO AND IAGO

35 *Iago*   Ha? I like not that.

 Othello What dost thou say?

 Iago   Nothing, my lord. Or if – I know not what.

 Othello Was not that Cassio parted[21] from my wife?

 Iago   Cassio, my lord? No, sure, I cannot think it

40 That he would steal away[22] so guilty-like,

 Seeing you coming.

 Othello   I do believe 'twas he.

 Desdemona How now, my lord?

 I have been talking with a suitor here,

 A man that languishes[23] in your displeasure.

45 *Othello* Who is't you mean?[24]

 Desdemona Why, your lieutenant, Cassio. Good my lord,

 If I have any grace or power to move[25] you,

 His present reconciliation[26] take.

 For if he be not one that truly loves you,

50 That errs in ignorance, and not in cunning,

 I have no judgment in[27] an honest face.

 I prythee, call him back.

 Othello   Went he hence now?[28]

 Desdemona Ay sooth,[29] so humbled

---

21 gone away, leaving
22 steal away = secretly / stealthily withdraw
23 droops, wastes away, pines
24 (is it really possible that Othello does not know this?)
25 change your mind
26 return to favor
27 judgment in = discernment / faculty of judging about / of
28 just now
29 truly

That he hath left part of his grief with me
To suffer[30] with him. Good love, call him back.   55
Othello   Not now, sweet Desdemon, some other time.
Desdemona But shall't be shortly?
Othello   The sooner, sweet, for[31] you.
Desdemona Shall't be tonight at supper?
Othello   No, not tonight.
Desdemona Tomorrow dinner then?
Othello   I shall not dine at home.
I meet the captains at the Citadel.   60
Desdemona Why then tomorrow night, on Tuesday morn,
On Tuesday noon, or night, on Wednesday morn.
I prythee, name the time, but let it not
Exceed three days. In faith, he's penitent.
And yet his trespass,[32] in our common reason –   65
Save that, they say, the wars[33] must make examples
Out of their best – is not almost[34] a fault[35]
To incur a private[36] check. When shall he come?
Tell me, Othello. I wonder in my soul
What you would ask me, that I should deny,   70
Or stand so mamm'ring on?[37] What? Michael Cassio,
That came a-wooing with you? And so many a time,
When I have spoke of you dispraisingly,

30 endure
31 because of
32 sin, offense
33 the wars = warfare
34 for the most part, usually
35 defect, imperfection, flaw
36 personal
37 mamm'ring on = hesitating about

Hath ta'en your part — to have so much to-do[38]

75   To bring him in? Trust me, I could do much —

Othello   Prythee, no more. Let him come when he will.

I will deny thee nothing.

Desdemona   Why, this is not a boon.[39]

'Tis as I should entreat you wear your gloves,

Or feed on nourishing dishes, or keep you warm,

80   Or sue to you to do a peculiar profit

To your own person. Nay, when I have a suit

Wherein I mean to touch your love indeed,

It shall be full of poise,[40] and difficult weight,

And fearful to be granted.

Othello   I will deny[41] thee nothing.

85   Whereon,[42] I do beseech thee, grant me this,

To leave me but a little to myself.

Desdemona Shall I deny you? No. Farewell, my lord.

Othello   Farewell, my Desdemona. I'll come to thee straight.

Desdemona Emilia, come. (*to Othello*) Be as your fancies[43] teach

you.

90   Whate'er you be, I am obedient.[44]

EXEUNT DESDEMONA AND EMILIA

Othello   Excellent wretch.[45] Perdition catch my soul,

---

38 to do = fuss
39 favor, gift
40 importance, gravity
41 say no to, refuse
42 whereupon
43 moods, imaginings, judgment
44 dutiful, submissive
45 miserable/unfortunate person/little creature

But I do love thee. And when I love thee not,
Chaos is come again.

Iago   My noble lord.

Othello What dost thou say, Iago?

Iago   Did Michael Cassio, when you wooed my lady,   95
Know of your love?

Othello He did, from first to last. Why dost thou ask?

Iago   But for a satisfaction of my thought;
No further harm.[46]

Othello   Why[47] of thy thought, Iago?

Iago   I did not think he had been acquainted with her.   100

Othello O yes, and went between us very oft.

Iago   Indeed?

Othello Indeed? Ay, indeed. Discern'st[48] thou aught in that?
Is he not honest?

Iago   Honest, my lord?

Othello Honest. Ay, honest.

Iago   My lord, for aught I know.   105

Othello What dost thou think?

Iago   Think, my lord?

Othello Think, my lord? Alas, thou echo'st me,
As if there were some monster in thy thought
Too hideous to be shown. Thou dost mean something.
I heard thee say even now, thou lik'dst not that,   110
When Cassio left my wife. What didst not like?
And when I told thee he was of[49] my counsel

46 evil
47 is it
48 perceive
49 in

In my whole course of wooing, thou criedst, "Indeed?"
And didst contract[50] and purse[51] thy brow together,
115 As if thou then hadst shut up in thy brain
Some horrible conceit.[52] If thou dost love me,
Show me thy thought.

Iago   My lord, you know I love you.

Othello   I think thou dost.
And for[53] I know thou'rt full of love and honesty
120 And weigh'st thy words before thou giv'st them breath,
Therefore these stops of thine fright me the more.
For such things in a false disloyal knave
Are tricks of custom.[54] But in a man that's just,
They're close dilations,[55] working from the heart,
That passion cannot rule.

125 *Iago*   For[56] Michael Cassio,
I dare be sworn, I think that he is honest.

Othello   I think so too.

Iago   Men should be what they seem,
Or those that be not, would they might seem none.

Othello   Certain, men should be what they seem.

130 *Iago*   Why then I think Cassio's an honest man.

Othello   Nay, yet there's more in this?
I prythee speak to me as to[57] thy thinkings,

50 draw together, knit
51 wrinkle
52 thought, idea
53 because
54 usual, ordinary, habitual
55 close dilations = hidden/private/secret postponements/delays
56 as for
57 as to = about

As thou dost ruminate,[58] and give thy worst of thoughts
The worst of words.

Iago   Good my lord, pardon me.
Though I am bound to every act of duty,   135
I am not bound to that[59] all slaves are free to.[60]
Utter my thoughts? Why, say they are vile and false?
As where's that palace,[61] whereinto foul things
Sometimes intrude not? Who has a breast so pure
But some uncleanly apprehensions[62]   140
Keep leets and law-days,[63] and in session[64] sit
With meditations[65] lawful?

Othello Thou dost conspire against thy friend,[66] Iago,
If thou but think'st[67] him wronged and mak'st his ear
A stranger to thy thoughts.

Iago   I do beseech you,   145
Though I perchance am vicious[68] in my guess –
As I confess it is my nature's plague
To spy into abuses,[69] and of[70] my jealousy

58 ponder, consider, chew over
59 that which
60 from (an old German song declares that, though tyrants may jail us, *Die
    Gedanken sind frei,* "Our thoughts are free")
61 palatial/heavenly mansion
62 uncleanly apprehensions = impure/wicked thoughts/feelings
63 leets and law-days = courts convened by the lords of manors and the sheriff
    ("local courts")
64 conference, meeting
65 contemplation, conversation
66 thy friend = Othello himself
67 but think'st = so much as/even think
68 depraved, wicked
69 deceits, wrongs
70 out of, from

Shape faults that are not[71] – that your wisdom

150 From one[72] that so imperfectly conceits[73]

Would take no notice, nor build yourself a trouble[74]

Out of his scattering[75] and unsure observance.[76]

It were not[77] for your quiet nor your good,

Nor for my manhood, honesty, or wisdom,

To let you know my thoughts.

155 *Othello*   What dost thou mean?

Iago   Good name in man and woman, dear my lord,

Is the immediate[78] jewel of their souls.[79]

Who steals my purse steals trash. 'Tis something, nothing,

'Twas mine, 'tis his, and has been slave to thousands.

160 But he that filches[80] from me my good name

Robs me of that which not[81] enriches him

And makes me poor indeed.

Othello By heaven, I'll know thy thoughts.

Iago   You cannot, if[82] my heart were in your hand;

165 Nor shall not, whilst 'tis in my custody.[83]

Othello Ha?

Iago   O, beware, my lord, of jealousy,

71 are not = (1) do not exist, (2) are not faults
72 someone (himself)
73 perceives, thinks, imagines
74 worry, distress, misfortune
75 erratic, rambling
76 observations, watching
77 were not = would not be
78 primary
79 is THE imMEdyut JEWel OF their SOULS
80 steals, robs
81 does not
82 even if
83 care, safekeeping, protection

It is the green-eyed[84] monster which doth mock
The meat it feeds on. That cuckold[85] lives in bliss
Who, certain of his fate,[86] loves not his wronger.[87]
But O, what damnèd minutes tells[88] he o'er   170
Who dotes, yet doubts, suspects, yet strongly loves?

Othello O misery!

Iago   Poor and content is rich, and rich enough,
But riches fineless[89] is as poor as winter
To him that ever fears he shall be poor.   175
Good heaven, the souls of all my tribe defend[90]
From jealousy!

Othello   Why? why is this?[91]
Think'st thou I'd make a life of jealousy,
To follow still the changes of the moon
With fresh suspicions? No. To be once in doubt   180
Is to be resolved.[92] Exchange me for a goat
When I shall turn[93] the business of my soul
To[94] such exsufflicate and blown[95] surmises,
Matching thy inference.[96] 'Tis not to make me jealous

---

84 green: traditionally associated with either (1) growth, health, or (2) putrid
   matter, fear, sickness, jealousy
85 man whose wife has been unfaithful
86 what has happened
87 the wife who wrongs him
88 counts
89 unlimited ("without end")
90 tribe defend = family avert/ward off/repel
91 why is this = why are you saying these things?
92 settled, convinced, free from doubt
93 center, revolve, construct
94 on
95 exsufflicate and blown = inflated/windy/puffed up and whispered/hinted
96 implied/suggested conclusion

185 To say my wife is fair, feeds[97] well, loves company,
Is free of speech,[98] sings, plays, and dances well.[99]
Where virtue is, these are more[100] virtuous.
Nor from mine own weak merits will I draw
The smallest fear, or doubt[101] of her revolt,
190 For she had eyes and chose me. No, Iago,
I'll see before I doubt; when I doubt, prove;
And on the proof, there is no more but this,
Away at once with love or jealousy.

Iago I am glad of it. For now I shall have reason
195 To show the love and duty that I bear you
With franker spirit. Therefore,[102] as I am bound,[103]
Receive it from me. I speak not yet of proof.
Look to your wife, observe her well with Cassio,
Wear[104] your eyes thus, not jealous nor secure.
200 I would not have your free and noble nature,
Out of self-bounty,[105] be abused. Look to't.
I know our country disposition[106] well.
In Venice they[107] do let heaven see the pranks

97 eats
98 free of speech = (1) well spoken, ready (2) unrestrained, spontaneous, frank
99 is FREE of SPEECH sings PLAYS and DANces WELL (sings PLAYS: a
   prosodic convention, not to be confused with how the line was actually
   spoken)
100 even more
101 uncertainty
102 in that way
103 obliged in duty
104 use
105 out of self-bounty = from its own goodness/kindness/virtue
106 our country disposition = (1) my native country's (Venice's)? or (2) the
   rural/rustic arrangement/manner? (the former parallels the next line, but
   the latter is in contrast to it)
107 women

They dare not show their husbands. Their best conscience[108]
Is not to leave undone,[109] but keep unknown.   205

Othello   Dost thou say so?

Iago   She did deceive her father, marrying you,
And when she seemed to shake and fear your looks,
She loved them most.

Othello   And so she did.

Iago   Why, go to then.   210
She that, so young, could give out such a seeming,
To seal her father's eyes up close[110] as oak,
He thought 'twas witchcraft. But I am much to blame.[111]
I humbly do beseech you of your pardon
For too much loving you.

Othello   I am bound to thee for ever.   215

Iago   I see this hath a little dashed[112] your spirits.

Othello   Not a jot,[113] not a jot.

Iago   Trust me, I fear it has.
I hope you will consider what[114] is spoke
Comes from my love. But I do see you're moved.
I am to pray you not to strain[115] my speech   220
To grosser issues, nor to larger reach[116]
Than to suspicion.

Othello   I will not.

108 idea, conviction
109 leave undone = refrain from doing
110 dense
111 to blame = to be censured/criticized
112 cast down, depressed, discouraged
113 the least little bit
114 that what
115 push, force, stretch, extend
116 range, application

Iago   Should you do so, my lord,
    My speech should fall into such[117] vile success
    Which[118] my thoughts aimed not. Cassio's my worthy friend.
    My lord, I see you're moved.

225 Othello   No, not much moved.
    I do not think but[119] Desdemona's honest.

    Iago   Long live she so, and long live you to think so.

    Othello And yet, how nature erring from itself –

    Iago   Ay, there's the point. As, to be bold with you,
230   Not to affect[120] many proposed matches,[121]
    Of her own clime,[122] complexion,[123] and degree,
    Whereto we see in all things nature tends.
    Foh! One may smell[124] in such a will[125] most rank,
    Foul disproportion, thoughts unnatural.
235   But pardon me, I do not in position[126]
    Distinctly speak of her, though I may fear
    Her will, recoiling[127] to her better judgment,
    May fall to match you[128] with her country forms,
    And happily[129] repent.

    Othello   Farewell, farewell.

---

117 the kind of
118 at which
119 do not think but = I think only that
120 seek, choose, like
121 marriages★
122 (1) region, (2) climate
123 (1) character, disposition, (2) skin color, appearance, face★
124 perceive, suspect, find
125 (1) nature, inclination, (2) passion, carnal appetite
126 affirmative statement / assertion
127 returning, going back
128 fall to match you = decline / descend to link / pair / compare you
129 perhaps ("haply")

If more thou dost perceive, let me know more.   240
Set on[130] thy wife to observe. Leave me, Iago.

Iago   My lord, I take my leave.

EXIT IAGO

Othello Why did I marry? This honest creature doubtless
Sees and knows more, much more, than he unfolds.

IAGO RETURNS

Iago   My lord, I would I might[131] entreat your honor   245
To scan[132] this thing no farther. Leave it to time,
Alhough 'tis fit that Cassio have his place,
For sure he fills it up with great ability.
Yet if you please to hold him off awhile,
You shall by that perceive[133] him, and his means.   250
Note if your lady strain his entertainment[134]
With any strong or vehement importunity:[135]
Much will be seen in that. In the meantime,
Let me be thought too busy[136] in my fears,
As worthy cause I have to fear I am,   255
And hold her free, I do beseech your honor.

Othello Fear not my government.[137]

Iago   I once more take my leave.

EXIT IAGO

130 set on = direct, arrange for, urge
131 I would I might = I want to, let me
132 analyze, test, examine
133 (1) become aware of, understand, (2) see through, recognize
134 his entertainment = her support of him
135 excessive zeal
136 (1) active, diligent, (2) meddling, nosy
137 (1) conduct, behavior, (2) discretion

Othello This fellow's of exceeding honesty,
     And knows all qualities,[138] with a learnèd spirit,
260   Of human dealings. If I do prove her haggard,[139]
     Though that her jesses[140] were my dear heartstrings,
     I'd whistle her off,[141] and let her down the wind[142]
     To prey at fortune.[143] Haply for[144] I am black,
     And have not those soft parts of conversation
265   That chamberers[145] have, or for I am declined[146]
     Into the vale[147] of years — yet that's[148] not much —
     She's gone.[149] I am abused, and my relief[150]
     Must be to loathe her. O curse of marriage,
     That we can call these delicate creatures ours,
270   And not their appetites! I had rather be a toad,
     And live upon the vapor of a dungeon,
     Than keep[151] a corner in the thing I love
     For others' uses. Yet, 'tis the plague of great ones,
     Prerogatived[152] are they less than the base.
275   'Tis destiny unshunnable, like death.

138 characters, natures
139 wild, untamable (from hawk training: adult females caught too late to be trained)
140 leg straps for leashing hawks
141 whistle her off = send her away, abandon her
142 down the wind = free
143 prey at fortune = hunt however she liked
144 haply for = maybe it is because
145 gallants
146 fallen, drooped, sunk
147 valley
148 yet that's = that's still/as yet
149 undone, ruined
150 (1) deliverance, alleviation, release, (2) help, assistance, support
151 maintain, preserve, retain, hold back
152 privileged

Even then this forkèd[153] plague is fated to us
When we do quicken.[154]

ENTER DESDEMONA AND EMILIA

                   Look where she comes.
If she be false, heaven mocked itself.
I'll not believe't.

Desdemona   How now, my dear Othello?
Your dinner, and the generous islanders[155]   280
By you invited, do attend[156] your presence.

Othello   I am to blame.

Desdemona   Why do you speak so faintly?[157]
Are you not well?

Othello   I have a pain upon[158] my forehead, here.

Desdemona Why, that's with watching,[159] 'twill away again.   285
Let me but bind it hard,[160] within this hour
It will be well.

Othello   Your napkin[161] is too little.

HE PUSHES THE HANDKERCHIEF AWAY, AND IT FALLS

Let it alone. Come, I'll go in with you.

Desdemona I am very sorry that you are not well.

EXEUNT OTHELLO AND DESDEMONA

153 horned (cuckolds wear horns)
154 when we do quicken = (1) when we are given life / conceived, (2) while we
    are alive
155 generous islanders = high-born / noble Cypriots
156 await, look forward to
157 (1) feebly, weakly, (2) almost imperceptibly
158 in
159 (1) being on guard / vigilant, (2) insufficient sleep
160 tightly
161 handkerchief

EMILIA PICKS UP THE HANDKERCHIEF

290 *Emilia* I am glad I have found this napkin.
       This was her first remembrance[162] from the Moor,
       My wayward[163] husband hath a hundred times
       Wooed[164] me to steal it. But she so loves the token[165] –
       For he conjured[166] her she should ever keep it –
295   That she reserves[167] it evermore about her
       To kiss and talk to. I'll have the work taken out,[168]
       And give't Iago. What he will do with it
       Heaven knows, not I,
       I nothing[169] but to please his fantasy.

ENTER IAGO

300 *Iago* How now? What do you here alone?
   Emilia Do not you chide. I have a thing for you.
   Iago You have a thing for me? It is a common thing.[170]
   Emilia Hah?
   Iago To have a foolish wife.
305 *Emilia* O, is that all? What will you give me now
       For that same handkerchief?
   Iago   What handkerchief?
   Emilia What handkerchief?

162 keepsake
163 stubborn, perverse, willful
164 entreated, solicited, tempted
165 gift, present★
166 charged, constrained
167 retains, holds back
168 work taken out = needlework / embroidery copied
169 (1) do nothing, (2) wish
170 female genitalia

Why that the Moor first gave to Desdemona,

That which so often you did bid me steal.

Iago   Hast stolen it from her?   310

Emilia No. But she let it drop by negligence,

And to th'advantage, I being here, took't up.

Look, here it is.

Iago   A good wench,[171] give it me.

Emilia (not giving it) What will[172] you do with't, that you have
been so earnest[173]

To have me filch it?

Iago   (snatches it) Why, what is that to you?   315

Emilia If it be not for some purpose of import,[174]

Give't me again. Poor lady, she'll run mad[175]

When she shall lack[176] it.

Iago   Be not acknown on't.[177]

I have use for it. Go, leave me.

EXIT EMILIA

I will in Cassio's lodging lose[178] this napkin,   320

And let him find it. Trifles light as air

Are to the jealous confirmations strong

As[179] proofs of holy writ. This may do[180] something.

---

171 a good wench = (1) you're a good girl, (2) be a good girl
172 do you wish
173 ardent, determined
174 significance, importance
175 run mad = go crazy
176 be without, miss, need
177 be not acknown on't = do not let anyone know about it
178 leave behind, forget, drop
179 confirmations strong as = proofs as strong as
180 accomplish, achieve, cause

The Moor already changes with my poison.[181]

325   Dangerous conceits are in their natures poisons,

Which at the first[182] are scarce found to distaste,[183]

But with a little act[184] upon the blood

Burn like the mines[185] of sulphur. (*seeing Othello approach*)

I did say so.

330   Look, where he comes. Not poppy,[186] nor mandragora,[187]

Nor all the drowsy syrups[188] of the world,

Shall ever medicine[189] thee to that sweet sleep

Which thou ow'dst yesterday.

ENTER OTHELLO

Othello   Ha, ha, false to me?

Iago   Why, how now, general? No more of that.

335   *Othello*   Avaunt,[190] be gone. Thou hast set me on the rack.[191]

I swear 'tis better to be much abused

Than but to know't a little.

Iago   How now, my lord?

Othello What sense had I of her stolen hours of lust?

I saw't not, thought it not, it harmed not me.

340   I slept the next night well, was free and merry.

I found not Cassio's kisses on her lips.

181 with my poison = from/because of my harmful/baleful influence
182 at the first = at first
183 scarce found to distaste = seldom experienced/met with dislike/disgust
184 with a little act = after brief action
185 like the mines = like mines
186 used as a sleeping potion ("opium")
187 mandrake: another much-used sleeping medicine
188 drowsy syrups = sleep-inducing liquids (herb plus sugar)
189 medicate
190 go away
191 torture rack

He that is robbed, not wanting[192] what is stolen,
Let him not know't, and he's not robbed at all.

Iago   I am sorry to hear this.

Othello I had been happy if the general camp,[193]   345
Pioneers[194] and all, had tasted her sweet body,
So[195] I had nothing known. O now, for ever
Farewell the tranquil mind, farewell content,
Farewell the plumèd[196] troops, and the big[197] wars,
That makes ambition[198] virtue! O farewell,   350
Farewell the neighing steed and the shrill trump,[199]
The spirit-stirring drum, th'ear-piercing fife,
The royal banner,[200] and all quality,
Pride, pomp, and circumstance of glorious war![201]
And O you mortal engines,[202] whose rude throats   355
The immortal Jove's dread clamors[203] counterfeit,
Farewell. Othello's occupation's[204] gone.

Iago   Is't possible, my lord?

Othello (seizing him) Villain, be sure thou prove my love a whore,
Be sure of it. Give me the ocular[205] proof,   360

192 lacking
193 troops*
194 infantrymen who dig, build, repair
195 as long as
196 wearing feathers on their headgear
197 great, mighty
198 make ambition = turn ambition into
199 shrill trump = sharp/high-pitched trumpet
200 ensign, flag
201 pride POMP and CIRcumSTANCE of GLORyus WAR
202 mechanical contrivances: cannon
203 loud outbursts ("thunder")
204 occupation's = calling/profession is
205 visual

Or by the worth of mine eternal soul

Thou hadst been better have been born a dog

Than answer my wakèd[206] wrath!

Iago   Is' t[207] come to this?

Othello Make me to see't, or at the least so prove it

365   That the probation[208] bear no hinge nor loop[209]

To hang a doubt on, or woe upon thy life!

Iago   My noble lord –

Othello If thou dost slander her, and torture me,

Never pray more.[210] Abandon all remorse,[211]

370   On horror's head horrors accumulate,[212]

Do deeds to make heaven weep, all earth amazed,

For nothing canst thou to damnation add

Greater than that.

Iago   O grace! O heaven forgive me!

Are you a man? Have you a soul or sense? –

375   God be wi' you.[213] Take[214] mine office. O wretchèd fool,[215]

That liv'st to make thine honesty a vice!

O monstrous world! Take note, take note, O world,

To be direct[216] and honest is not safe.

---

206 wakened

207 is't = has it

208 proof

209 no hinge nor loop = neither that which turns/moves nor that which
    contains an opening

210 again (for a faithful Christian, spiritual death)

211 contrition, repentance

212 on horror's head horrors accumulate = on top of/in addition to horror pile
    up even more horrors

213 God be wi' you = good-bye

214 remove/receive back/accept

215 himself, for trying to "help" Othello

216 straightforward

I thank you for this profit, and from hence
I'll love no friend, sith[217] love breeds such offense.   380
Othello   Nay, stay. Thou shouldst[218] be honest.
Iago   I should be wise, for honesty's a fool,
And loses that[219] it works for.
Othello   By the world,[220]
I think my wife be honest, and think she is not.
I think that thou art just, and think thou art not.   385
I'll have[221] some proof. My name, that was as fresh
As Dian's[222] visage, is now begrimed and black
As mine own face. If[223] there be cords or knives,
Poison or fire, or suffocating streams,[224]
I'll not endure it.[225] Would I were satisfied!   390
Iago   I see, sir, you are eaten up[226] with passion.
I do repent me that I put it to you.
You would be satisfied?
Othello   Would? Nay, and I will.
Iago   And may. But how? How[227] satisfied, my lord?
Would you, the supervisor,[228] grossly gape on?[229]   395

217 since
218 ought to
219 that which
220 by the world: a common oath
221 I'll have = I want to have
222 Diana: the moon
223 whether ("whatever it takes / requires")
224 suffocating streams = drowning
225 I'll not endure it = I will not go on like this
226 devoured, consumed, gnawed
227 in what way
228 spectator, observer (from the Quarto)
229 gape on = stare, watch

Behold her topped?[230]

Othello   Death and damnation. O!

Iago   It were a tedious[231] difficulty, I think,
        To bring them to that prospect.[232] Damn them then,
        If ever mortal eyes do see them bolster[233]
400   More[234] than their own. What then? How then?
        What shall I say? Where's satisfaction?
        It is impossible you should see this
        Were they[235] as prime[236] as goats, as hot as monkeys,
        As salt[237] as wolves in pride,[238] and fools as gross[239]
405   As ignorance made drunk. But yet, I say,
        If imputation[240] and strong circumstances,
        Which lead directly to the door of truth,
        Will give you satisfaction, you may have't.

Othello Give me a living reason[241] she's disloyal.

410 Iago   I do not like the office.
        But sith I am entered[242] in this cause so far,
        Pricked[243] to it by foolish honesty and love,
        I will go on. I lay[244] with Cassio lately;

230 copulated with ("covered/tupped")
231 (1) wearisome, (2) irksome, disagreeable, painful
232 view, spectacle
233 lie on the same pillow ("have sex together")
234 any eyes more/other
235 were they = even if they were
236 in heat, sexually excited
237 salacious, lecherous
238 heat
239 glaring, total, stupefied
240 attribution, logical analysis
241 living reason = current ("valid") fact ("evidence")
242 involved
243 goaded, spurred, driven
244 shared a bed (for reasons of convenience, lack of space, etc.)

And, being troubled with a raging[245] tooth,
I could not sleep. There are a kind of men,   415
So loose[246] of soul, that in their sleeps will mutter
Their affairs. One of this kind is Cassio.
In sleep I heard him say, "Sweet Desdemona,
Let us be wary, let us hide our loves,"
And then, sir, would he gripe[247] and wring my hand,   420
Cry, "O sweet creature,"[248] then kiss me hard,[249]
As if he plucked[250] up kisses by the roots
That grew upon my lips, lay his leg o'er my thigh,
And sigh, and kiss, and then cry "Cursèd fate
That gave thee to the Moor!"

Othello   O monstrous! monstrous!   425

Iago   Nay, this was but his dream.

Othello But this denoted a foregone[251] conclusion.
  'Tis a shrewd[252] doubt, though it be but a dream.

Iago   And this may help to thicken[253] other proofs
  That do demonstrate thinly.   430

Othello I'll tear her all to pieces.

Iago   Nay, but be wise. Yet[254] we see nothing done,
  She may be honest yet.[255] Tell me but this,

245 violently painful
246 unrestrained, disconnected, slack, indulgent
247 grasp, clutch
248 CREEaTYUR
249 vigorously, intensely
250 pulled, gathered
251 already accomplished/occurring
252 depraved, wicked
253 fill the gaps in
254 as yet
255 still

Have you not sometimes seen a handkerchief
435   Spotted with strawberries in your wife's hand?

Othello I gave her such a one, 'twas my first gift.

Iago   I know not that. But such a handkerchief –
I am sure it was your wife's – did I today
See Cassio wipe his beard with.

Othello   If it be that –

440 *Iago*   If it be that, or any that was hers,
It speaks against her with the other proofs.

Othello O, that the slave[256] had forty thousand lives.
One is too poor, too weak for my revenge!
Now do I see 'tis true. Look here, Iago,
445   All my fond love thus do I blow to heaven.
'Tis gone.
Arise, black vengeance, from thy[257] hollow[258] hell!
Yield up, O love, thy crown and hearted[259] throne
To tyrannous[260] hate! Swell, bosom, with thy fraught,[261]
For 'tis of aspics'[262] tongues!

450 *Iago*   Yet be content.

Othello O, blood, Iago, blood!

Iago   Patience, I say. Your mind perhaps may change.

Othello Never, Iago. Like to the Pontic Sea,[263]
Whose icy current and compulsive[264] course

256 Desdemona? Cassio?
257 (from the Quarto)
258 deep-buried, open, empty
259 fixed in the heart
260 relentless, inexorable, overpowering
261 load, burden
262 asps'
263 Pontic Sea = Black Sea
264 driving/forcing forward

Ne'er feels retiring ebb, but keeps due on   455
To the Propontic[265] and the Hellespont,
Even so my bloody thoughts, with violent pace,[266]
Shall ne'er look back, ne'er ebb to humble[267] love,
Till that a capable and wide[268] revenge
Swallow them[269] up. Now, by yond marble[270] heaven,   460
In the due reverence of a sacred vow

OTHELLO KNEELS

I here engage[271] my words.

Iago   Do not rise yet.

IAGO KNEELS

Witness, you ever-burning lights[272] above,
You elements that clip[273] us round about,
Witness that here Iago doth give up[274]
The execution[275] of his wit, hands, heart,   465
To wronged Othello's service. Let him command,
And to obey shall be in me remorse,[276]
What bloody business ever.[277]

265 Sea of Marmora
266 speed
267 modestly satisfied
268 capable and wide = capacious/roomy and broad
269 probably (1) his thoughts, but conceivably (2) Desdemona and Cassio
270 stone-hard, inflexible
271 pledge
272 stars
273 clasp, hug, embrace
274 give up = commit, bestow, grant
275 operation, action, performance
276 without mitigation, solemn obligation
277 what bloody business ever = whatever the bloody business

Othello   I greet[278] thy love

470   Not with vain thanks, but with acceptance bounteous,
      And will upon the instant put thee to't.
      Within these three days let me hear thee say
      That Cassio's not alive.

Iago   My friend is dead.
      'Tis done at your request. But let her live.

475 Othello Damn her, lewd minx![279] O, damn her! damn her!
      Come, go with me apart, I will withdraw
      To furnish me with some swift means of death
      For the fair devil. Now art thou my lieutenant.

Iago   I am your own for ever.

EXEUNT

278 receive, welcome
279 lewd mix = evil / worthless / lascivious woman

SCENE 4

A street

ENTER DESDEMONA, EMILIA, AND CLOWN

Desdemona Do you know, sirrah,[1] where Lieutenant Cassio
lies?[2]

Clown I dare not say he lies[3] anywhere.

Desdemona Why, man?

Clown He's a soldier; and for one to say a soldier lies is[4]
stabbing.

Desdemona Go to. Where lodges he?

Clown To tell you where he lodges is to tell you where I
lie.[5]

Desdemona Can anything be made of[6] this?

Clown I know not where he lodges, and for me to devise a
lodging, and say he lies here, or he lies there, were to lie in
mine own throat.

Desdemona Can you inquire[7] him out, and be edified[8] by report?

Clown I will catechize[9] the world for him, that is, make
questions and by[10] them answer.

Desdemona Seek him, bid him come hither. Tell him I have
moved my lord on his behalf, and hope all will be well.

---

1 form of address used for servants and children
2 lives, lodges
3 tells lies
4 may cause, risks
5 where I lie = what I would be telling lies about
6 made of = derived from, understood by
7 search, seek
8 informed, instructed
9 question, examine, interrogate
10 by means of

Clown   To do this is within the compass of man's wit, and
20   therefore I will attempt the doing it.[11]

EXIT CLOWN

Desdemona Where should I lose[12] that handkerchief, Emilia?

Emilia   I know not, madam.

Desdemona Believe me, I had rather have lost my purse
Full of crusadoes.[13] And but my noble Moor
25   Is true of mind and made of no such baseness
As jealous creatures are, it were enough
To put him to ill thinking.

Emilia   Is he not jealous?

Desdemona Who, he? I think the sun where he was born
Drew all such humors[14] from him.

Emilia   Look where he comes.
30 *Desdemona* I will not leave him now till Cassio
Be called to him.

ENTER OTHELLO

            How is't with you, my lord?

Othello   Well, my good lady. (*aside*) O hardness[15] to
dissemble!
    How do you, Desdemona?

Desdemona   Well, my good lord.

Othello   Give me your hand. This hand is moist, my lady.
35 *Desdemona* It yet hath felt no age nor known no sorrow.

11 of it
12 where should I lose = where must I have lost
13 Portuguese coins (cruSEYdoze)
14 moods
15 (1) how difficult it is, (2) may I be granted the severity/rigor/endurance

[handwritten margin note: this would be enough to make a husband suspicious but Othello is not the jealous type]

Othello   This argues[16] fruitfulness[17] and liberal heart.

Hot, hot, and moist. This hand of yours requires[18]

A sequester[19] from liberty, fasting,[20] and prayer,

Much castigation,[21] exercise devout,[22]

For here's a young and sweating[23] devil, here,   40

That commonly[24] rebels. 'Tis a good hand,

A frank one.

Desdemona   You may, indeed, say so,

For 'twas that hand that gave away my heart.

Othello   A liberal hand. The hearts of old gave hands.

But our new heraldry[25] is hands, not hearts.   45

Desdemona I cannot speak of this. Come now, your promise.

Othello   What promise, chuck?[26]

Desdemona I have sent to bid Cassio come speak with you.

Othello   (*fit of coughing?*) I have a salt and sorry rheum[27]

offends[28] me.

Lend me thy handkerchief.

16 this argues = (1) this hand, and/or (2) this feature/line of your hand
   indicates (Othello was surely familiar with the practice of "reading" hands
   by interpretation of their specific and individual characteristics)
17 fertility
18 hot HOT and MOIST this HAND of YOURS reQUIRES
19 isolation, seclusion
20 and also requires fasting
21 correction, discipline, purification
22 pious/religious activity/employment
23 (because hot and moist, as active devils are)
24 usually, ordinarily
25 method/way of showing/exhibiting rank/precedence (the rights
   accompanying rank)
26 term of endearment
27 salt and sorry rheum = irritating/vexatious and dismal/distressing mucous
   nasal discharge ("a running cold")
28 which attacks

50	*Desdemona*	Here, my lord.
	Othello	(*rejecting it*) That which I gave you.
	Desdemona	I have it not
	about[29] me.	
	Othello	Not?
	Desdemona	No indeed, my lord.
	Othello	That is a fault.

That handkerchief *[handwritten: Origin of the handkerchief very special - magical]*
Did an Egyptian[30] to my mother give.
55 She was a charmer,[31] and could almost read
The thoughts of people. She told her,[32] while she kept it
'Twould make her amiable[33] and subdue my father
Entirely to her love. But if she lost it,
Or made a gift of it, my father's eye
60 Should hold her loathèd, and his spirits[34] should[35] hunt
After new fancies. She, dying, gave it me,
And bid me, when my fate would have me wive,
To give it her.[36] I did so, and take heed on't,[37]
Make it a darling,[38] like your precious eye.
65 To lose't or give't away were such perdition *[handwritten: This is the worst thing you could lose]*
As nothing else could match. *[handwritten: loosing it will break spell of love]*

Desdemona   Is't possible?

29 with
30 gypsy? Egyptian?
31 enchanter, magician
32 Othello's mother
33 lovable
34 impulses, emotions
35 would necessarily / be obliged to
36 my wife
37 heed on't = careful attention / regard of it
38 object of your love

Othello   'Tis true. There's magic in the web[39] of it.
A sibyl,[40] that had numbered[41] in the world
The sun to course[42] two hundred compasses,[43]
In her prophetic fury[44] sewed the work.   70
The worms[45] were hallowed[46] that did breed[47] the silk,
And it was dyed in mummy,[48] which the skillful
Conserved of [49] maiden's hearts.

Desdemona   Indeed? Is't true?

Othello   Most veritable,[50] therefore look to't well.

Desdemona Then would to heaven that I had never seen't!   75

Othello   Ha? Wherefore?

Desdemona Why do you speak so startingly and rash?[51]

Othello   Is't lost? Is't gone? Speak, is it out of the way?[52]

Desdemona Bless us!

Othello   Say you?[53]   80

Desdemona It is not lost. But what an if[54] it were?

Othello   How?

Desdemona I say, it is not lost.

39 weaving, fabric
40 prophetess, fortune-teller, witch
41 been able to count
42 run
43 circles around the earth ("years")
44 frenzy, passion
45 silkworms/caterpillars
46 consecrated, sanctified
47 generate, produce
48 medicinal substance prepared from mummified bodies
49 conserved of = preserved from
50 truthful, genuine
51 startlingly and rash = abruptly and urgently/hastily/impetuously
52 out of the way = lost, missing, astray
53 say you = what do you say/respond/answer
54 what an if = what if

Othello   Fetch't, let me see't.

Desdemona   Why, so I can. But I will not now.

85   This is a trick to put[55] me from my suit.

     Pray you, let Cassio be received again.   *← Trying to change subject*

Othello   Fetch me the handkerchief. My mind misgives.[56]

Desdemona   Come, come.

     You'll never meet[57] a more sufficient[58] man.   *is where the dramatic*

Othello   The handkerchief!

90   Desdemona   I pray, talk[59] me of Cassio.   *effect*

Othello   The handkerchief!

Desdemona   A man that all his time

     Hath founded[60] his good fortunes on your love,

     Shared dangers with you.

Othello   The handkerchief!

95   Desdemona   In sooth, you are to blame.

Othello   Away![61]

EXIT

Emilia   Is not this man jealous?

Desdemona   I ne'er saw this before.

     Sure there's some wonder[62] in this handkerchief.

100   I am most unhappy in the loss of it.

Emilia   'Tis not[63] a year or two shows us[64] a man.

55 turn, divert
56 is apprehensive/suspicious
57 find, come across
58 satisfactory, competent, capable★
59 talk to
60 all his time hath founded = has always based
61 get away
62 some wonder = something miraculous/marvelous
63 'tis not = it is not just ("it takes more than")
64 we women

They are all but stomachs and we all but food,
They eat us hungerly,[65] and when they are full
They belch us. Look you, Cassio and my husband.

ENTER CASSIO AND IAGO

Iago   There is no other way. 'Tis she must do't.   105
And lo the happiness.[66] Go and importune her.

Desdemona How now, good Cassio, what's the news with you?

Cassio   Madam, my former suit. I do beseech you
That by your virtuous means I may again
Exist, and be a member of[67] his love,   110
Whom I, with all the office of my heart,
Entirely honor. I would not[68] be delayed.
If my offense be of such mortal[69] kind
That nor[70] my service past, nor present sorrows,
Nor purposed[71] merit in futurity   115
Can ransom[72] me into his love again,
But[73] to know so must be my benefit.
So shall I clothe me in a forced[74] content,
And shut myself up in some other course
To fortune's alms.[75]

Desdemona   Alas, thrice-gentle Cassio,   120

65 hungrily, greedily
66 good luck (seeing Desdemona)
67 a member of = one who participates in ("a part")
68 would not = do not wish/want
69 fatal, destructive, deadly
70 neither
71 intended
72 redeem, restore
73 just, only
74 involuntary
75 benefactions, gifts

Tells Cassio it is not a good time to discuss his suit with Othello. He is in a bad mood & not acting himself

My advocation[76] is not now in tune.[77]

My lord is not my lord, nor should I know him

Were he in favor as in humor[78] altered.

So help me every spirit sanctified

125 As[79] I have spoken for you all my best,

And stood within the blank[80] of his displeasure

For my free speech. You must awhile be patient.

What I can do I will. And more I will

Than for myself I dare. Let that suffice you.

Iago   Is my lord angry?

130 *Emilia*   He went hence but now,

And certainly in strange unquietness.[81]

Iago   Can he be angry? I have seen the cannon,

When it hath blown his ranks[82] into the air,

And like the devil from his very arm

135 Puffed[83] his own brother. And is he angry?

Something of moment, then. I will go meet him,

There's matter in't indeed, if he be angry.

Desdemona I prythee do so.

EXIT IAGO

Something sure of state,[84]

Either from Venice or some unhatched[85] practice

76 appeal, pleading
77 in tune = according to Othello's mood
78 mood, disposition
79 that
80 point-blank range
81 turbulence, disturbance
82 soldiers
83 blown away
84 something sure of state = surely some matter of state / government business
85 not yet begun / brought into being

Made demonstrable[86] here in Cyprus to him,   140
Hath puddled[87] his clear spirit, and in such cases
Men's natures wrangle[88] with inferior[89] things,
Though great ones[90] are their object. 'Tis even so.
For let our finger ache, and it indues[91]
Our other healthful members even to that sense   145
Of pain. Nay, we[92] must think men[93] are not gods,
Nor of[94] them look for such observancy[95]
As fits the bridal.[96] Beshrew me much, Emilia.
I was, unhandsome[97] warrior[98] as I am,
Arraigning[99] his unkindness[100] with[101] my soul.   150
But now I find I had suborned[102] the witness,
And he's indicted falsely.

Emilia Pray heaven it be state matters, as you think,
And no conception[103] nor no jealous toy[104]
Concerning you.   155

86 evident, apparent
87 muddled, confused
88 bicker, argue
89 lesser, lower
90 things/matters
91 brings, introduces
92 we women
93 males
94 from
95 observance of forms/customs
96 the bridal = marriage
97 faulty, inexperienced, unskillful
98 "O my fair warrior" are Othello's first words to her to her, in act 2, scene 1
99 accusing
100 absence of affection/consideration
101 from, by the perspective of
102 unlawfully secured false testimony
103 notion, imagination
104 trifle, crotchet, fancy

Desdemona Alas the day, I never gave him cause.

Emilia But jealous souls will not be answered[105] so.

They are not ever jealous for the cause,

But jealous for they are jealous. It is a monster

160 Begot upon itself, born on itself.

Desdemona Heaven keep that monster from Othello's mind!

Emilia Lady, amen.

Desdemona I will go seek him. Cassio, walk hereabout.

If I do find him fit, I'll move your suit,

165 And seek to effect it to my uttermost.

Cassio I humbly thank your ladyship.

EXEUNT DESDEMONA AND EMILIA

ENTER BIANCA

Bianca Save[106] you, friend Cassio!

Cassio What make you from[107] home?

How is it with you, my most fair Bianca?

170 Indeed, sweet love, I was coming to your house.

Bianca And I was going to your lodging, Cassio.

What? Keep a week away? Seven days and nights?

Eight score[108] eight hours? And lovers' absent hours,

More tedious than the dial,[109] eight score times?

O weary reckoning.[110]

175 *Cassio* Pardon me, Bianca.

105 rebutted, satisfied
106 may God deliver/protect (a conventional greeting)
107 make you from = are you doing away from
108 a score = 20
109 dial of a clock
110 calculation, computation

I have this while with leaden thoughts been pressed,
But I shall in a more continuate[111] time
Strike off this score[112] of absence. Sweet Bianca,
Take me this work out.

HE GIVES HER DESDEMONA'S HANDKERCHIEF

Bianca   O Cassio, whence came this?
This is some token from a newer friend.   180
To the felt[113] absence now I feel a cause.
Is't[114] come to this? Well, well.

Cassio   Go to, woman!
Throw your vile guesses in the devil's teeth,
From whence you have[115] them. You are jealous now
That this is from some mistress, some remembrance.   185
No, in good troth, Bianca.

Bianca   Why, whose is it?

Cassio I know not neither.[116] I found it in my chamber,
I like the work well. Ere it be demanded,[117]
As like enough it will, I'd have it copied.
Take it, and do't, and leave me for this time.[118]   190

Bianca Leave you? Wherefore?

Cassio I do attend here on the general,
And think it no addition,[119] nor my wish,

111 more continuate = more lasting/less interrupted
112 strike off this score = cancel/pay off this reckoning/tally mark
113 perceived, experienced
114 is't = has it
115 got
116 either
117 asked for, requested
118 this time = now
119 added honor

To have him see me womaned.

Bianca   Why, I pray you?

195 *Cassio* Not that I love you not.

Bianca But that you do not love me.

I pray you bring me on the way a little,[120]

And say if I shall see you soon at night.

Cassio 'Tis but a little way[121] that I can bring you,

200 For I attend here. But I'll see you soon.

Bianca 'Tis very good. I must be circumstanced.[122]

EXEUNT

---

120 bring me on the way a little = escort me along the road a bit
121 distance
122 be circumstanced = accept/be governed by circumstances/realities

Act 4

SCENE I

A street

ENTER OTHELLO AND IAGO

Iago   Will you think so?
Othello   Think so, Iago?
Iago   What,
  To kiss in private?
Othello   An unauthorized[1] kiss?
Iago   Or to be naked with her friend in bed,
  An hour or more, not meaning any harm?
Othello Naked in bed, Iago, and not mean harm?   5
  It is hypocrisy against[2] the devil.
  They that mean virtuously and yet do so,[3]
  The devil their virtue tempts, and they tempt heaven.

---

1 illicit, unsanctioned
2 with? in active opposition / resistance to? in the face / presence of? in
  preparation for?
3 things like this ("thus")

Iago   So[4] they do nothing, 'tis a venial slip.[5]

10   But if I give my wife a handkerchief –

Othello What then?

Iago   Why, then, 'tis hers, my lord, and being hers,

She may, I think, bestow't on any man.

Othello She is protectress of her honor too.

15   May she give that?

Iago   Her honor is an essence[6] that's not seen:

They have it very oft that have it not.[7]

But for the handkerchief –

Othello By heaven, I would most gladly have forgot it.

20   Thou said'st – O, it comes o'er[8] my memory,

As doth the raven o'er the infected[9] house,

Boding[10] to all – he had my handkerchief.

Iago   Ay. What of that?

Othello   That's not so good now.[11]

Iago   What if I had said I had seen him do you wrong?

25   Or heard him say – as knaves be such abroad,[12]

Who having, by their own importunate[13] suit,

Or voluntary dotage[14] of some mistress,

Convinced or supplied[15] them, cannot choose

---

4 if

5 venial slip = forgivable / unimportant (1) error / fault, (2) evasion

6 element, substance, characteristic

7 they often have it by reputation, though not in fact

8 to, across

9 tainted / contaminated with (1) disease / infected properties, (2) evil / diseased morality

10 portending, presaging

11 now that is not so good

12 at large, all over

13 troublesome, persistent

14 foolishness, infatuation, stupidity

15 convinced or supplied = firmly persuaded or fulfilled / satisfied

But they must blab[16] –

Othello   Hath he said anything?

Iago   He hath, my lord, but be you well assured,   30
    No more than he'll unswear.

Othello   What hath he said?

Iago   Why, that he did – I know not what he did.

Othello   What? what?

Iago   Lie.

Othello   With her?

Iago   With her, on her, what you will.

Othello   Lie with her? Lie on her? We say lie on her,[17] when   35
they belie[18] her. Lie with her. That's fulsome.[19] Handkerchief
– confessions – handkerchief! To confess, and be hanged for
his labor, first to be hanged, and then to confess. I tremble at
it. Nature would not invest[20] herself in such shadowing[21]
passion without some instruction.[22] It is not words that shake   40
me thus. – Pish – Noses, ears, and lips. Is't possible? Confess –
handkerchief! O devil! –

OTHELLO FALLS IN A TRANCE

Iago   Work on.
    My medicine works. Thus credulous fools are caught,
    And many worthy. And chaste dames even thus,   45
    All guiltless, meet reproach. – What ho? my lord?
    My lord, I say. Othello!

16 reveal indiscreetly, tell, chatter
17 say lie on her = accuse her of lying
18 they belie = her words contradict/give the lie to
19 rank, overgrown
20 clothe, wrap, enclose
21 boding, prefiguring
22 information, knowledge

ENTER CASSIO

How now, Cassio!

Cassio What's the matter?

Iago My lord is fallen into an epilepsy,
50 This is his second fit. He had one yesterday.

Cassio Rub him about the temples.

Iago The lethargy[23] must have his[24] quiet course.
  If not, he foams at[25] mouth, and by and by
  Breaks out to[26] savage madness. Look, he stirs,
55 Do you withdraw yourself a little while,
  He will recover straight. When he is gone,
  I would on great occasion[27] speak with you.

EXIT CASSIO

How is it, general? Have you not hurt your head?

Othello Dost thou mock me?

Iago   I mock you not, by heaven.
60 Would you would bear your fortune like a man.

Othello A hornèd[28] man's a monster and a beast.

Iago There's many a beast, then, in a populous city,
  And many a civil[29] monster.

Othello Did he confess it?[30]

Iago   Good sir, be a man.

23 torpor, inertness
24 its
25 at the
26 in, into
27 circumstances, matters
28 cuckolded
29 citizen? civilized? refined?
30 (?) is it certain, then?

Think[31] every bearded fellow that's but yoked[32]   65
May draw[33] with you. There's millions now alive
That nightly lie in those unproper[34] beds
Which they dare swear peculiar.[35] Your case is better.
O, 'tis the spite of hell, the fiend's arch-mock,
To lip[36] a wanton in a secure couch,   70
And to suppose her chaste. No, let me know,
And knowing what I am, I know what she shall be.[37]

Othello O, thou art wise, 'tis certain.

Iago   Stand you awhile apart,
Confine yourself but in a patient list.[38]   75
Whilst you were here o'erwhelmèd with your grief –
A passion most unsuiting such a man –
Cassio came hither. I shifted[39] him away,
And laid[40] good 'scuses upon your ecstasy,[41]
Bade him anon return, and here speak with me,   80
The which he promised. Do but encave[42] yourself,
And mark the fleers[43] the gibes,[44] and notable scorns[45]

31 consider/realize that
32 (1) coupled, with a yoke, like a draught animal, (2) married
33 pull, haul
34 (1) improper, indecent, (2) common, universal
35 their own private property
36 kiss
37 (1) and knowing what kind of man I am (bold, brave, strong), I know what
   she will be (dead), (2) and knowing what kind of man I am (burdened with
   original sin/inherently imperfect), I know what she must be (unfaithful)
38 boundary, limit
39 I shifted = by means of indirect/evasive methods, I sent
40 placed, set
41 frenzy, fit
42 enclose, cover up ("hide")
43 notable scorns = striking/obvious sneers/gibes/mockery
44 scoffing, taunting, flouting
45 notable scorns = remarkable/striking/conspicuous contempt

That dwell[46] in every region[47] of his face.
For I will make him tell the tale anew,
85   Where, how, how oft, how long ago, and when
He hath, and is again to cope[48] your wife.
I say, but mark his gesture. Marry, patience,
Or I shall say you're all in all in spleen,[49]
And nothing of a man.

Othello   Dost thou hear, Iago?
90   I will be found most cunning in my patience,
But – dost thou hear? – most bloody.

Iago   That's not amiss,[50]
But yet keep time[51] in all. Will you withdraw?

OTHELLO WITHDRAWS

Now will I question Cassio of[52] Bianca,
A housewife that, by selling her desires,
95   Buys herself bread and clothes. It is a creature
That dotes on Cassio – as 'tis the strumpet's[53] plague
To beguile many and be beguiled by one.
He, when he hears of her, cannot refrain
From the excess of laughter. – Here he comes.
100   As he shall smile, Othello shall go mad,

46 abide, inhabit
47 area, part
48 have intercourse with
49 all in all in spleen = altogether / completely in a hot / capricious / peevish
   temper
50 wrong, out of order
51 the proper pace / speed / tempo
52 about
53 harlot, prostitute★

And his unbookish[54] jealousy must construe[55]
Poor Cassio's smiles, gestures, and light[56] behavior
Quite in the wrong.

ENTER CASSIO

      How do you now, lieutenant?

Cassio The worser that you give me the addition[57]
 Whose want[58] even kills me.   105

I*ago* Ply[59] Desdemona well, and you are[60] sure on't.
 Now, if this suit lay in Bianca's power, (*Iago lowers his voice*)
 How quickly should you speed![61]

Cassio   Alas, poor caitiff![62]

Othello (*aside*) Look how he laughs already.

Iago I never knew woman love man so.   110

Cassio Alas, poor rogue, I think indeed she loves me.

Othello (*aside*) Now he denies it faintly, and laughs it out.

Iago Do you hear, Cassio?

Othello   (*aside*) Now he importunes him
 To tell it o'er. Go to, well said, well said.

Iago She gives it out that you shall marry her.   115
 Do you intend it?

Cassio   Ha, ha, ha!

54 unlearnèd
55 analyze, interpret (conSTRUE)
56 trivial, unimportant, venial, of no weight
57 title, "lieutenant"
58 lack
59 apply to, work away at, solicit, importune, press
60 will be
61 succeed, prosper
62 wretch

Othello (aside) Do you triumph, Roman?[63] Do you triumph?

Cassio I marry. What? A customer?[64] Prythee, bear[65] some charity to my wit,[66] do not think it so unwholesome.[67] Ha,

120   ha, ha!

Othello (aside) So, so, so, so. They laugh that win.

Iago Why, the cry[68] goes that you shall marry her.

Cassio Prythee, say true.

Iago   I am a very villain else.

Othello (aside) Have you scored[69] me? Well.

125 Cassio This is the monkey's own giving out. She is persuaded I will marry her, out of her own love and flattery, not out of my promise.

Othello (aside) Iago beckons me; now he begins the story.

Cassio She was here even now. She haunts me in every place. I

130   was the other day talking on the sea bank with certain Venetians, and thither comes the bauble,[70] and falls thus about my neck.

Othello (aside) Crying, "O dear Cassio," as it were. His gesture imports it.

135 Cassio So hangs, and lolls,[71] and weeps upon me. So shakes and pulls me. Ha, ha, ha!

63 triumphant Roman generals were welcomed back to Rome in a great parade: triumphs
64 (1) a whore (if Cassio refers to Bianca), (2) a purchaser, client (if he refers to himself)
65 profess, pretend, maintain
66 mind, reason
67 noxious, infirm, sick, corrupted
68 rumor
69 whipped me and left marks
70 (1) plaything, pretty toy / gewgaw, (2) fool
71 droops, dangles

Othello (*aside*) Now he tells how she plucked him to my
    chamber. O, I see that nose of yours, but not that dog I shall
    throw it to.

Cassio   Well, I must leave[72] her company.   140

Iago   Before me! Look where she comes.

Cassio   'Tis such[73] another fitchew.[74] Marry, a perfumed one.

ENTER BIANCA

What do you mean by this haunting of me?

Bianca   Let the devil and his dam[75] haunt you! What did you
    mean by that same[76] handkerchief you gave me even[77] now?   145
    I was a fine[78] fool to take it. I must take out the work? A
    likely piece of work that you should find it in your chamber
    and not know who left it there. This is some minx's token,
    and I must take out the work? There, give it[79] your hobby-
    horse,[80] wheresoever you had it, I'll take out no work on't.[81]   150

Cassio   How now, my sweet Bianca? How now? how now?

Othello (*aside*) By heaven, that should[82] be my handkerchief.

Bianca   An[83] you'll come to supper to-night, you may; an you
    will not, come when you are next prepared[84] for.

72 quit, give up
73 just
74 polecat
75 mother
76 identical (in a vexed sense: "that blankety-blank")
77 just
78 perfect, absolute, sheer
79 it to
80 loose woman, whore
81 on't = off/from it
82 must
83 if
84 ready

EXIT BIANCA

155 *Iago*   After her, after her.

    Cassio   I must, she'll rail[85] in the street else.[86]

    Iago   Will you sup there?

    Cassio   Yes, I intend so.

    Iago   Well, I may chance to see you, for I would very fain

160   speak with you.

    Cassio   Prythee, come. Will you?

    Iago   Go to. Say no more.

EXIT CASSIO

    Othello (*coming forward*) How shall I murder him, Iago?

    Iago   Did you perceive how he laughed at his vice?[87]

165 *Othello* O Iago!

    Iago   And did you see the handkerchief?

    Othello Was that mine?

    Iago   Yours, by this hand. And to see how he prizes the

    foolish woman your wife! She gave it[88] him, and he hath

170   given it his whore.

    Othello I would have him nine years a-killing. A fine[89] woman,

    a fair woman, a sweet woman?

    Iago   Nay, you must forget that.

    Othello Ay, let her rot, and perish, and be damned tonight, for

175   she shall not live. No, my heart is turned to stone. I strike it,

    and it hurts my hand. O, the world hath not a sweeter

85 curse
86 otherwise
87 depravity, corruption
88 it to
89 (1) superior, pure, (2) delicate, exquisite, refined

creature. She might lie by an emperor's side, and command
him tasks.

Iago   Nay, that's not your way.[90]

Othello Hang her, I do but say what she is – so delicate with her 180
needle, an admirable musician. O, she will sing the savageness
out of a bear. Of so high and plenteous wit and invention.

Iago   She's the worse for all this.

Othello O, a thousand, a thousand times. And then, of so gentle
a condition.   185

Iago   Ay, too gentle.

Othello Nay, that's certain. But yet the pity of it, Iago. O Iago,
the pity of it, Iago!

Iago   If you are so fond over[91] her iniquity,[92] give her
patent[93] to offend, for if it touch not you, it comes near   190
nobody.

Othello I will chop her into messes.[94] Cuckold me?

Iago   O, 'tis foul in her.

Othello With mine officer?

Iago   That's fouler.   195

Othello Get me some poison, Iago, this night. I'll not
expostulate[95] with her, lest her body[96] and beauty
unprovide[97] my mind again. This night, Iago.

Iago   Do it not with poison, strangle her in her bed, even the

---

90 road, path, course
91 about
92 wickedness, unrighteous deeds
93 license, authority
94 food
95 remonstrate, reason/argue with
96 personal being, individuality
97 make unready/unequipped/unprepared

200 bed she hath contaminated.[98]

Othello   Good, good. The justice of it pleases. Very good.

Iago   And for Cassio, let me be his undertaker.[99] You shall
      hear more by midnight.

Othello   Excellent[100] good.

A TRUMPET WITHIN

                        What trumpet is that same?[101]

205 Iago   I warrant something from Venice.
      'Tis Lodovico, this, comes from the Duke.
      See, your wife is with him.

ENTER LODOVICO, DESDEMONA, AND ATTENDANTS

Lodovico   Save you, worthy general!

Othello   With all my heart, sir.

210 Lodovico   The Duke and senators of Venice greet you.

GIVES OTHELLO LETTERS

Othello   I kiss the instrument[102] of their pleasures.

READS

Desdemona And what's the news, good cousin Lodovico?

Iago   I am very glad to see you, signior.
      Welcome to Cyprus.

215 Lodovico   I thank you. How does Lieutenant Cassio?

Iago   Lives,[103] sir.

---

98 sullied, defiled
99 be his undertaker = take care of him
100 exceptionally
101 that same = that
102 agent
103 he lives/is alive

Desdemona Cousin, there's fall'n between him, and my lord,
    An unkind breach.[104] But you shall make all well.

Othello   Are you sure of that?

Desdemona   My lord?

Othello   (*reads aloud*) "This fail you not to do, as you will."[105]   220

Lodovico   He did not call.[106] He's busy in the paper.[107]
    Is there division[108] 'twixt my lord and Cassio?

Desdemona A most unhappy one. I would do much
    To atone them,[109] for the love I bear to Cassio.

Othello   Fire and brimstone![110]

Desdemona   My lord?

Othello   (*to Desdemona*) Are
    you wise?[111]   225

Desdemona What, is he angry?

Lodovico   May be the letters moved him.
    For, as I think, they do command him home,
    Deputing[112] Cassio in his government.[113]

Desdemona Trust me, I am glad on't.[114]

Othello   Indeed?

Desdemona   My lord?

---

104 unkind breach = strange / unnatural / unpleasant rupture / separation
105 as you will = (1) as you will not fail to do, (2) in what manner / way you
    wish
106 he did not call = Othello did not address / speak to us (Lodovico wrongly
    explains away Othello's remark to Desdemona)
107 in the paper = with / reading the letters
108 separation, discord, variance
109 atone them = reconcile them (Othello and Cassio)
110 (to be found in hell)
111 sane / right in the head
112 appointing, substituting
113 office, authority, rule
114 on't = of it

Othello   I am glad to see you mad.[115]

230 Desdemona   Why, sweet Othello –

OTHELLO STRIKES HER

Othello   Devil!

Desdemona I have not deserved this.

Lodovico   My lord, this would not be believed in Venice,
    Though I should swear I saw't. 'Tis very much,[116]
    Make her amends. She weeps.

235 Othello   O devil, devil!
    If that the earth could teem[117] with woman's tears,
    Each drop she falls would prove a crocodile.[118]
    Out of my sight!

Desdemona (going) I will not stay to offend you.

240 Lodovico   Truly, an obedient lady.
    I do beseech your lordship, call her back.

Othello   Mistress![119]

Desdemona   My lord?

Othello   What would you[120] with her,
    sir?

Lodovico   Who, I, my lord?

Othello   Ay; you did wish that I would make her turn.[121]

245   Sir, she can turn, and turn, and yet go on,

115 out of your mind
116 very much = truly excessive ("too much")
117 bring forth, produce, swarm
118 (legends described crocodiles weeping (1) to trick men into being eaten, (2) after eating men)
119 (a frigidly distant way of addressing his wife)
120 would you = do you want
121 (1) come back, (2) change/transform/reverse positions/directions, (3) be fickle/inconstant, (4) betray, (5) infatuate/drive crazy

And turn again. And she can weep, sir, weep.
And she's obedient. As you say, obedient.
Very obedient. (*to Desdemona*) Proceed you in your tears.
(*to Lodovico*) Concerning this, sir. (*to* Desdemona) O well-
painted[122] passion.
(*to Lodovico*) I am commanded[123] home. (*to Desdemona*) Get   250
you away;
I'll send for you anon. (*to Lodovico*) Sir, I obey the mandate,[124]
And will return to Venice. (*to Desdemona*) Hence, avaunt!

EXIT DESDEMONA

Cassio shall have my place. And, sir, tonight
I do entreat that we may sup together.
You are welcome, sir, to Cyprus.   255
Goats and monkeys![125]

EXIT OTHELLO

Lodovico Is this the noble Moor whom our full senate
Call all in all[126] sufficient? Is this the nature
Whom passion could not shake? Whose solid virtue
The shot[127] of accident nor dart[128] of chance   260
Could neither graze[129] nor pierce?
Iago   He is much changed.

---

122 feigned, pretended, artificial
123 ordered
124 command
125 (Iago's words at 3.3.000: "as prime as goats, as hot as monkeys")
126 all in all = completely, in every respect
127 bullets, shells
128 spears, javelins
129 touch

Lodovico Are his wits safe?[130] Is he not light[131] of brain?

Iago He's that he is. I may not breathe my censure

What he might be. If what he might, he is not,

I would to heaven he were![132]

265 *Lodovico* What, strike his wife!

Iago 'Faith,[133] that was not so well. Yet would I knew[134]

That stroke would prove the worst.

Lodovico Is it his use?[135]

Or did the letters work upon his blood,

And new create this fault?

Iago Alas, alas!

270 It is not honesty in me to speak

What I have seen and known. You shall[136] observe him,

And his own courses will denote[137] him so[138]

That I may save my speech. Do but go after,

And mark how he continues.

275 *Lodovico* I am sorry that I am deceived in him.

EXEUNT

130 sound
131 deficient
132 (?) (this speech is in outline comprehensible, but in detail obscure)
133 in faith
134 would I knew = I wish I knew
135 habit, custom
136 (1) must, (2) will
137 make known, mark
138 in such a way

SCENE 2

The Citadel

ENTER OTHELLO AND EMILIA

Othello You have seen nothing, then?

Emilia Nor ever heard. Nor ever did suspect.

Othello Yes, you have seen Cassio and she together.

Emilia But then I saw no harm. And then I heard

    Each syllable that breath made up between them.   5

Othello What? Did they never whisper?

Emilia   Never, my lord.

Othello Nor send you out o' the way?

Emilia Never.

Othello To fetch her fan, her gloves, her mask,[1] nor nothing?

Emilia Never, my lord.   10

Othello That's strange.

Emilia I durst, my lord, to wager she is honest,

    Lay down[2] my soul at stake.[3] If you think other,[4]

    Remove[5] your thought. It doth abuse your bosom.

    If any wretch have put this in your head,   15

    Let heaven requite[6] it with the serpent's curse!

    For if she be not honest, chaste, and true,

    There's no man happy. The purest of their wives

    Is foul as slander.

1 (worn to keep off the sun, protect the face from dust)
2 durst ... lay down = dare bet
3 at stake = at risk ("as a bet")
4 otherwise, differently
5 withdraw, abandon, dismiss, change
6 repay, reward, revenge

Othello	Bid her come hither. Go.

EXIT EMILIA

20   She says enough. Yet she's[7] a simple bawd[8]
      That cannot say as much. This[9] is a subtle[10] whore,
      A closet[11] lock and key of villainous secrets.
      And yet she'll kneel and pray. I have seen her do't.

ENTER EMILIA WITH DESDEMONA

Desdemona My lord, what is your will?
Othello   Pray, chuck, come hither.
Desdemona What is your pleasure?
25 *Othello*   Let me see your eyes.
      Look in my face.
Desdemona   What horrible fancy's[12] this?
Othello   (*to Emilia*) Some[13] of your function,[14] mistress.
      Leave procreants[15] alone and shut the door.
      Cough, or cry hem, if anybody come.

EXIT EMILIA

30   Your mystery,[16] your mystery. Nay, dispatch.[17]
Desdemona Upon my knees, what doth your speech import?

---

  7 she's = she (any woman) would be
  8 simple bawd = foolish / stupid procurer (female for "pimp")
  9 Desdemona
 10 elusive, expert, clever
 11 hidden / secret place
 12 fancy's = whim is
 13 give me / let me have
 14 your function = the business of your trade (as a bawd)
 15 those who make babies / have sex
 16 hidden / secret matter
 17 hurry, quick

    I understand a fury in your words,

    But not the words.[18]

Othello   Why, what art thou?

Desdemona Your wife, my lord. Your true and loyal wife.

Othello   Come, swear it. Damn thyself,   35

    Lest being like one of heaven,[19] the devils themselves

    Should fear to seize thee. Therefore be double damned.

    Swear thou art honest.

Desdemona   Heaven doth truly know it.

Othello   Heaven truly knows that thou art false[20] as hell.

Desdemona To whom, my lord? With whom? How am I false?   40

Othello   Ah Desdemona, away, away, away!

Desdemona Alas the heavy day. Why do you weep?

    Am I the motive[21] of these tears, my lord?

    If haply you my father do suspect

    An instrument of this your calling back,   45

    Lay not your blame on me. If you have lost him,

    Why, I have lost him too.

Othello   Had it pleased heaven

    To try[22] me with affliction, had they rained

    All kinds of sores and shames on my bare head,

    Steeped me in poverty to the very lips,   50

    Given to captivity me and my utmost[23] hopes,

    I should have found in some place of my soul

    A drop of patience. But alas, to make me

18 ("but not the words": from the Quarto)
19 being like one of heaven = looking as you do like an angel
20 treacherous
21 cause, reason
22 test
23 final

       A fixèd[24] figure for the time, for scorn

55   To point his slow unmoving finger at!

       Yet could I bear that too, well, very well.

       But there where I have garnered[25] up my heart,

       Where either I must live, or bear[26] no life,

       The fountain[27] from the which my current[28] runs,

60   Or else dries up – to be discarded[29] thence!

       Or keep[30] it as a cistern[31] for foul toads

       To knot and gender[32] in. Turn thy complexion there,

       Patience,[33] thou young and rose-lipp'ed cherubin.[34]

       Ay, here[35] look grim as hell.

65   *Desdemona* I hope my noble lord esteems[36] me honest.

     Othello   O ay, as summer flies are in the shambles,[37]

       That quicken even with blowing.[38] O thou weed,[39]

       Who art so lovely fair, and smell'st so sweet

       That the sense[40] aches at thee, would thou hadst ne'er been

       born!

24 lasting, permanent
25 stored, deposited
26 have, own
27 spring, source, well
28 flowing stream ("life")
29 rejected, cast off
30 or keep = or else to maintain / preserve
31 water tank / reservoir / pond
32 knot and gender = entangle and beget / copulate
33 turn thy complexion there, Patience = look at that (complexion = countenance, face), Patience
34 (a description of Patience)
35 at Desdemona
36 thinks
37 meat stall / market
38 quicken even with blowing = are conceived / given life the moment the male fly deposits semen in the female (oviposition = blowing)
39 wild / rank plant (the blossoming of plants also = blowing)
40 the sense = perception

Desdemona Alas, what ignorant[41] sin have I committed?   70

Othello   Was this fair paper, this most goodly book,

Made to write "whore" upon? What committed,

Committed? O thou public commoner![42]

I should[43] make very forges of my cheeks,

That would to cinders burn up modesty,   75

Did I but speak thy deeds. What committed?

Heaven stops[44] the nose at it, and the moon winks.

The bawdy wind, that kisses all it meets,

Is hushed within the hollow mine[45] of earth

And will not hear it. What committed?   80

Impudent strumpet!

Desdemona   By heaven, you do me wrong.

Othello   Are not you a strumpet?

Desdemona No, as I am[46] a Christian.

If to preserve this vessel[47] for my lord

From any other foul unlawful touch   85

Be not to be a strumpet, I am none.

Othello   What, not a whore?

Desdemona   No, as I shall be saved.

Othello   Is't possible?

Desdemona   O, heaven forgive us!

Othello   I cry you mercy[48] then.

I took you for that cunning whore of Venice   90

41 unknowing, unconscious, innocent
42 common whore
43 would
44 plugs, blocks/stuffs up
45 subterranean cavity
46 as I am = in the name of my being
47 her body
48 cry you mercy = beg your pardon

That married with Othello. (*calling to Emilia*) You, mistress,

That have the office opposite[49] to Saint Peter,

And keeps[50] the gate of hell![51]

ENTER EMILIA

You, you. Ay, you!

We have done our course.[52] There's money for your pains.

95   I pray you turn the key, and keep our counsel.

EXIT OTHELLO

Emilia   Alas, what does this gentleman conceive?[53]

How do you, madam? How do you, my good lady?

Desdemona Faith, half asleep.[54]

Emilia   Good madam, what's the matter with my lord?

Desdemona With who?[55]

100 *Emilia*   Why, with my lord, madam.

Desdemona Who is thy lord?

Emilia   He that is yours, sweet lady.

Desdemona I have none. Do not talk to me, Emilia.

I cannot weep, nor answer have I none

But what should go by water.[56] Prythee, tonight

105   Lay on my bed my wedding sheets – remember –

---

49 the office opposite = the employment/function/task directly opposed/
    contrary to
50 take care of, guard, watch over
51 (as opposed to St. Peter, who is the gatekeeper of heaven)
52 bout, gallop ("what we were supposed to have done")
53 does this gentleman conceive = what is this man thinking/imagining
54 dormant, numb, stunned
55 (in spoken English, the "who"/"whom" controversy was won, at least 300
    years ago, by "who")
56 go by water = be transmitted by tears

And call thy husband hither.

Emilia   Here's a change indeed.

EXIT EMILIA

Desdemona 'Tis meet I should be used so, very meet.
 How have I been behaved, that he might stick
 The small'st opinion[57] on my least misuse?[58]

ENTER EMILIA AND IAGO

Iago   What is your pleasure, madam? How is't with you? 110
Desdemona I cannot tell. Those that do teach young babes
 Do it with gentle means and easy tasks.
 He might have chid me so, for in good faith,
 I am a child[59] to chiding.
Iago   What is the matter, lady?
Emilia   Alas, Iago, my lord hath so bewhored[60] her, 115
 Thrown such despite[61] and heavy terms upon her,
 As true hearts cannot bear.
Desdemona   Am I that name, Iago?
Iago   What name, fair lady?
Desdemona Such as she says my lord did say I was.
Emilia   He called her whore. A beggar in his drink[62] 120
 Could not have laid such terms upon his callet.[63]
Iago   Why did he so?

57 stick the small'st opinion = fix/fasten/attach the most minor/trivial
 judgment/belief/estimate
58 wrong/wicked conduct
59 inexperienced ("unaccustomed")
60 used the word "whore" against
61 contempt, scorn, disdain
62 in his drink = when drunk
63 strumpet, lewd woman

Desdemona   I do not know. I am sure I am none such.

Iago   Do not weep, do not weep. Alas the day!

125 Emilia   Hath she forsook so many noble matches,
　　　　　Her father, and her country, and her friends,
　　　　　To be called whore? Would it not make one weep?

Desdemona   It is my wretchèd fortune.

Iago   Beshrew him for't.
　　　　　How comes this trick[64] upon him?

Desdemona   Nay, heaven doth know.[65]

130 Emilia   I will be hanged, if some eternal[66] villain,
　　　　　Some busy and insinuating[67] rogue,
　　　　　Some cogging, cozening[68] slave, to get some office,[69]
　　　　　Have not devised this slander. I will be hanged else.

Iago   Fie, there is no such man. It is impossible.

135 Desdemona   If any such there be, heaven pardon him!

Emilia   A halter[70] pardon him, and hell gnaw his bones!
　　　　　Why should he call her whore? Who keeps her company?
　　　　　What place? What time? What form?[71] What likelihood?
　　　　　The Moor's abused by some most villainous knave,
140　　　　Some base notorious knave, some scurvy[72] fellow.
　　　　　O heaven, that such companions thou'dst unfold,[73]

64 crafty / fraudulent / sham act
65 heaven knows; we don't
66 (1) infinite, endless, perpetual, (2) infinitely disgusting
67 wily, wheedling, artful
68 cogging, cozening = cheating, fraudulent
69 (1) attention (2) post
70 hangman's rope
71 manner, way
72 shabby, worthless, contemptible
73 thou'dst unfold = you (heaven) would disclose / make clear / lay open to
　　view

And put in every honest hand a whip
To lash the rascals naked through the world
Even from the east to th'west.

Iago   Speak within door.[74]

Emilia   O, fie upon them![75] Some such squire[76] he was   145
   That turned your wit the seamy side[77] without,
   And made you to suspect me with the Moor.

Iago   You are a fool. Go to.

Desdemona   Alas, Iago,
   What shall I do to win my lord again?
   Good friend, go to him. For by this light of heaven,   150
   I know not how I lost him. Here I kneel.
   If e'er my will did trespass[78] 'gainst his love,
   Either in discourse[79] of thought or actual deed,
   Or that mine eyes, mine ears, or any sense,
   Delighted them[80] in any other form,[81]   155
   Or that I do not yet,[82] and ever did
   And ever will – though he do shake me off
   To beggarly[83] divorcement – love him dearly,
   Comfort forswear me![84] Unkindness may do much,

---

74 speak within door = softly, so that no one outside this room hears
75 such rascals
76 follower, servant (negative connotation)
77 seamy side = under-/rough side of a garment (seams having visible,
   protruding hard edges)
78 sin, offend
79 course
80 delighted them = took pleasure
81 body ("man")
82 do not yet = still do not so take pleasure
83 sordid, mean
84 comfort forswear me = may (1) support/help (2) gladness/solace abandon
   me if I have done such things

160 And his unkindness may defeat[85] my life,

But never taint my love. I cannot say whore.

It does abhor me now I speak the word.

To do the act that might the addition earn

Not the world's mass[86] of vanity could make me.

165 *Iago*   I pray you, be content. 'Tis but his humor.

The business of the state does him offense,

And he does chide with you.[87]

Desdemona   If 'twere no other.[88]

Iago   'Tis but so, I warrant.

TRUMPETS WITHIN

Hark, how these instruments summon to supper.[89]

170 The messengers of[90] Venice stay[91] the meat,[92]

Go in,[93] and weep not. All things shall be well.

EXEUNT DESDEMONA AND EMILIA

ENTER RODERIGO

How now, Roderigo!

Roderigo   I do not find that thou deal'st justly with me.

Iago   What in[94] the contrary?

85 destroy, ruin, nullify
86 whole bulk
87 (this line from the Quarto)
88 if 'twere no other = if only it might be that, and nothing more
89 (?) what a great deal of noise they make
90 from
91 are coming to
92 meal, repast, dinner
93 go in = go into dinner ("join the company")
94 to

Roderigo Every day thou daffest me[95] with some device, Iago, 175
and rather, as it seems to me now, keep'st from me all
conveniency[96] than suppliest me with the least advantage[97]
of hope. I will indeed no longer endure it, nor am I yet
persuaded to put up[98] in peace what already I have foolishly
suffered.[99] 180

Iago Will you hear me, Roderigo?

Roderigo I have heard too much. And your words and
performances[100] are no kin together.[101]

Iago You charge[102] me most unjustly.

Roderigo With naught but truth. I have wasted[103] myself out of 185
my means.[104] The jewels you have had from me to deliver to
Desdemona would half[105] have corrupted[106] a votarist.[107]
You have told me she hath received them, and returned
me[108] expectations and comforts of sudden respect[109] and
acquaintance,[110] but I find none. 190

Iago Well, go to. Very well.

Roderigo Very well, go to! I cannot go to, man, nor 'tis not very

95 daffest me = put me off
96 opportunity
97 circumstance, position, chance
98 up with
99 endured, submitted to
100 actions, deeds
101 no kin together = not from the same family
102 accuse
103 consumed, exhausted
104 resources
105 only a half of them
106 defiled, perverted
107 devotee ("nun")
108 returned me = given me back
109 sudden respect = speedy regard/favor
110 intimacy

well. Nay, I think 'tis very scurvy,[111] and begin to find myself
fobbed[112] in it.

195 *Iago*   Very well.

Roderigo I tell you 'tis not very well. I will make myself known
to Desdemona. If she will return me my jewels, I will give
over my suit and repent my unlawful solicitation. If not, assure
yourself I will seek satisfaction[113] of you.

200 *Iago*   You have said[114] now.

Roderigo Ay, and said nothing but what I protest[115] intendment
of doing.

Iago   Why, now I see there's mettle[116] in thee, and even from
this instant do build on thee a better opinion than ever

205 before. Give me thy hand, Roderigo. Thou hast taken against
me a most just exception.[117] But yet I protest I have dealt
most directly in thy affair.

Roderigo It hath not appeared.[118]

Iago   I grant indeed it hath not appeared, and your suspicion

210 is not without wit and judgment. But, Roderigo, if thou hast
that in thee indeed, which I have greater reason to believe
now than ever – I mean purpose, courage, and valor[119] – this
night show it. If thou the next night following enjoy[120] not
Desdemona, take me from this world with treachery and

111 shabby, contemptible
112 cheated
113 (1) compensation, amends, (2) a duel of honor
114 you have said = you're finished
115 declare most formally / solemnly
116 spirit, vigor, courage
117 complaint
118 shown itself, become apparent / visible
119 worth, manliness, boldness
120 possess, have sexual intercourse with

devise engines[121] for my life.   215

Roderigo Well, what is it? Is it within reason and compass?[122]

Iago   Sir, there is especial commission[123] come from Venice
to depute[124] Cassio in Othello's place.

Roderigo Is that true? Why then Othello and Desdemona return
again to Venice.   220

Iago   O no. He goes into Mauritania,[125] and taketh away
with him the fair Desdemona, unless his abode be lingered[126]
here by some accident. Wherein none can be so
determinate[127] as the removing of Cassio.

Roderigo How do you mean removing of him?   225

Iago   Why, by making him uncapable of Othello's place.
Knocking out his brains.

Roderigo And that you would have me to do?

Iago   Ay, if you dare do yourself a profit and a right.[128] He
sups tonight with a harlotry,[129] and thither will I go to him.   230
He knows not yet of his honorable[130] fortune. If you will
watch his going thence – which I will fashion[131] to fall
out[132] between twelve and one – you may take[133] him at

121 plots
122 reach
123 order, instruction, command
124 appoint
125 (the population of Mauritania is largely Moorish)
126 protracted, continued
127 definitive, decisive
128 that which is proper/a duty
129 harlot
130 distinguished
131 shape, contrive
132 fall out = occur
133 lay hold of, strike, catch by surprise

your pleasure. I will be near to second[134] your attempt, and

235   he shall fall between us. Come, stand not amazed at it, but

go[135] along with me. I will show you such a necessity in his

death that you shall think yourself bound to put it on[136] him.

It is now high[137] supper time, and the night grows to

waste.[138] About it.[139]

240 *Roderigo* I will[140] hear further reason for this.

    Iago   And you shall be satisfied.

EXEUNT

134 support
135 walk
136 put it on = attack, proceed against
137 well advanced/along to
138 grows to waste = is coming to/approaching its end
139 about it = set about it ("do it")
140 wish/want to

SCENE 3

The Citadel

ENTER OTHELLO, LODOVICO, DESDEMONA, EMILIA,
AND ATTENDANTS

Lodovico	I do beseech you, sir, trouble yourself no further.
Othello	O, pardon me. 'Twill do me good to walk.
Lodovico	Madam, good night. I humbly thank your ladyship.
Desdemona	Your honor is most welcome.
Othello	Will you walk, sir? O, Desdemona.
Desdemona	My lord?
Othello	Get you to bed on th'instant. I will be returned

forthwith.[1] Dismiss your attendant there. Look't be done.

Desdemona I will, my lord.

EXEUNT OTHELLO, LODOVICO, AND ATTENDANTS

Emilia How goes it now? He looks gentler[2] than he did. 10

Desdemona He says he will return incontinent.[3]

He hath commanded me to go to bed,

And bade me to dismiss you.

Emilia Dismiss me?

Desdemona It was his bidding.[4] Therefore, good Emilia,

Give me my nightly wearing,[5] and adieu. 15

We must not now displease him.

Emilia I would[6] you had never seen him.

1 without delay, directly
2 quieter, softer, milder
3 straightway, without delay
4 order, command
5 clothing
6 wish

Desdemona So would not I. My love doth so approve him,

That even his stubbornness, his checks, his frowns –

20   Prythee, unpin me[7] – have grace and favor in them.

Emilia   I have laid those sheets you bade me on the bed.

Desdemona All's one.[8] Good Father, how foolish are our minds!

If I do die before thee, prythee, shroud me

In one of those same sheets.

Emilia   Come, come. You talk.[9]

25 *Desdemona* My mother had a maid[10] called Barbary,[11]

She was in love. And he she loved proved mad,

And did forsake her. She had a song of "willow,"

An old thing 'twas. But it expressed[12] her fortune,

And she died singing it. That song tonight

30   Will not go from my mind. I have much to do[13]

But to go hang[14] my head all at one side[15]

And sing it like poor Barbary. Prythee dispatch.

Emilia   Shall I go fetch your nightgown?

Desdemona No, unpin me here.

35   This Lodovico[16] is a proper man.

Emilia   A very handsome man.

Desdemona He speaks well.

Emilia   I know a lady in Venice would have walked barefoot

7 unpin me = hair? dress?

8 all's one = it's all one ("all right")

9 speak trivially, prate

10 servant (a word also meaning "slave," as in Latin *servus*)

11 (northern coast of Africa: was the maid a Moor? was she black?)

12 represented, portrayed

13 I have much to do = it is hard to keep myself from

14 bend, droop (in sadness)

15 all at one side = all the way down

16 (Lodovico is her cousin; some editors assign this line to Emilia)

to Palestine for a touch of his nether[17] lip.

Desdemona (*singing*)

> The poor soul sat sighing, by a sycamore tree,   40
>   Sing all a green willow.[18]
> Her hand on her bosom, her head on her knee,
>   Sing willow, willow, willow.
> The fresh[19] streams ran by her, and murmured her moans,
>   Sing willow, willow, willow.   45
> Her salt tears fell from her, and softened the stones,
>   Sing willow, willow, willow.

(*to Emilia*) Lay by[20] these.

> Sing willow, willow –

Prythee, hie[21] thee. He'll come anon.[22]   50

> Sing all a green willow must be my garland.
> Let nobody blame him, his scorn I approve –

Nay, that's not next. Hark! who is't that knocks?

Emilia   It's the wind.

Desdemona   (*singing*)

> I call'd my love false love. But what said he then?   55
>   Sing willow, willow, willow.

17 lower
18 green willow: symbolic of grief for loss of a lover or the failure of love to be reciprocated
19 not saltwater
20 put away, store
21 hurry
22 immediately

If I court mo[23] women, you'll couch[24] with mo men.

So get thee gone, good night. Mine eyes do itch.
Doth that bode[25] weeping?

Emilia   'Tis neither here nor there.

60   *Desdemona* I have heard it said so. O, these men, these men!
Dost thou in conscience think – tell me, Emilia –
That there be women do abuse[26] their husbands
In such gross kind?

Emilia   There be some such, no question.

65   *Desdemona* Wouldst thou do such a deed for all the world?

Emilia   Why, would not you?

Desdemona No, by this heavenly light!

Emilia   Nor I neither by this heavenly light.
I might do't as well i' the dark.

70   *Desdemona* Wouldst thou do such a deed for all the world?

Emilia   The world's a huge thing.
It is a great price for a small vice.

Desdemona In troth, I think thou wouldst not.

Emilia   In troth, I think I should, and undo't[27] when I had
75   done. Marry, I would not do such a thing for a joint-ring,[28]
nor for measures of lawn,[29] nor for gowns, petticoats, nor
caps, nor any petty exhibition.[30] But for all the whole world
– why, who would not make her husband a cuckold to make

23 more
24 sleep
25 foretell, predict
26 deceive, cheat
27 undo't = annul, cancel ("disregard")
28 made of two separable halves
29 measures of lawn = a good deal of fine linen
30 gift, present

him a monarch? I should venture[31] purgatory for't.

Desdemona Beshrew me, if I would do such a wrong for the   80
whole world.

Emilia   Why, the wrong is but a wrong i' the world. And
having the world for your labor,[32] 'tis a wrong in your own
world,[33] and you might[34] quickly make it right.

Desdemona I do not think there is any such woman.   85

Emilia   Yes, a dozen, and as many to the vantage[35] as would
store[36] the world they played for.

But I do think it is their husbands' faults
If wives do fall. Say that they slack their duties
And pour our treasures into foreign laps,   90
Or else break out in peevish jealousies,
Throwing restraint upon us. Or say they strike us,
Or scant[37] our former having, in despite.
Why, we have galls.[38] And though we have some grace,[39]
Yet have we some revenge. Let husbands know   95
Their wives have sense like them. They see and smell
And have their palates both for sweet and sour,
As husbands have. What is it that they do
When they change us for others? Is it sport?

31 risk
32 having the world for your labor = earning/winning the world for the work
   you've done
33 your own world = the world you own/possess
34 could
35 to the vantage = more
36 stock, supply
37 diminish, limit
38 things that irritate, distress, harass
39 we have some grace = (?) we have gotten ourselves some illicit favor? made
   it necessary that we be divinely forgiven?

100   I think it is. And doth affection[40] breed it?
       I think it doth. Is't frailty that thus errs?
       It is so too. And have not we affections,
       Desires for sport, and frailty, as men have?
       Then let them[41] use us well. Else let them know
105   The ills[42] we do their ills instruct[43] us so.
   Desdemona Goodnight, goodnight. Heaven me such usage[44]
       send,
       Not to pick bad from bad,[45] but by[46] bad mend.[47]

                        EXEUNT

40 (1) feeling, emotion, (2) passion, lust
41 men
42 ills that we do to men (ills = sinful actions)
43 train, educate, teach
44 practices, procedures, ways
45 pick bad from bad = choose one sinful thing rather than another sinful thing
46 because of
47 improve

Act 5

A street

ENTER IAGO AND RODERIGO

Iago   Here, stand behind this bulk,[1] straight will he come.

    Wear[2] thy good rapier[3] bare, and put it home.[4]

    Quick, quick, fear nothing. I'll be at thy elbow.

    It makes us, or it mars[5] us, think on that,

    And fix most firm thy resolution.[6]   5

Roderigo Be near at hand, I may miscarry[7] in't.

Iago   Here,[8] at thy hand. Be bold, and take thy stand.[9]

IAGO STEPS ASIDE

1 framework projecting from a shop front
2 carry
3 pointed, two-edged sword
4 put it home = thrust it as far in as it will go
5 ruins
6 REsoLUseeON
7 be unsuccessful
8 I am / will be here
9 ambush position

Roderigo I have no great devotion[10] to the deed,

And yet he hath given me satisfying reasons.

10 'Tis but a man gone. Forth, my sword. He dies.

Iago (*aside*) I have rubbed this young quat[11] almost to the sense,[12]

And he grows angry. Now, whether he kill Cassio,

Or Cassio him, or each do kill the other,

Every way makes my gain. Live Roderigo,[13]

15 He calls me to a restitution large

Of gold and jewels that I bobbed from[14] him,

As gifts to Desdemona.

It must not be. If Cassio do remain,

He hath a daily beauty[15] in his life

20 That makes me ugly. And besides, the Moor

May unfold me to him. There stand I in much peril.

No, he must die. But, so, I hear him coming.

ENTER CASSIO

Roderigo I know his gait, 'tis he. Villain, thou diest!

THRUSTS AT CASSIO

Cassio That thrust had been mine enemy[16] indeed,

25 But that my coat[17] is better than thou know'st.

I will make proof of thine.

---

10 dedication, enthusiasm
11 pimple, boil
12 quick, flesh
13 if Roderigo lives
14 bobbed from = fished/cheated out of
15 daily beauty = habitual graciousness
16 death
17 a mail-coat?

CASSIO DRAWS, AND WOUNDS RODERIGO

Roderigo   O, I am slain!

IAGO FROM BEHIND STABS CASSIO IN THE LEG, AND EXITS

Cassio   I am maimed[18] forever. Help, ho! Murder! Murder!

ENTER OTHELLO TO THE SIDE

Othello   The voice of Cassio, Iago keeps his word.
Roderigo O, villain that I am!
Othello   It is even so.
Cassio   O, help, ho! Light, a surgeon!   30
Othello   'Tis he. O brave Iago, honest and just,
      That hast such noble sense of thy friend's wrong,
      Thou teachest me. Minion,[19] your dear[20] lies dead,
      And your unbless'd[21] fate hies. Strumpet, I come.
      Forth of [22] my heart those charms, thine eyes, are blotted.[23]   35
      Thy bed, lust-stained, shall with lust's blood be spotted.[24]

EXIT OTHELLO

ENTER LODOVICO AND GRATIANO AT A DISTANCE

Cassio   What ho? No watch? No passage?[25] Murder, murder!
Gratiano 'Tis some mischance,[26] the cry is very direful.[27]

18 crippled
19 paramour, illicit mistress (Desdemona)
20 Cassio
21 miserable ("unholy")
22 from, out of
23 effaced, obliterated ("made illegible")
24 stained, disfigured
25 passersby
26 disaster, calamity
27 terrible, dreadful

Cassio	O help!
Lodovico	Hark!
Roderigo	O wretched villain!
Lodovico	Two or three[28] groan. It is a heavy[29] night,

These may be counterfeits.[30] Let's think't[31] unsafe
To come into[32] the cry without more help.

Roderigo	Nobody come? Then shall I[33] bleed to death.
Lodovico	Hark!

ENTER IAGO

Gratiano	Here's one comes in his shirt,[34] with light and weapons.
Iago	Who's there? Whose noise is this that cries on murder?
Lodovico	We do not know.
Iago	Did not you hear a cry?
Cassio	Here, here! For heaven's sake, help me!
Iago	What's the matter?[35]
Gratiano	This is Othello's ancient, as I take it.[36]
Lodovico	The same indeed, a very valiant[37] fellow.
Iago	(*holding up his lantern*) What are you here that cry so grievously?
Cassio	Iago? O, I am spoiled, undone by villains!

28 two or three = there are two or three who
29 overcast, gloomy, dark
30 pretended, sham
31 think't = consider it
32 come into = go to
33 shall I = I must
34 nightshirt
35 what's the matter = what's going on
36 take it = think
37 bold, stout-hearted, worthy

Give me some help.

Iago   O me, lieutenant! What villains have done this?

Cassio   I think that one of them is hereabout,
And cannot make away.

Iago   O treacherous villains!
(*to Lodovico and Gratiano*) What are you there? Come in and
give some help.   60

Roderigo O, help me here!

Cassio   That's one of them.

Iago   (*to Roderigo*) O murderous slave! O villain!

Iago stabs Roderigo

Roderigo O damned Iago! O inhuman dog!

Iago   Kill men i' the dark! Where be these bloody thieves?   65
How silent is this town! Ho, murder, murder!
(*to Gratiano and Lodovico*) What may you be? Are you of good
or evil?

Lodovico As you shall prove us, praise[38] us.

Iago   Signior Lodovico?

Lodovico He, sir.

Iago   I cry you mercy. Here's Cassio hurt by villains.   70

Gratiano Cassio?

Iago   How is't, brother?

Cassio   My leg is cut in two.

Iago   Marry, heaven forbid!
Light,[39] gentlemen, I'll bind it with my shirt.

enter Bianca

38 appraise, set a price / value on
39 give me light, hold the light up for me

75   *Bianca*   What is the matter, ho? who is't that cried?

       Iago   (*mocking her*) Who is't that cried!

     Bianca   O my dear Cassio,

       My sweet Cassio! O Cassio, Cassio, Cassio!

       Iago   O notable strumpet! Cassio, may you suspect

       Who they should be that have thus mangled[40] you?

80   *Cassio*   No.

   Gratiano   I am sorry to find you thus. I have been to seek you.[41]

       Iago   Lend me a garter.[42] So. O for a chair,[43]

       To bear him easily hence!

     Bianca   Alas, he faints! O Cassio, Cassio, Cassio!

85   *Iago*   Gentlemen all, I do suspect this trash[44]

       To be a party[45] in this injury.[46] –

       Patience awhile, good Cassio. – Come, come,

       Lend me a light. – (*looking at Roderigo*) Know we this face

       or no?

       Alas, my friend and my dear countryman

90   Roderigo? No. Yes, sure. Yes, 'tis Roderigo.

   Gratiano   What, of[47] Venice?

       Iago   Even he, sir. Did you know him?

   Gratiano   Know him? Ay.

       Iago   Signior Gratiano? I cry you gentle pardon.

       These bloody accidents must excuse my manners

---

40 wounded, hacked at
41 been to seek you = gone to your lodgings in search of
42 not a leg garter, but one worn over the shoulder as a belt/sash/scarf
43 (1) a chair for sitting, (2) an enclosed chair on poles, for carrying ("litter," "palanquin")
44 disreputable/worthless person
45 participant, accessory
46 mischief, wrongful act
47 from

That so neglected you.

Gratiano   I am glad to see you.   95

Iago   How do you, Cassio? (*calling*) O, a chair, a chair!

Gratiano Roderigo?

Iago   He, he, 'tis he. – O, that's well said.[48] The chair.

A CHAIR IS BROUGHT IN

Some good man bear him carefully from hence,

I'll fetch the general's surgeon. (*to Bianca*) For[49] you, mistress,   100

Save you[50] your labor.[51] (*to Cassio*) He that lies slain here,

Cassio,

Was my dear friend. What malice was between you?

Cassio   None in the world. Nor do I know the man.

Iago   (*to Bianca*) What? Look you pale? — O, bear him out

o' the air.[52]

CASSIO AND RODERIGO ARE CARRIED OUT

Stay you, good gentlemen. – Look you pale, mistress? –   105

Do you perceive the gastness[53] of her eye? –

(*to Bianca*) Nay, if you stare,[54] we shall hear more anon. –

Behold her well. I pray you, look upon her.

Do you see, gentlemen? Nay, guiltiness will speak,

Though tongues were out of use.[55]   110

48 (?) assayed? ("done")
49 as for
50 save you = spare you
51 exertion, trouble
52 night air was "vaporous" and dangerous to the health
53 terrified appearance
54 in astonishment?
55 were out of use = are not being used

ENTER EMILIA

Emilia 'Las, what's the matter? What's the matter, husband?

Iago Cassio hath here been set on in the dark

By Roderigo and fellows that are 'scap'd.

He's almost slain, and Roderigo quite dead.

115 *Emilia* Alas, good gentleman. Alas, good Cassio.

Iago This is the fruits of whoring. Prythee, Emilia,

Go know of Cassio where he supped tonight.

(*to Bianca*) What, do you shake at that?

Bianca He supped at my house, but I therefore[56] shake not.

120 *Iago* O, did he so? I charge you go with me.

Emilia O fie upon thee, strumpet!

Bianca I am no strumpet, but of life as honest

As you that thus abuse me.

Emilia   As I? Fie upon thee!

Iago Kind gentlemen, let's go see poor Cassio dressed.[57]

125 (*to Bianca*) Come, mistress, you must tell's[58] another tale.[59]

Emilia, run you to the Citadel,

And tell my lord and lady what hath happed.

(*to Gratiano, Lodovico*) Will you go on afore? (*aside*) This is the night

That either makes[60] me or fordoes[61] me quite.

EXEUNT

56 for that
57 taken care of
58 tell us
59 another tale = a different sequence of events / narrative
60 sets me up, brings me success / fortune
61 destroys, ruins

SCENE 2

DESDEMONA ASLEEP; A CANDLE BURNS

ENTER OTHELLO

Othello It is the cause,[1] it is the cause, my soul.
　　Let me not name it to you, you chaste[2] stars,
　　It is the cause. Yet I'll not shed her blood,
　　Nor scar that whiter skin of hers, than snow,[3]
　　And smooth as monumental[4] alabaster.　　　　　　　　　5
　　Yet she must die, else she'll betray more men.
　　Put out the light,[5] and then put out the light.[6]
　　(*to candle*) If I quench thee, thou flaming minister,[7]
　　I can again thy former light restore,
　　Should I repent me. (*to Desdemona*) But once put out
　　thy light,　　　　　　　　　　　　　　　　　　　　10
　　Thou cunning'st pattern[8] of excelling nature,[9]
　　I know not where is that Promethean[10] heat
　　That can thy light relume.[11] When I have plucked thy rose,
　　I cannot give it vital[12] growth again,

1 reason/ground for action (the "offense")
2 virtuous, innocent
3 whiter skin of hers, than snow = skin of hers, whiter than snow
4 tomb/funeral/memorial
5 the candle
6 of her life
7 servant, attendant
8 cunning'st pattern = most ingenious model
9 excelling nature = (1) a superior kind/sort, (2) surpassing/great Nature
10 Prometheus = the fire giver
11 rekindle, relight
12 living

15   It must needs[13] wither. I'll smell thee on the tree.[14]

KISSES HER

O balmy[15] breath, that dost almost persuade
Justice[16] to break her sword. One more, one more.[17]
Be thus when thou art dead, and I will kill thee,
And love thee after. One more, and that's the last.
20   So sweet was ne'er so fatal.[18] I must weep,
But they are cruel tears. This sorrow's heavenly,[19]
It strikes where it doth love. – She wakes.

Desdemona Who's there? Othello?

Othello   Ay, Desdemona.

Desdemona Will you come to bed, my lord?

Othello   Have you prayed tonight, Desdemona?

25 *Desdemona*   Ay, my lord.

Othello   If you bethink[20] yourself of any crime[21]
Unreconciled as yet[22] to heaven and grace,[23]
Solicit[24] for it straight.

Desdemona Alack, my lord, what may you mean by that?

---

13 necessarily, of necessity
14 (roses were said to grow on plants/bushes/shrubs/trees: "tree" included single-stemmed bushes)
15 delicately/deliciously fragrant
16 a female goddess, holding either balanced scales or a sword, for cutting the thread of life (Justitia)
17 one more = one more kiss
18 doomed, condemned by fate
19 divine, like the punishment/revenge of God
20 remember, recollect
21 offense, sin
22 unreconciled as yet = not yet absolved/set right
23 heaven's grace/mercy
24 beg, seek ("pray")

Othello   Well, do it, and be brief, I will walk by.[25]   30

  I would not kill thy unprepared spirit,

  No, heaven forfend,[26] I would not kill thy soul.

Desdemona Talk you of killing?

Othello   Ay, I do.

Desdemona   Then heaven

  Have mercy on me!

Othello   Amen, with all my heart.

Desdemona If you say so,[27] I hope you will not kill me.   35

Othello   Humph.

Desdemona And yet I fear you. For you are fatal then

  When[28] your eyes roll so. Why I should fear I know not,

  Since guiltiness I know not. But yet I feel I fear.

Othello   Think on[29] thy sins.

Desdemona   They are loves I bear to you.[30]   40

Othello   Ay, and for that thou diest.

Desdemona That death's unnatural that kills for loving.[31]

  Alas, why gnaw you so your nether lip?

  Some bloody passion shakes your very frame.[32]

  These are portents.[33] But yet I hope, I hope,   45

  They do not point on[34] me.

25 nearby, close by
26 forbid, prevent
27 say so = speak like that
28 then when = when
29 about
30 (her love should be directed to God; to the extent that it is not, she sins
   against God by loving Othello)
31 ("it is against Nature to kill what you love")
32 very frame = (1) entire body, (2) actual body (very = an intensifier)
33 omens, signs
34 at

Othello   Peace, and be still.[35]

Desdemona I will so. What's the matter?

Othello   That handkerchief which I so loved and gave thee,
Thou gav'st to Cassio.

Desdemona   No, by my life and soul!
Send for the man, and ask him.

50 *Othello*   Sweet soul, take heed,
Take heed of perjury; thou art on thy death-bed.

Desdemona Ay, but not yet to die.

Othello   Presently.
Therefore confess thee freely of thy sin.
For to deny each article[36] with oath[37]
55 Cannot remove nor choke[38] the strong conception[39]
That I do groan withal.[40] Thou art to die.

Desdemona O heaven have mercy on me!

Othello   I say, amen.

Desdemona And have you[41] mercy too. I never did
Offend you in my life, never loved Cassio
60 But with such general warranty[42] of heaven
As I might love. I never gave him token.

Othello   By heaven, I saw my handkerchief in 's hand.
O perjured woman, thou dost stone my heart,
And mak'st me call what I intend to do

35 peace, and be still = be silent, and stay silent
36 charge, accusation, indictment
37 an oath
38 smother, stop, kill
39 idea, opinion
40 with, from
41 have you = you have
42 authorization

A murder, which I thought a sacrifice.   65
I saw the handkerchief.
Desdemona   He found it then.
I never gave it him. Send for him hither.
Let him confess a truth.
Othello   He hath confessed.
Desdemona What, my lord?
Othello   That he hath used[43] thee.
Desdemona How? Unlawfully?
Othello   Ay.
Desdemona   He will not say so.   70
Othello   No, his mouth is stopped.
Honest Iago hath ta'en order[44] for't.
Desdemona O, my fear interprets![45] What, is he dead?
Othello   Had all his hairs been lives, my great revenge
Had stomach[46] for them all.   75
Desdemona Alas, he is betrayed,[47] and I undone![48]
Othello   Out,[49] strumpet! Weep'st thou for him to my face?
Desdemona (*trying to rise*) O, banish me, my lord, but kill me not!
Othello   Down, strumpet!
Desdemona Kill me tomorrow, let me live tonight!   80
Othello   Nay, if you strive[50] –
Desdemona But half an hour!

43 had sexual intercourse with
44 ta'en order = undertaken the arrangement/accomplishment
45 explains it to me
46 relish, desire, disposition
47 is betrayed = has been treacherously brought down
48 destroyed, ruined
49 (vehement, indignant exclamation)
50 struggle, fight

Othello	Being done,[51] there is no pause.
Desdemona	But while I say one prayer!
Othello	It is too late.

HE SMOTHERS HER

Emilia (*at the door*) My lord, my lord? What, ho? My lord, my lord.

Othello What noise is this? (*to Desdemona*) Not dead? Not
85 yet quite dead?

I that am cruel[52] am yet merciful,

I would not have thee linger in thy pain.

(*smothering her again*) So, so.

Emilia What ho? My lord, my lord?

Othello Who's there?

90 *Emilia* O good my lord, I would speak a word with you.

Othello (*to Emilia*) Yes. (*to himself*) 'Tis Emilia. (*to Emilia*) By
and by. (*looking at Desdemona*) She's dead.

'Tis like she[53] comes to speak of Cassio's death.

The noise[54] was high. – Ha, no more moving?

Still as the grave. – Shall she[55] come in? Were't good? –

95 I think she[56] stirs again. No. What's best to do?

If she come in, she'll sure speak to my wife.

My wife, my wife. What wife? I have no wife.

O insupportable![57] O heavy hour!

Methinks it[58] should be now a huge eclipse

51 performed, executed, accomplished
52 CRUel
53 'tis like she = it's likely she (Emilia)
54 outcry, clamor
55 shall she = should Emilia
56 Desdemona
57 unbearable, unendurable
58 there

Of sun and moon, and that the affrighted globe   100
Should yawn at alteration.[59]

Emilia   I do beseech you
That I may speak with you. O good my lord.

Othello   I had forgot thee. O come in, Emilia.
Soft, by and by, let me the curtains draw.[60]
(*to Desdemona*) Where art thou?[61] What's the matter[62] with
thee now?   105

HE UNLOCKS THE DOOR

ENTER EMILIA

Emilia   O my good lord, yonder's foul murders done.

Othello   What? Now?

Emilia   But now, my lord.

Othello   It is the very error[63] of the moon,
She comes more nearer earth than she was wont   110
And makes men mad.

Emilia   Cassio, my lord, hath killed a young Venetian
Called Roderigo.

Othello   Roderigo killed?
And Cassio killed?

Emilia   No, Cassio is not killed.

Othello   Not Cassio killed? Then murder's out of tune,   115
And sweet revenge grows harsh.

Desdemona O, falsely, falsely murdered!

Emilia   Alas, what cry is that?

---

59 yawn at alteration = break out in chasms at the/this change
60 curtains draw = close the bed curtains
61 in heaven or in hell?
62 the matter = going on
63 wandering, roaming

Othello	That? What?
Emilia	Out and alas, that was my lady's voice.

EMILIA OPENS THE BED CURTAINS

120 Help, help ho, help! O lady, speak again,
Sweet Desdemona, O sweet mistress, speak!

Desdemona A guiltless death I die.

Emilia O who hath done this deed?

Desdemona Nobody. I myself. Farewell.

125 Commend me to my kind lord. O farewell!

SHE DIES

Othello	Why, how should she be murdered?
Emilia	Alas, who

knows?

Othello	You heard her say herself it was not I.
Emilia	She said so. I must needs report the truth.
Othello	She's like a liar gone to burning hell.

'Twas I that killed her.

130 *Emilia* O the more angel she,
And you the blacker[64] devil!

Othello	She turned to folly.[65] And she was a whore.
Emilia	Thou dost belie[66] her, and thou art a devil.
Othello	She was false as water.[67]
Emilia	Thou art rash[68] as fire, to

say

135 That she was false. O she was heavenly true.

64 more foul/soiled
65 sin, wickedness, lewdness
66 slander
67 (water betrays those who try to stand or walk on it; it is always in flux)
68 reckless

Othello   Cassio did top[69] her. Ask thy husband else.[70]

  O I were damned beneath all depth in hell,

  But that I did proceed upon just grounds

  To this extremity.[71] Thy husband knew it all.

Emilia   My husband?

Othello   Thy husband.

Emilia   That she was false to

  wedlock?[72]   140

Othello   Ay, with Cassio. Nay, had she been true,

  If heaven would make me such another world

  Of one entire and perfect chrysolite,[73]

  I'd not have sold her for it.

Emilia   My husband?

Othello   Ay, 'twas he that told me on her first,   145

  An honest man he is, and hates the slime

  That sticks on filthy deeds.

Emilia   My husband?

Othello   What needs this iterance,[74] woman? I say thy husband.

Emilia   O mistress, villainy hath made mocks with love.

  My husband say she was false?

Othello   He, woman.   150

  I say thy husband. Dost understand the word?

  My friend, thy husband, honest, honest Iago.

Emilia   If he say so, may his pernicious[75] soul

  Rot half a grain[76] a day! He lies to th'heart,

69 have sexual intercourse with
70 if she did not
71 (1) final penalty, (2) severe/rigorous measure
72 her marriage vow
73 green-colored gem (topaz, zircon, etc.)
74 repetition
75 wicked, villainous, destructive
76 a small piece/bit

155 She was too fond of her most filthy bargain.[77]

Othello　Ha?

Emilia　Do thy worst.

This deed of thine is no more worthy heaven

Than thou wast worthy[78] her.

Othello　　　　　　　　　　Peace, you were best.[79]

160 *Emilia*　Thou hast not half that power to do me harm

As I have[80] to be hurt. O gull,[81] O dolt,[82]

As ignorant as dirt! Thou hast done a deed –

OTHELLO REACHES TO HIS SWORD

I care not[83] for thy sword, I'll make thee known,

Though I lost twenty lives. Help, help, ho, help!

165 The Moor hath killed my mistress! Murder, murder!

ENTER MONTANO, GRATIANO, AND IAGO

Montano　What is the matter? How now, general?

Emilia　O, are[84] you come, Iago? You have done well,

That men must lay their murders on your neck.[85]

Gratiano　What is the matter?

170 *Emilia*　(*to Iago*) Disprove[86] this villain, if thou be'st a man.

He says thou told'st him that his wife was false.

77 marriage to Othello
78 worthy of
79 you were best = it would be the most advantageous / desirable thing for
　　you
80 have the endurance
81 dupe, simpleton, fool
82 blockhead, numskull
83 care not = couldn't care less
84 have
85 on your neck = on your head / you
86 refute, contradict

I know thou didst not. Thou'rt not such a villain.

Speak, for my heart is full.

Iago I told him what I thought, and told no more

Than what he found himself was apt and true.   175

Emilia But did you ever tell him she was false?

Iago I did.

Emilia You told a lie, an odious, damnèd lie.

Upon my soul, a lie, a wicked lie.

She false with Cassio! Did you say with Cassio?   180

Iago With Cassio, mistress. Go to, charm[87] your tongue.

Emilia I will not charm my tongue, I am bound to speak.

My mistress here lies murdered in her bed.

All   O heavens forfend!

Emilia And your reports[88] have set the murder on.[89] 185

Othello Nay stare not, masters. It is true, indeed.

Gratiano 'Tis a strange truth.

Montano O monstrous act!

Emilia Villainy, villainy, villainy!

I think upon't, I think – I smell't – O villainy!   190

I thought so then. I'll kill myself for grief.

O villainy, villainy!

Iago What, are you mad? I charge you, get you home.

Emilia Good gentlemen, let me have leave to speak.

'Tis proper I obey him, but not now.   195

Perchance, Iago, I will ne'er go home.

OTHELLO FALLS ONTO THE BED

87 control, subdue
88 statements, accounts, testimony
89 set . . . on = incited, encouraged, arranged

Othello   O! O! O!

Emilia   Nay, lay thee down and roar.
    For thou hast killed the sweetest innocent
    That e'er did lift up eye.

Othello   (*rising*) O, she was foul!
200   I scarce did know you, uncle.[90] There lies your niece,
    Whose breath, indeed, these hands have newly stopped.
    I know this act shows[91] horrible and grim.

Gratiano Poor Desdemona. I am glad thy father's dead.
    Thy match was mortal[92] to him, and pure grief
205   Shore[93] his old thread[94] in twain.[95] Did he live[96] now,
    This sight would make him do a desperate turn,[97]
    Yea, curse his better angel from his side,[98]
    And fall to reprobance.[99]

Othello   'Tis pitiful.[100] But yet Iago knows
210   That she with Cassio hath the act of shame
    A thousand times committed. Cassio confessed it,
    And she did gratify[101] his amorous works[102]
    With that recognizance[103] and pledge of love

90 (custom made a spouse's relatives one's own relatives)
91 looks, appears
92 deadly, fatal
93 cut (past tense of "shear")
94 thread of life
95 two
96 did he live = were he alive
97 desperate turn = despairing change in direction ("life reversal")
98 his better angel from his side = his good guardian angel away from him
99 state of being lost in sin
100 lamentable
101 reward
102 deeds, doings
103 token, acknowledgment

Which I first gave her. I saw it in his hand.
It was a handkerchief, an antique token   215
My father gave my mother.

Emilia   O heaven! O heavenly powers!

Iago   Come, hold your peace.

Emilia   'Twill out, 'twill out. I peace?
No, I will speak as liberal as the north.[104]
Let heaven and men and devils, let them all,   220
All, all, cry shame against me, yet I'll speak.

Iago   Be wise, and get you home.

Emilia   I will not.

IAGO TRIES TO STAB HIS WIFE

Gratiano Fie! Your sword upon[105] a woman?

Emilia   O thou dull[106] Moor, that handkerchief thou speak'st of
I found by fortune and did give my husband.   225
For often with a solemn earnestness —
More than, indeed, belonged to such a trifle —
He begged of me to steal it.

Iago   Villainous whore!

Emilia   She give it Cassio? No, alas I found it,
And I did give't my husband.

Iago   Filth, thou liest!   230

Emilia   By heaven, I do not, I do not, gentlemen.
(*to Othello*) O murd'rous coxcomb,[107] what should such a
fool

---

104 liberal as the north = free as the north wind
105 against
106 foolish, stupid
107 simpleton

Do with so good a wife?

Othello   Are there not stones[108] in heaven

But what serve for thunder? (*to Iago*) Precious[109] villain!

> OTHELLO RUNS AT IAGO, WHO EVADES HIM,
> STABS EMILIA, AND RUNS OUT

> MONTANO DISARMS OTHELLO

235 *Gratiano* The woman falls. Sure, he hath killed his wife.

      Emilia   Ay, ay. O lay me by my mistress' side.

      Gratiano He's gone, but his wife's killed.

      Montano 'Tis a notorious[110] villain. Take you this weapon,

      Which I have here recovered from the Moor.

240 Come, guard[111] the door without,[112] let him[113] not pass,

      But kill him rather. I'll after[114] that same villain,

      For 'tis a damnèd slave.

> EXIT MONTANO AND GRATIANO

Othello   I am not valiant[115] neither,[116]

But every puny whipster[117] gets[118] my sword.

But why should honor outlive honesty?

Let it go all.

---

108 missiles, thunderbolts
109 out and out, total
110 obvious
111 you guard
112 door without = door outside this room
113 Othello
114 follow, pursue
115 (1) strong, sturdy, (2) bold, brave
116 either
117 puny whipster = insignificant/inferior/little fellow/boy (whipping a top)
118 takes possession of

Emilia	What did thy song bode, lady?	245

Hark, canst thou hear me? I will play the swan,
And die in music.[119] (*sings*) "Willow, willow, willow."
Moor, she was chaste. She loved thee, cruel Moor.
So come my soul[120] to bliss, as I speak true.
So speaking as I think, alas, I die.   250

SHE DIES

Othello   I have another weapon in this chamber,
It was a sword of Spain, the ice-brook's temper.[121]
O, here it is. (*calling*) Uncle, I must come forth.
Gratiano (*within*) If thou attempt it, it will cost thee dear.
Thou hast no weapon, and perforce[122] must suffer.[123]   255
Othello   Look in upon me then, and speak with me,
Or naked[124] as I am I will assault thee.

ENTER GRATIANO

Gratiano What is the matter?
Othello   Behold, I have a weapon.
A better never did itself sustain[125]
Upon a soldier's thigh. I have seen the day   260
That with this little[126] arm and this good sword
I have made my way through more impediments

---

119 (the swan was thought never to sing until just before its death)
120 come my soul = let/may my soul come
121 ice-brook's temper = made of steel tempered/cooled in a frigid stream
    (Spanish steel was considered second only to that of Damascus)
122 of necessity
123 endure bodily injury
124 unarmored? unarmed? (as Gratiano believes)
125 hang steadily/firmly/consistently
126 bare (*O.E.D.,* s.v. "little," 6b)

Than twenty times your stop.[127] But, O vain boast,
Who can control his fate? 'Tis not so now.
265 Be not afraid, though you do see me weaponed.
Here is my journey's end, here is my butt[128]
And very sea-mark[129] of my utmost sail.
Do you go back dismayed?[130] 'Tis a lost[131] fear.
Man but a rush[132] against Othello's breast,
270 And he retires. Where should Othello go?
(*approaches Desdemona*) Now. How dost thou look now? O ill-
starred[133] wench,[134]
Pale as thy smock.[135] When we shall meet at compt,[136]
This look of thine will hurl my soul from heaven,
And fiends will snatch at it. (*touches her*) Cold, cold, my girl?
275 Even like thy chastity.[137] (*to himself*) O cursèd, cursèd slave!
Whip me, ye devils,
From[138] the possession[139] of this heavenly[140] sight![141]

127 obstruction, obstacle, prohibition
128 terminal point, boundary mark
129 (1) something highly visible from the sea, as a guide to navigation, (2) high
    tide
130 overwhelmed by fear
131 vain, groundless
132 man but a rush = (1) use only a reed-stalk (as in mock tournaments)
    against? (2) simply dash at?
133 ill-fated, unlucky
134 girl (familiar/affectionate)
135 shift, chemise (undergarment)
136 Judgment Day (compt = count/account = reckoning)
137 utter, devout purity (see *As You Like It* 3.4.15—17: "A nun ... kisses not
    more religiously, the very ice of chastity is in them [his kisses]")
138 away from
139 physical/actual vision
140 divine
141 (hell's devils were said to whip/drive condemned sinners away from
    anything sanctified, which might re-sanctify them)

Blow me about in winds, roast me in sulphur,
Wash me in steep-down[142] gulfs of liquid fire!
O Desdemon! Dead Desdemon! Dead! O! O!   280

ENTER LODOVICO, MONTANO, CASSIO IN A CHAIR,
AND, BEHIND THEM, OFFICERS WITH IAGO, PRISONER

Lodovico   Where is this rash, and most unfortunate man?
Othello   That's he that was Othello. Here I am.
Lodovico   Where is that viper? Bring the villain forth.
Othello   I look down towards his feet.[143] But that's a fable.
  (*to Iago*) If that thou be'st a devil, I cannot kill thee.   285

HE STABS IAGO

Lodovico   Wrench his sword from him.
Iago   (*to Othello, sarcastically*) I bleed, sir – but not killed.
Othello   I am not sorry neither. I'd have thee live.
  For in my sense,[144] 'tis happiness to die.
Lodovico   O thou Othello, that wert once so good,   290
  Fallen in the practice[145] of a cursèd slave,
  What shall[146] be said to thee?
Othello   Why, anything.
  An honorable murderer, if you will.
  For naught did I in[147] hate, but all in honor.
Lodovico   This wretch hath part confessed his villainy.   295
  Did you and he consent in Cassio's death?

142 precipitous, sheer
143 (the Devil was thought to have a cloven foot)
144 in my sense = to my mind
145 brought low by the practices/scheming/treachery
146 ought to be
147 out/because of, with

Othello   Ay.

Cassio   Dear general, I never gave you cause.

Othello   I do believe it, and I ask your pardon.

300   Will you, I pray, demand[148] that demi-devil[149]

        Why he hath thus ensnared my soul and body?

Iago   Demand me nothing. What you know, you know.

        From this time forth, I never will speak word.

Lodovico   What? Not[150] to pray?

Gratiano   Torments[151] will ope your lips.

305 *Othello*   (*to Iago*) Well, thou dost best.

Lodovico   (*to Othello*) Sir, you shall[152] understand what hath

        befallen,

        Which, as I think, you know not. Here is a letter

        Found in the pocket of the slain Roderigo,

        And here another. The one of them imports

310   The death of Cassio to be undertook

        By Roderigo.

        Othello O villain!

Cassio   Most heathenish[153] and most gross!

Lodovico   Now here's another discontented[154] paper,

        Found in his pocket too. And this, it seems,

315   Roderigo meant to have sent this damnèd villain,

        But that, belike,[155] Iago in the interim

148 ask (French *demander,* "to ask")
149 (continuing the sarcastic wordplay between Othello and Iago?)
150 not even
151 torture
152 must
153 un-Christian/civilized, barbarous
154 irritated, vexed
155 probably, possibly

Came in and satisfied him.

Othello   O thou pernicious caitiff![156]

How came you, Cassio, by that handkerchief

That was my wife's?

Cassio   I found it in my chamber.

And he himself confessed't but even now   320

That there he dropped it for a special purpose

Which wrought to[157] his desire.

Othello   (*to himself*) O fool! fool! fool!

Cassio   There is besides, in Roderigo's letter,

How he upbraids[158] Iago that he[159] made him

Brave[160] me upon[161] the watch. Whereon[162] it came[163]   325

That I was cast. And even but now he spake –

After long seeming dead – Iago hurt[164] him,

Iago set him on.[165]

Lodovico   (*to Othello*) You must forsake[166] this room,[167] and go

with us.

Your power and your command[168] is taken off,[169]   330

And Cassio rules in Cyprus. For[170] this slave,

156 despicable wretch, villain
157 wrought to = worked toward
158 reproaches, criticizes
159 Iago
160 challenge, defy
161 on, during
162 at which time
163 came about, happened
164 wounded? insulted?
165 set him on = attacked him? incited him?
166 withdraw from, leave
167 (1) chamber, (2) office, post
168 power and ... command = authority, rule
169 taken off = removed
170 as for

If there be any cunning cruelty
That can torment him much and hold[171] him long,
It shall be his. You shall close prisoner rest,[172]

335   Till that the nature of your fault be known
To the Venetian state. Come, bring[173] away.
  Othello Soft you,[174] a word or two before you go.
    I have done the state some service, and they know't.
    No more of that. I pray you, in your letters,

340   When you shall these unlucky deeds relate,
    Speak of me as I am. Nothing extenuate,[175]
    Nor set down aught in malice. Then must you speak
    Of one that loved not wisely, but too well.
    Of one not easily jealous but, being wrought,[176]

345   Perplexed[177] in the extreme. Of one whose hand,
    Like the base Judean,[178] threw a pearl away
    Richer than all his tribe. Of one whose subdued[179] eyes,
    Albeit unusèd to the melting mood,
    Drop tears as fast as the Arabian trees

350   Their medicinal gum. Set you down this.
    And say besides, that in Aleppo[180] once,
    Where a malignant[181] and a turbaned Turk

---

171 preserve ("keep alive")
172 shall close prisoner rest = must confined/strictly guarded prisoner remain
173 let yourself be brought/taken
174 soft you = wait
175 weaken, lessen
176 agitated
177 was entangled/bewildered
178 (Quarto: Indian; there being no specific reference, one non-Christian will do as well as another)
179 overcome
180 (a city in NW Syria)
181 malcontent, rebellious

Beat a Venetian and traduced the state,[182]
I took by th'throat the circumcisèd dog
And smote him (*pulls out hidden dagger*) thus.   355

OTHELLO STABS HIMSELF

Lodovico   O bloody period![183]
Gratiano   All that's spoke[184] is marred.[185]
Othello   I kissed thee ere I killed thee. No way but this,
   (*falling on Desdemona*) Killing myself, to die upon a kiss.

OTHELLO DIES

Cassio   This did I fear, but thought he had no weapon,
   For he was great of heart.
Lodovico   (*to Iago*) O Spartan dog,[186]   360
   More fell[187] than anguish, hunger, or the sea.
   Look on the tragic loading of[188] this bed.
   This is thy work. The object[189] poisons sight,
   Let it be hid. Gratiano, keep[190] the house,
   And seize upon[191] the fortunes[192] of the Moor,   365

---

182 traduced the state = verbally slandered/defamed Venice
183 ending, conclusion, completion
184 that's spoke = that has been said
185 ruined
186 Spartan dog = fiercely predatory animal (Theseus and Hippolyta, in *A
   Midsummer Night's Dream,* act 4, scene 1, discuss the famous virtues of
   Spartan hunting dogs; Iago is clearly not Spartan-like, nor is Lodovico
   praising him)
187 cruel, ruthless, savage
188 loading of = load on ("cargo")
189 spectacle, sight
190 attend to, take care of
191 seize upon = take possession of
192 estate, wealth

For they succeed on[193] you. (*to Cassio*) To you, lord governor,
Remains the censure[194] of this hellish villain.
The time, the place, the torture, O enforce it![195]
Myself will[196] straight aboard,[197] and to the state
370   This heavy act[198] with heavy heart relate.

EXEUNT

193 succeed on = pass by way of heredity (Othello's deceased wife's family
    being his only known heirs)
194 sentence and punishment
195 enforce it = impose / compel it, press it hard
196 will go / proceed
197 aboard ship ("sail")
198 outcome, thing done

AN ESSAY BY HAROLD BLOOM

"The character of Iago . . . belongs to a class of characters common to Shakespeare, and at the same time peculiar to him—namely, that of great intellectual activity, accompanied with a total want of moral principle, and therefore displaying itself at the constant expense of others, and seeking to confound the practical distinctions of right and wrong, by referring them to some overstrained standard of speculative refinement.—Some persons, more nice than wise, have thought the whole of the character of Iago unnatural. Shakespeare, who was quite as good a philosopher as he was a poet, thought otherwise. He knew that the love of power, which is another name for the love of mischief, was natural to man. He would know this as well or better than if it had been demonstrated to him by a logical diagram, merely from seeing children paddle in the dirt, or kill flies for sport. We might ask those who think the character of Iago not natural, why they go to see it performed, but from the interest it excites, the sharper edge which it sets on their curiosity and imagination? Why do we go to see tragedies in general? Why do we always read the accounts in the newspapers of dreadful fires and shocking murders, but for the same reason? Why do so many persons frequent executions and trials, or why do the lower classes almost universally take delight in barbarous sports and cruelty to animals, but because there is a natural tendency in the mind to strong excitement, a desire to have its faculties roused and stimulated to the utmost? Whenever this principle is not under the restraint of humanity, or the sense of moral obligation, there are no excesses to which it will not of itself give rise, without the assistance of any other motive, either of passion or self-interest. Iago is only an extreme instance of the kind; that is, of diseased intellectual activity, with a preference of the latter, because it falls more in with his favourite propensity, gives greater zest to his thoughts, and scope to his actions.—Be it observed, too, (for the sake of those who are for squaring all human actions by the maxims of Rochefoucault), that he is quite or nearly as indifferent to his own fate as to that of others; that he runs all risks for a trifling and doubtful advantage; and is himself the dupe and victim of his ruling passion—an incorrigible love of mischief—an insatiable craving after action of the most difficult and dangerous kind. Our 'Ancient' is a philosopher, who fancies that a lie that kills has more point in it than an alliteration or an antithesis; who thinks a fatal experiment on the peace of a family a better thing than watching the palpitations in the heart of a flea in an air-pump; who plots the ruin of his friends as an exercise for his understanding, and stabs men in the dark to prevent *ennui*."—William Hazlitt

S ince it is Othello's tragedy, even if it is Iago's play (not even Hamlet or Edmund seem to compose so much of their dramas), we need to restore some sense of Othello's initial dignity and glory. A bad modern tradition of criticism that goes from T. S. Eliot and F. R. Leavis through current New Historicism has divested the hero of his splendor, in effect doing Iago's work so that, in Othello's words, "Othello's occupation's gone." Since 1919 or so, generals have lost esteem among the elite, though not always among the groundlings. Shakespeare himself subjected chivalric valor to the superb comic critique of Falstaff, who did not leave intact very much of the nostalgia for military prowess. But Falstaff, although he still inhabited a corner of Hamlet's consciousness, is absent from *Othello.*

The clown scarcely comes on stage in *Othello,* though the Fool in *Lear,* the drunken porter at the gate in *Macbeth,* and the fig-and-asp seller in *Antony and Cleopatra* maintain the persistence of tragicomedy in Shakespeare after *Hamlet.* Only *Othello* and *Coriolanus* exclude all laughter, as if to protect two great captains from the Falstaffian perspective. When Othello, doubtless the fastest sword in his profession, wants to stop a street fight, he need only utter the one massive and menacingly monosyllabic line "Keep up your bright swords, for the dew will rust them."

To see Othello in his unfallen splendor, within the play, becomes a little difficult, because he so readily seems to become Iago's dupe. Shakespeare, as before in *Henry IV, Part One,* and directly after in *King Lear,* gives us the responsibility of foregrounding by inference. As the play opens, Iago assures his gull, Roderigo, that he hates Othello, and he states the only true motive for his hatred, which is what Milton's Satan calls "a Sense of Injured Merit." Satan (as Milton did not wish to know) is the legitimate son of Iago, begot by Shakespeare upon Milton's Muse. Iago, long Othello's "ancient" (his ensign, or flag officer, the third-in-command), has been passed over for promotion, and Cassio has become Othello's lieutenant. No reason is given for Othello's decision; his regard for "honest Iago," bluff veteran of Othello's "big wars," remains undiminished. Indeed, Iago's position as flag officer, vowed to die rather than let Othello's colors be captured in battle, testifies both to Othello's trust and to Iago's former devotion. Paradoxically, that quasi-religious worship of the war god Othello by his true believer Iago can be inferred as the cause of Iago's having been passed over. Iago, as Harold Goddard finely remarked, is always at war; he is a moral pyromaniac setting fire to all of reality. Othello, the skilled professional who maintains the purity of arms by sharply dividing the camp of war from that of peace, would have seen in his brave and zealous ancient someone who could not replace him were he to be killed or wounded. Iago cannot stop fighting, and so cannot be preferred to Cassio, who is relatively inexperienced (a kind of staff officer) but who is courteous and diplomatic and knows the limits of war.

Sound as Othello's military judgment clearly was, he did not know Iago, a very free artist of himself. The catastrophe that foregrounds Shakespeare's play is what I would want to call the Fall of Iago, which sets the paradigm for Satan's Fall in Milton. Milton's God, like Othello, pragmatically demotes his most ardent devotee, and the wounded Satan rebels. Unable to bring down the Supreme Being, Satan ruins Adam and Eve instead, but the subtler Iago can do far better, because his only God is Othello himself, whose fall becomes the appropriate revenge for Iago's evidently sickening loss of being at rejection, with consequences including what may be sexual impotence, and what certainly is a sense of nullity, of no longer being what one was. Iago is Shakespeare's largest study in ontotheological absence, a sense of the void that theologue and as advanced dramatic poet. Shakespeare endowed only Hamlet, Falstaff, and Rosalind with more wit and intellect than he gave to Iago and Edmund, while in aesthetic sensibility, only Hamlet overgoes Iago. Grant Iago his Ahab-like obsession— Othello is the Moby-Dick who must be harpooned—and Iago's salient quality rather outrageously is his freedom. A great improviser, he works with gusto and mastery of timing, adjusting his plot to openings as they present themselves. If I were a director of *Othello,* I would instruct my Iago to manifest an ever-growing wonder and confidence in the diabolic art. Unlike Barabas and his progeny, Iago is an inventor, an experimenter always willing to try modes heretofore unknown. Auden, in a more inspired moment, saw Iago as a scientist rather than a practical joker. Satan, exploring the untracked Abyss in *Paradise Lost,* is truly in Iago's spirit. Who before Iago, in literature or in life, perfected the arts of disinformation, disorientation, and derangement? All these combine in Iago's grand program of uncreation, as Othello is returned to original chaos, to the Tohu and Bohu from which we came.

Even a brief glance at Shakespeare's source in Cinthio reveals the extent to which Iago is essentially Shakespeare's radical invention, rather than an adaptation of the wicked Ensign in the original story. Cinthio's Ensign falls passionately in love with Desdemona, but wins no favor with her, since she loves the Moor. The unnamed Ensign decides that his failure is due to Desdemona's love for an unnamed Captain (Shakespeare's Cassio), and so he determines to remove this supposed rival, by inducing jealousy in the Moor and then plotting with him to murder both Desdemona and the Captain. In Cinthio's version, the Ensign beats Desdemona to death, while the Moor watches approvingly. It is only afterward, when the Moor repents and desperately misses his wife, that he dismisses the Ensign, who thus is first moved to hatred against his general. Shakespeare transmuted the entire story by giving it, and Iago, a different starting point, the foreground in which Iago has been passed over for promotion. The ontological shock of that rejection is Shakespeare's original invention and is the trauma that truly creates Iago, no mere wicked Ensign but rather a genius of evil who has engendered himself from a great Fall.

Milton's Satan owes so much to Iago that we can be tempted to read the Christian Fall of Adam into Othello's catastrophe, and to find Lucifer's decline into Satan a clue to Iago's inception. But though Shakespeare's Moor has been baptized, *Othello* is no more a Christian drama than *Hamlet* was a doctrinal tragedy of guilt, sin, and pride. Iago playfully invokes a "Divinity of Hell," and yet he is no mere diabolist. He is War Everlasting (as Jean-Luc Goddard sensed) and inspires in me the same uncanny awe and fright that Cormac McCarthy's Judge Holden arouses each time I reread *Blood Meridian, Or, The Evening Redness in the West* (1985). The Judge, though based on a historic filibuster who massacred and scalped Indians in the post–Civil War Southwest and in Mexico, is War Incarnate. A reading of his formidable pronunciamentos provides a theology-in-little of Iago's enterprise, and betrays perhaps a touch of Iago's influence upon *Blood Meridian,* an American descendant of the Shakespeare-intoxicated Herman Melville and William Faulkner. "War," says the Judge, "is the truest form of divination. . . . War is god," because war is the supreme game of will against will. Iago is the genius of will reborn from war's slighting of the will. To have been passed over for Cassio is to have one's will reduced to nullity, and the self's sense of power violated. Victory for the will therefore demands a restoration of power, and power for Iago can only be war's power: to maim, to kill, to humiliate, to destroy the godlike in another, the war god who betrayed his worship and his trust. Cormac McCarthy's Judge Holden is Iago come again when he proclaims war as the game that defines us:

> Wolves cull themselves, man. What other creature could? And is the race of man not more predacious yet? The way of the world is to bloom and flower and die but in the affairs of men there is no waning and the moon of his expression signals the onset of night. His spirit is exhausted at the peak of its achievement. His meridian is at once his darkening and the evening of his day. He loves games? Let him play for stakes.

In Iago, what was the religion of war, when he worshiped Othello as its god, has now become the game of war, to be played everywhere except upon the battlefield. The death of belief becomes the birth of invention, and the passed-over officer becomes the poet of street brawls, stabbings in the dark, disinformation, and above all else, the uncreation of Othello, the sparagmos of the great captain-general so that he can be returned to the original abyss, the chaos that Iago equates with the Moor's African origins. That is not Othello's view of his heritage (or Shakespeare's), but Iago's interpretation wins, or almost wins, since I will argue that Othello's much-maligned suicide speech is something very close to a recovery of dignity and coherence, though not of lost greatness. Iago, forever beyond Othello's understanding, is not beyond ours, because we are more like Iago than we resemble Othello; Iago's views on war, on the will, and on the aesthetics of re-

Devil himself—in Milton, Marlowe, J. W. van Goethe, Dosto-yevsky, Melville, or any other writer—cannot compete with Iago, whose American descendants range from Nathaniel Hawthorne's Chillingworth and Melville's Claggart through Mark Twain's Mysterious Stranger on to Nathanael West's Shrike and Cormac McCarthy's Judge Holden. Modern literature has not surpassed Iago; he remains the perfect Devil of the West, superb as psychologist, playwright, dramatic critic, and negative theologian. G. B. Shaw, jealous of Shakespeare, argued that "the character defies all consistency," being at once "a coarse blackguard" and also refined and subtle. Few have agreed with Shaw, and those who question Iago's persuasiveness tend also to find Othello a flawed representation. A. C. Bradley, an admirable critic always, named Falstaff, Hamlet, Iago, and Cleopatra as Shakespeare's "most wonderful" characters. If I could add Rosalind and Macbeth to make a sixfold wonder, then I would agree with Bradley, for these are Shakespeare's grandest inventions, and all of them take human nature to some of its limits, without violating those limits. Falstaff's wit, Hamlet's ambivalent yet charismatic intensity, Cleopatra's mobility of spirit find their rivals in Macbeth's proleptic imagination, Rosalind's control of all perspectives, and Iago's genius for improvisation. Neither merely coarse nor merely subtle, Iago constantly re-creates his own personality and character: "I am not what I am." Those who question how a twenty-eight-year-old professional soldier could harbor so sublimely negative a genius might just as soon question how the thirty-nine-year-old professional actor, Shakespeare, could imagine so convincing a "demi-devil" (as Othello finally terms Iago). We think that Shakespeare abandoned acting just before he composed *Othello;* he seems to have played his final role in *All's Well That Ends Well.* Is there some link between giving up the player's part and the invention of Iago? Between *All's Well That Ends Well* and *Othello,* Shakespeare wrote *Measure for Measure,* a farewell to stage comedy. *Measure for Measure's* enigmatic Duke Vincentio, as I have observed, seems to have some Iago-like qualities, and may also relate to Shakespeare's release from the burden of performance. Clearly a versatile and competent actor, but never a leading one, Shakespeare perhaps celebrates a new sense of the actor's energies in the improvisations of Vincentio and Iago.

Bradley, in exalting Falstaff, Hamlet, Iago, and Cleopatra, may have been responding to the highly conscious theatricalism that is fused into their roles. Witty in himself, Falstaff provokes wit in others through his performances. Hamlet, analytical tragedian, discourses with everyone he encounters, driving them to self-revelation. Cleopatra is always on stage—living, loving, and dying—and whether she ceases to perform, when alone with Antony, we will never know, because Shakespeare never shows them alone together, save once, and that is very brief. Perhaps Iago, before the Fall of his rejection by Othello, had not yet discovered his own dramatic genius; it seems the largest pragmatic consequence of his Fall, once his sense of nullity has passed through an initial trauma. When we first hear him, at the start of the play, he already indulges his actor's freedom:

O, sir, content you,
I follow him to serve my turn upon him.
We cannot all be masters, nor all masters
Cannot be truly followed. You shall mark
Many a duteous and knee-crooking knave
That, doting on his own obsequious bondage,

Wears out his time, much like his master's ass,
For nought but provender, and when he's old, cashiered.
Whip me such honest knaves! Others there are
Who, trimmed in forms and visages of duty,
Keep yet their hearts attending on themselves,
And throwing but shows of service on their lords,
Do well thrive by them, and when they have lined their coats
Do themselves homage. These fellows have some soul
And such a one do I profess myself.

[1.1.39–53]

Only the actor, Iago assures us, possesses "some soul"; the rest of us wear our hearts upon our sleeves. Yet this is only the start of a player's career; at this early point, Iago is merely out for mischief, rousing up Brabantio, Desdemona's father, and conjuring up street brawls. He knows that he is exploring a new vocation, but he has little sense as yet of his own genius. Shakespeare, while Iago gathers force, centers instead upon giving us a view of Othello's precarious greatness, and of Desdemona's surpassing human worth. Before turning to the Moor and his bride, I wish further to foreground Iago, who requires quite as much inferential labor as do Hamlet and Falstaff.

Richard III and Edmund have fathers; Shakespeare gives us no antecedents for Iago. We can surmise the ancient's previous relationship to his superb captain. What can we infer of his marriage to Emilia? There is Iago's curious mistake in his first mention of Cassio: "A fellow almost damned in a fair wife." This seems not to be Shakespeare's error but a token of Iago's obsessive concern with marriage as a damnation, since Bianca is plainly Cassio's whore and not his wife. Emilia, no better than she should be, will be the ironic instrument that undoes Iago's triumphalism, at the cost of her life. As to the relationship between this singular couple, Shakespeare allows us some pungent hints. Early in the play, Iago tells us what neither he nor we believe, not because of any shared regard for Emilia but because Othello is too grand for this:

> And it is thought abroad that 'twixt my sheets
> He has done my office. I know not if 't be true,
> But I, for mere suspicion in that kind,
> Will do as if for surety.
>
> [1.3.380–83]

Later, Iago parenthetically expresses the same "mere suspicion" of Cassio: "For I fear Cassio with my night-cap too." We can surmise that Iago, perhaps made impotent by his fury at being passed over for promotion, is ready to suspect Emilia with every male in the play, while not particularly caring one way or the other. Emilia, comforting Desdemona after Othello's initial rage of jealousy against his blameless wife, sums up her own marriage also:

> 'Tis not a year or two shows us a man.
> They are all but stomachs and we all but food,
> They eat us hungerly, and when they are full
> They belch us.
>
> [3.4.101–4]

That is the erotic vision of *Troilus and Cressida,* carried over into a greater realm, but not a less rancid one, because the world of *Othello* belongs to Iago. It is not persuasive to say that Othello is a normal man and Iago abnormal; Iago is the genius of his time and place, and is all will. His passion for destruction is the only creative passion in the play. Such a judgment is necessarily very somber, but then this is surely Shakespeare's most painful play. *King Lear* and *Macbeth* are even darker, but theirs is the darkness of the negative sublime. The only sublimity in *Othello* is Iago's. Shakespeare's conception of him was so definitive that the revisions made between the Quarto's text and the Folio's enlarge and sharpen our sense primarily of Emilia, and secondly of Othello and Desdemona, but hardly touch Iago. Shakespeare rightly felt no need to revise Iago, already the perfection of malign will and genius for hatred. There can be no question concerning Iago's primacy in the play: he speaks eight soliloquies, Othello only three.

Edmund outthinks and so outplots everyone else in *King Lear*, and yet is destroyed by the recalcitrant endurance of Edgar, who develops from credulous victim into inexorable revenger. Iago, even more totally the master of his play, is at last undone by Emilia, whom Shakespeare revised into a figure of intrepid outrage, willing to die for the sake of the murdered Desdemona's good name. Shakespeare had something of a tragic obsession with the idea of a good name living on after his protagonists' deaths. Hamlet, despite saying that no man can know anything of whatever he leaves behind him, nevertheless exhorts Horatio to survive so as to defend what might become of his prince's wounded name. We will hear Othello trying to recuperate some shred of reputation in his suicidal final speech, upon which critical agreement no longer seems at all possible. If the *Funeral Elegy* for Will Peter indeed was Shakespeare's (I think this probable), then the poet-dramatist in 1612, four years before his own death at fifty-two, was much preoccupied with his own evidently blemished name.

Emilia's heroic victory over Iago is one of Shakespeare's grandest ironies, and appropriately constitutes the play's most surprising dramatic moment:

Emilia   O heaven! O heavenly powers!

Iago   Come, hold your
    peace!

Emilia   'Twill out, 'twill out. I peace?
    No, I will speak as liberal as the north.
    Let heaven and men and devils, let them all,
    All, all, cry shame against me, yet I'll speak.

Iago   Be wise, and get you home.

Emilia   I will not.

IAGO TRIES TO STAB HIS WIFE

Gratiano Fie! Your sword upon a woman?

Emilia   O thou dull Moor, that handkerchief thou speak'st of
    I found by fortune and did give my husband.
    For often with a solemn earnestness—
    More than, indeed, belonged to such a trifle—
    He begged of me to steal it.

Iago   Villainous whore!

Emilia   She give it Cassio? No, alas I found it,
    And I did give't my husband.

Iago   Filth, thou liest!

Emilia   By heaven, I do not, I do not, gentlemen.
    O murd'rous coxcomb, what should such a fool
    Do with so good a wife?

Othello   Are there not stones in heaven
    But what serve for thunder? (*to Iago*) Precious villain!

OTHELLO RUNS AT IAGO, WHO EVADES HIM,
STABS EMILIA, AND RUNS OUT

MONTANO DISARMS OTHELLO

Gratiano The woman falls. Sure, he hath killed his wife.
Emilia Ay, ay. O lay me by my mistress' side.
Gratiano He's gone, but his wife's killed.

[5.2.217−37]

We are surprised, but Iago is shocked; indeed it is his first reversal since being passed over for Cassio. That Emilia should lose
her worldly wisdom, and become as free as the north wind, was
the only eventuality that Iago could not foresee. And his failure to
encompass his wife's best aspect—her love for and pride in Desdemona—is the one lapse for which he cannot forgive himself.
That is the true undersong of the last lines he ever will allow himself to utter, and which are directed as much to us as to Othello or
to Cassio:

Othello Will you, I pray, demand that demi-devil
    Why he hath thus ensnared my soul and body?
Iago Demand me nothing. What you know, you know.
    From this time forth, I never will speak word.

[5.2.300−3]

What is it that we know, beyond what Othello and Cassio
know? Shakespeare's superb dramatic irony transcends even that
question into the subtler matter of allowing us to know something about Iago that the ancient, despite his genius, is incapable
of knowing. Iago is outraged that he could not anticipate, by dramatic imagination, his wife's outrage that Desdemona should be

not only murdered but perhaps permanently defamed. The aesthete's web has all of war's gamelike magic, but no place in it for Emilia's honest indignation. Where he ought to have been at his most discerning—within his marriage—Iago is blank and blind. The superb psychologist who unseamed Othello, and who deftly manipulated Desdemona, Cassio, Roderigo, and all others, angrily falls into the fate he arranged for his prime victim, the Moor, and becomes another wife murderer. He has, at last, set fire to himself.

Since the world is Iago's, I scarcely am done expounding him, and will examine him again in an overview of the play, but only after brooding upon the many enigmas of Othello. Where Shakespeare granted Hamlet, Lear, and Macbeth an almost continuous and preternatural eloquence, he chose instead to give Othello a curiously mixed power of expression, distinct yet divided, and deliberately flawed. Iago's theatricalism is superb, but Othello's is troublesome, brilliantly so. The Moor tells us that he has been a warrior since he was seven, presumably a hyperbole but indicative that he is all too aware his greatness has been hard won. His professional self-awareness is extraordinarily intense; partly this is inevitable, since he is technically a mercenary, a black soldier of fortune who honorably serves the Venetian state. And yet his acute sense of his reputation betrays what may well be an uneasiness, sometimes manifested in the baroque elaborations of his language, satirized by Iago as "a bombast circumstance, / Horribly stuffed with epithets of war."

A military commander who can compare the movement of his mind to the "icy current and compulsive course" of the Pontic (Black) Sea, Othello seems incapable of seeing himself except in grandiose terms. He presents himself as a living legend or walking myth, nobler than any antique Roman. The poet Anthony Hecht thinks that we are meant to recognize "a ludicrous and nervous vanity" in Othello, but Shakespeare's adroit perspectivism evades so single a recognition. Othello has a touch of Shakespeare's Julius Caesar in him; there is an ambiguity in both figures that makes it very difficult to trace the demarcations between their vainglory and their grandeur. If you believe in the war god Caesar (as Antony does) or in the war god Othello (as Iago once did), then you lack the leisure to contemplate the god's failings. But if you are Cassius, or the postlapsarian Iago, then you are at pains to behold the weaknesses that mask as divinity. Othello, like Caesar, is prone to refer to himself in the third person, a somewhat unnerving habit; whether in literature or in life. And yet, again like Julius Caesar, Othello believes his own myth, and to some extent we must also, because there is authentic nobility in the language of his soul. That there is opacity also, we cannot doubt; Othello's tragedy is precisely that Iago should know him better than the Moor knows himself.

Othello is a great commander, who knows war and the limits of war but who knows little else, and cannot know that he does not know. His sense of himself is very large, in that its scale is vast, but he sees himself from afar as it were; up close, he hardly confronts the void at his center. Iago's apprehension of that abyss is sometimes compared to Montaigne's; I sooner would compare it to Hamlet's, because like one element in the infinitely varied Prince of Denmark, Iago is well beyond skepticism and has crossed into nihilism. Iago's most brilliant insight is that if *he* was reduced to nothingness by Cassio's preferment, then how much more vulnerable Othello must be, lacking Iago's intellect and game-playing will. Anyone can be pulverized, in Iago's view, and in this drama he is right. There is no one in the play with the irony and wit that alone could hold off Iago: Othello is consciously theatrical but quite humorless, and Desdemona is a miracle of sincerity. The terrible painfulness of *Othello* is that Shakespeare shrewdly omits any counterforce to Iago. In *King Lear,* Edmund also confronts no one with the intellect to withstand him, until he is annihilated by the exquisite irony of having created the nameless avenger who was once his gull, Edgar. First and last, Othello is powerless against Iago; that helplessness is the most harrowing element in the play, except perhaps for Desdemona's double powerlessness, in regard both to Iago and to her husband.

It is important to emphasize the greatness of Othello, despite all his inadequacies of language and of spirit. Shakespeare implicitly celebrates Othello as a giant of mere being, an ontological splendor, and so a natural man self-raised to an authentic if precarious eminence. Even if we doubt the possibility of the purity of arms, Othello plausibly represents that lost ideal. At every point, he is the antithesis of Iago's "I am not what I am," until he begins to come apart under Iago's influence. Manifestly, Desdemona has made a wrong choice in a husband, and yet that choice testifies to Othello's hard-won splendor. These days, when so many academic critics are converted to the recent French fashion of denying the self, some of them happily seize upon Othello as a fit instance. They undervalue how subtle Shakespeare's art can be; Othello indeed may seem to prompt James Calderwood's Lacanian observation: "Instead of a self-core discoverable at the center of his being, Othello's 'I am' seems a kind of internal repertory company, a 'we are.'"

If Othello, at the play's start, or at its close, is only the sum of his self-descriptions, then indeed he could be judged a veritable picnic of souls. But his third-person relation to his own images of self testifies not to a "we are" but to a perpetual romanticism at seeing and describing himself. To some degree, he is a self-enchanter, as well as the enchanter of Desdemona. Othello desperately wants and needs to be the protagonist of a Shakespearean romance, but alas he is the hero-victim of this most painful Shakespearean domestic tragedy of blood. John Jones makes the fine observation that Lear in the Quarto version is a romance figure, but then is revised by Shakespeare into the tragic being of the Folio text. As Iago's destined gull, Othello presented Shakespeare with enormous problems in representation. How are we to believe in the essential heroism, largeness, and loving nature of so catastrophic a protagonist? Since Desdemona is the most admirable image of love in all Shakespeare, how are we to sympathize with her increasingly incoherent destroyer, who renders her the unluckiest of all wives? Romance, literary and human, depends on partial or imperfect knowledge. Perhaps Othello never gets beyond that, even in his final speech, but Shakespeare shrewdly frames the romance of Othello within the tragedy of *Othello,* and thus solves the problem of sympathetic representation.

Othello is not a "poem unlimited," beyond genre, like *Hamlet,* but the romance elements in its three principal figures do make it a very uncommon tragedy. Iago is a triumph because he is in exactly the right play for an ontotheological villain, while the charitable Desdemona is superbly suited to this drama also. Othello cannot quite fit, but then that is his sociopolitical dilemma, the heroic Moor commanding the armed forces of Venice, sophisticated in its decadence then as now. Shakespeare mingles commercial realism and visionary romance in his portrait of Othello, and the mix necessarily is unsteady, even for this greatest of all makers. Yet we do Othello wrong to offer him the show of violence, whether by unselfing him or by devaluing his goodness. Iago, nothing if not critical, has a keener sense of Othello than most of us now tend to achieve:"The Moor is of a free and open nature / That thinks men honest that but seem to be so."

There are not many in Shakespeare, or in life, that are "of a free and open nature": to suppose that we are to find Othello ludicrous or paltry is to mistake the play badly. He is admirable, a tower among men, but soon enough he becomes a broken tower. Shakespeare's own Hector, Ulysses, and Achilles, in his *Troilus and Cressida,* were all complex travesties of their Homeric originals (in George Chapman's version), but Othello is precisely Homeric, as close as Shakespeare desired to come to Chapman's heroes. Within his clear limitations, Othello indeed is "noble": his consciousness, prior to his fall, is firmly controlled, just, and massively dignified, and has its own kind of perfection. Reuben Brower admirably said of Othello that "his heroic simplicity was also heroic blindness. That too is part of the 'ideal' hero, part of Shakespeare's metaphor." The metaphor, no longer quite Homeric, had to extend to the professionalism of a great mercenary soldier and a heroic black in the service of a highly decadent white society. Othello's superb professionalism is at once his extraordinary strength and his tragic freedom to fall. The love between Desdemona and Othello is authentic, yet might have proved catastrophic even in the absence of the daemonic genius of Iago. Nothing in Othello is marriageable: his military career fulfills him completely. Desdemona, persuasively innocent in the highest of senses, falls in love with the pure warrior in Othello, and he falls in love with her love for him, her mirroring of his legendary career. Their romance is his own pre-existent romance; the marriage does not and cannot change him, though it changes his relationship to Venice, in the highly ironic sense of making him more than ever an outsider.

Othello's character has suffered the assaults of T. S. Eliot and F. R. Leavis and their various followers, but fashions in Shakespeare criticism always vanish, and the noble Moor has survived his denigrators. Yet Shakespeare has endowed Othello with the authentic mystery of being a radically flawed hero, an Adam too free to fall. In some respects, Othello is Shakespeare's most wounding representation of male vanity and fear of female sexuality, and so of the male equation that makes the fear of cuckoldry and the fear of mortality into a single dread. Leontes, in *The Winter's Tale,* is partly a study in repressed homosexuality, and thus his virulent jealousy is of another order than Othello's. We wince when Othello, in his closing apologia, speaks of himself as one not easily jealous, and we wonder at his blindness. Still we never doubt his valor, and this makes it even stranger that he at least matches Leontes in jealous madness. Shakespeare's greatest insight into male sexual jealousy is that it is a mask for the fear of being castrated by death. Men imagine that there never can be enough time and space for themselves, and they find in cuckoldry, real or imaginary, the image of their own vanishing, the realization that the world will go on without them.

Othello sees the world as a theater for his professional reputation; this most valiant of soldiers has no fear of literal death-in-battle, which only would enhance his glory. But to be cuckolded by his own wife, and with his subordinate Cassio as the other offender, would be a greater, metaphorical death-in-life, for his reputation would not survive it, particularly in his own view of his mythic renown. Shakespeare is sublimely daemonic, in a mode transcending even Iago's genius, in making Othello's vulnerability exactly consonant with the wound rendered to Iago's self-regard by being passed over for promotion. Iago says, "I am not what I am"; Othello's loss of ontological dignity would be even greater, had Desdemona "betrayed" him (I place the word between quotation marks, because the implicit metaphor involved is a triumph of male vanity). Othello all too self-consciously has risked his hard-won sense of his own being in marrying Desdemona, and he has an accurate foreboding of chaotic engulfment should that risk prove a disaster:

> Excellent wretch. Perdition catch my soul,
> But I do love thee. And when I love thee not,
> Chaos is come again.
>
> [3.3.91−93]

An earlier intimation of Othello's uneasiness is one of the play's subtlest touches:

> For know, Iago,
> But that I love the gentle Desdemona,
> I would not my unhousèd free condition
> Put into circumscription and confine
> For the sea's worth.
>
> [1.2.23−27]

Othello's psychological complexity has to be reconstructed by the audience from his ruins, as it were, because Shakespeare does not supply us with the full foreground. We are given the hint that but for Desdemona, he never would have married, and indeed he himself describes a courtship in which he was essentially passive:

These things to hear
Would Desdemona seriously incline,
But still the house affairs would draw her thence,
Which ever as she could with haste dispatch,
She'd come again, and with a greedy ear
Devour up my discourse. Which I observing,
Took once a pliant hour, and found good means
To draw from her a prayer of earnest heart
That I would all my pilgrimage dilate,
Whereof by parcels she had something heard,
But not intentively. I did consent,
And often did beguile her of her tears,
When I did speak of some distressful stroke
That my youth suffered. My story being done,
She gave me for my pains a world of kisses.
She swore, in faith, 'twas strange, 'twas passing strange,
'Twas pitiful, 'twas wondrous pitiful.
She wished she had not heard it, yet she wished
That heaven had made her such a man. She thanked me,
And bade me, if I had a friend that loved her,
I should but teach him how to tell my story,
And that would woo her. Upon this hint I spake:
She loved me for the dangers I had passed,
And I loved her that she did pity them.

[1.3.145−68]

That is rather more than a "hint," and nearly constitutes a boldly direct proposal, on Desdemona's part. With the Venetian competition evidently confined to the likes of Roderigo, Desdemona is willingly seduced by Othello's naive but powerful romance of the self, provocative of that "world of kisses." The Moor is not only noble; his saga brings "a maiden never bold" (her father's testimony) "to fall in love with what she feared to look on." Desdemona, a High Romantic centuries ahead of her time, yields to the fascination of quest, if *yields* can be an accurate word for so active a surrender. No other match in Shakespeare is so fabulously unlikely, or so tragically inevitable. Even in a Venice and a Cyprus without Iago, how does so improbable a romance domesticate itself? The high point of passion between Othello and Desdemona is their reunion on Cyprus:

Othello   O my fair warrior.
Desdemona   My dear Othello.
Othello   It gives me wonder great as my content
   To see you here before me. O my soul's joy.
   If after every tempest come such calms,
   May the winds blow till they have wakened death,
   And let the laboring bark climb hills of seas
   Olympus-high, and duck again as low
   As hell's from heaven. If it were now to die,
   'Twere now to be most happy, for I fear
   My soul hath her content so absolute
   That not another comfort like to this
   Succeeds in unknown fate.
Desdemona   The heavens forbid
   But that our loves and comforts should increase
   Even as our days do grow.
Othello   Amen to that, sweet powers.
   I cannot speak enough of this content,
   It stops me here. It is too much of joy.

And this, and this, the greatest discords be

HE KISSES HER

That e'er our hearts shall make.

[2.1.177–94]

From such an apotheosis one can only descend, even if the answering chorus were not Iago's aside that he will loosen the strings now so well tuned. Shakespeare (as I have ventured before, following my master, Dr. Johnson) came naturally to comedy and to romance, but violently and ambivalently to tragedy. *Othello* may have been as painful for Shakespeare as he made it for us. Placing the precarious nobility of Othello and the fragile romanticism of Desdemona upon one stage with the sadistic aestheticism of Iago (ancestor of all modern literary critics) was already an outrageous coup of self-wounding on the poet-dramatist's part. I am delighted to revive the now scoffed-at romantic speculation that Shakespeare carries a private affliction, an erotic vastation, into the high tragedies, *Othello* in particular. Shakespeare is, of course, not Lord Byron, scandalously parading before Europe the pageant of his bleeding heart, yet the incredible agony we rightly undergo as we observe Othello murdering Desdemona has a private as well as public intensity informing it. Desdemona's murder is the crossing point between the overflowing cosmos of Hamlet and the cosmological emptiness of Lear and of Macbeth.

The play *Hamlet* and the mind of Hamlet verge upon an identity, since everything that happens to the Prince of Denmark already seems to be the prince. We cannot quite say that the mind of Iago and the play *Othello* are one, since his victims have their own greatness. Yet, until Emilia confounds him, the drama's action is Iago's; only the tragedy of their tragedy belongs to Othello and Desdemona. In 1604, an anonymous storyteller reflected upon "Shakespeare's tragedies, where the Comedian rides, when the Tragedian stands on Tip-toe." This wonderful remark was made of Prince Hamlet, who "pleased all," but more subtly illuminates *Othello,* where Shakespeare-as-comedian rides Iago, even as the dramatist stands on tip-toe to extend the limits of his so painful art. We do not know who in Shakespeare's company played Iago against Burbage's Othello, but I wonder if it was not the great clown Robert Armin, who would have played the drunken porter at the gage in *Macbeth,* the Fool in *King Lear,* and the asp bearer in *Antony and Cleopatra.* The dramatic shock in Othello is that we delight in Iago's exuberant triumphalism, even as we dread his villainy's consequences. Marlowe's self-delighting Barabas, echoed by Aaron the Moor and Richard III, seems a cruder Machiavel when we compare him with the refined Iago, who confounds Barabas with aspects of Hamlet, in order to augment his own growing inwardness. With Hamlet, we confront the ever-growing inner self, but Iago has no inner self, only a fecund abyss, precisely like his descendant, Milton's Satan, who in every deep found a lower deep opening wide. Satan's discovery is agonized; Iago's is diabolically joyous. Shakespeare invents in Iago a sublimely sadistic comic poet, an archon of nihilism who delights in returning his war god to an uncreated night. Can you invent Iago without delighting in your invention, even as we delight in our ambivalent reception of Iago?

Iago is not larger than his play; he perfectly fits it, unlike Hamlet, who would be too large even for the most unlimited of plays. I have noted already that Shakespeare made significant revisions to what is spoken by Othello, Desdemona, and Emilia (even Roderigo) but not by Iago; it is as though Shakespeare knew he had gotten Iago right the first time round. No villain in all literature rivals Iago as a flawless conception, who requires no improvement. Swinburne was accurate: "the most perfect evildom, the most potent demi-devil," and "a reflection by hell-fire of the figure of Prometheus." A Satanic Prometheus may at first appear too High Romantic, yet the pyromaniac Iago encourages Roderigo to a

> dire yell
> As when, by night and negligence, the fire
> Is spied in populous cities.

> [1.1.73–75]

According to the myth, Prometheus steals fire to free us; Iago steals us, as fresh fodder for the fire. He is an authentic Promethean, however negative, because who can deny that Iago's fire is poetic? The hero-villains of John Webster and Cyril Tourneur are mere names on the page when we contrast them with Iago; they lack Promethean fire. Who else in Shakespeare, except for Hamlet and Falstaff, is so creative as Iago? These three alone can read your soul, and read everyone they encounter. Perhaps Iago is the recompense that the Negative demanded to counterbalance Hamlet, Falstaff, and Rosalind. Great wit, like the highest irony, needs an inner check in order not to burn away everything else: Hamlet's disinterestedness, Falstaff's exuberance, Rosalind's graciousness. Iago is nothing at all, except critical; there can be no inner check when the self is an abyss. Iago has the single affect of sheer gusto, increasingly aroused as he discovers his genius for improvisation.

Since the plot of *Othello* essentially is Iago's plot, improvisation by Iago constitutes the tragedy's heart and center. Hazlitt's review of Edmund Kean's performance as Iago in 1814, from which I have drawn my epigraph for this essay, remains the finest analysis of Iago's improvisatory genius, and is most superb when it observes that Iago "stabs men in the dark to prevent *ennui*." That prophetic insight advances Iago to the Age of Charles Baudelaire, Nietzsche, and Dostoyevsky, an Age that in many respects remains our own. Iago is not a Jacobean Italian malcontent, another descendant of Marlowe's Machiavels. His greatness is that he is out ahead of us, though every newspaper and television newscast brings us accounts of his disciples working on every scale, from individual crimes of sadomasochism to international terrorism and massacre. Iago's followers are everywhere: I have watched, with great interest, many of my former students, undergraduate and graduate, pursue careers of Iagoism, both in and out of the academy. Shakespeare's great male intellectuals (as contrasted to Rosalind and Beatrice, among his women) are only four all together: Falstaff and Hamlet, Iago and Edmund. Of these, Hamlet and Iago are also aesthetes, critical consciousnesses of near-preternatural power. Only in Iago does the aesthete predominate, in close alliance with nihilism and sadism.

I place particular emphasis upon Iago's theatrical and poetic genius, as an appreciation of Iago that I trust will be aesthetic without also being sadomasochistic, since that danger always mingles with any audience's enjoyment of Iago's revelations to us. There is no major figure in Shakespeare with whom we are less likely to identify ourselves, and yet Iago is as beyond vice as he is beyond virtue, a fine recognition of Swinburne's. Robert B. Heilman, who perhaps undervalued Othello (the hero, not the play), made restitution by warning that there was no single way into Iago: "As the spiritual have-not, Iago is universal, that is, many things at once, and of many times at once." Swinburne, perhaps tinged with his usual sadomasochism in his high regard for Iago, prophesied that Iago's stance in hell would be like that of Farinata, who stands upright in his tomb: "as if of Hell he had a great disdain." There is hardly a circle in Dante's *Inferno* that Iago could not inhabit, so vast is his potential for ill.

By interpreting Iago as a genius for improvising chaos in others, a gift born out of his own ontological devastation by Othello, I am in some danger of giving us Iago as a negative theologian, perhaps too close to the Miltonic Satan whom he influenced. As I have tried to emphasize, Shakespeare does not write Christian or religious drama; he is not Pedro Calderón de la Barca or (to invoke lesser poet-playwrights) Paul Claudel or T. S. Eliot. Nor is Shakespeare (or Iago) any kind of a heretic; I am baffled when critics argue as to whether Shakespeare was Protestant or Catholic, since the plays are neither. There are gnostic heretical elements in Iago, as there will be in Edmund and in Macbeth, but Shakespeare was not a gnostic, or a hermeticist, or a Neoplatonic occultist. In his extraordinary way, he was the most curious and universal of gleaners, possibly even of esoteric spiritualities, yet here too he was primarily an inventor or discoverer. Othello is a Christian, by conversion; Iago's religion is war, war everywhere—in the streets, in the camp, in his own abyss. Total war is a religion, whose best literary theologian I have cited already, Judge Holden in Cormac McCarthy's frightening *Blood Meridian*. The Judge imitates Iago by expounding a theology of the will, whose ultimate expression is war, against everyone. Iago says that he has never found a man who knew how to love himself, which means that self-love is the exercise of the will in murdering others. That is Iago's self-education in the will, since he does not start out with the clear intention of murder. In the beginning was a sense of having been outraged by a loss of identity, accompanied by the inchoate desire to be revenged upon the god Iago had served.

Shakespeare's finest achievement in *Othello* is Iago's extraordinary mutations, prompted by his acute self-overhearing as he moves through his eight soliloquies, and their supporting asides. From tentative, experimental promptings on to excited discoveries, Iago's course develops into a triumphal march, to be ended only by Emilia's heroic intervention. Much of the theatrical greatness of *Othello* inheres in this triumphalism, in which we unwillingly participate. Properly performed, *Othello* should be a momentary trauma for its audience. *Lear* is equally catastrophic, where Edmund triumphs consistently until the duel with Edgar, but *Lear* is vast, intricate, and varied, and not just in its double plot. In *Othello,* Iago is always at the center of the web, ceaselessly weaving his fiction, and snaring us with dark magic: Only Prospero is comparable, a luminous magus who in part is Shakespeare's answer to Iago.

You can judge Iago to be, in effect, a misreader of Montaigne, as opposed to Hamlet, who makes of Montaigne the mirror of nature. Kenneth Gross shrewdly observes that "Iago is at best a nightmare image of so vigilant and humanizing a pyrrhonism as Montaigne's." Pyrrhonism, or radical skepticism, is transmuted by Hamlet into disinterestedness; Iago turns it into a war against existence, a drive that seeks to argue that there is no reason why anything should be, at all. The exaltation of the will, in Iago, emanates from an ontological lack so great that no human emotion possibly could fill it:

Virtue: A fig! 'Tis in ourselves that we are thus or thus. Our bodies are gardens, to the which our wills are gardeners. So that if we will plant nettles or sow lettuce, set hyssop and weed up thyme, supply it with one gender of herbs or distract it with many, either to have it sterile with idleness or manured with industry, why, the power and corrigible authority of this lies in our wills. If the balance of our lives had not one scale of reason to poise another of sensuality, the blood and baseness of our natures would conduct us to most preposterous conclusions. But we have reason to cool our raging motions, our carnal stings, our unbitted lusts, whereof I take this, that you call love, to be a sect or scion.

[1.3.319–31]

"Virtue" here means something like "manly strength," while by "reason" Iago intends only his own absence of significant emotion. This prose utterance is the poetic center of *Othello,* presaging Iago's conversion of his leader to a reductive and diseased vision of sexuality. We cannot doubt that Othello loves Desdemona; Shakespeare also may suggest that Othello is amazingly reluctant to make love to his wife. As I read the play's text, the marriage is never consummated, despite Desdemona's eager desires. Iago derides Othello's "weak function"; that seems more a hint of Iago's impotence than of Othello's, and yet nothing that the Moorish captain-general says or does reflects an authentic lust for Desdemona. This certainly helps explain his murderous rage, once Iago has roused him to jealousy, and also makes that jealousy more plausible, since Othello literally does not know whether his wife is a virgin, and is afraid to find out, one way or the other. I join here the minority view of Graham Bradshaw, and of only a few others, but this play, of all Shakespeare's, seems to me the most weakly misread, possibly because its villain is the greatest master of misprision in Shakespeare, or in literature. Why did Othello marry anyway, if he does not sexually desire Desdemona? Iago cannot help us here, and Shakespeare allows us to puzzle the matter out for ourselves, without ever giving us sufficient information to settle the question. But Bradshaw is surely right to say that Othello finally testifies Desdemona died a virgin:

> Now. How dost thou look now? O ill-starred wench,
> Pale as thy smock. When we shall meet at compt,
> This look of thine will hurl my soul from heaven,
> And fiends will snatch at it. (*touches her*) Cold, cold, my girl?
> Even like thy chastity.

> [5.2.271–75]

Unless Othello is merely raving, we at least must believe he means what he says: she died not only faithful to him but "cold . . . Even like thy chastity." It is a little difficult to know just what Shakespeare intends Othello to mean, unless his victim had never become his wife, even for the single night when their sexual union was possible. When Othello vows not to "shed her blood," he means only that he will smother her to death, but the frightening irony is there as well: neither he nor Cassio nor anyone else has ever ended her virginity. Bradshaw finds in this a "ghastly tragicomic parody of an erotic death," and that is appropriate for Iago's theatrical achievement.

I want to shift the emphasis from Bradshaw's in order to question a matter upon which Iago had little influence: Why was Othello reluctant, from the start, to consummate the marriage? When, in act 1, scene 3, the Duke of Venice accepts the love match of Othello and Desdemona, and then orders Othello to Cyprus, to lead its defense against an expected Turkish invasion, the Moor asks only that his wife be housed with comfort and dignity during his absence. It is the ardent Desdemona who requests that she accompany her husband:

> So that, dear lords, if I be left behind,
> A moth of peace, and he go to the war,
> The rites for which I love him are bereft me,
> And I a heavy interim shall support
> By his dear absence. Let me go with him.
>
> [1.3.256–60]

Presumably by "rites" Desdemona means consummation, rather than battle, and though Othello seconds her, he rather gratuitously insists that desire for her is not exactly hot in him:

> Let her have your voice.
> Vouch with me, heaven, I therefore beg it not
> To please the palate of my appetite,
> Nor to comply with heat – the young affects
> In me defunct – and proper satisfaction,
> But to be free and bounteous to her mind.
> And heaven defend your good souls, that you think
> I will your serious and great business scant
> For she is with me. No, when light-winged toys
> Of feathered Cupid seel with wanton dullness
> My speculative and officed instruments,

That my disports corrupt and taint my business,
Let housewives make a skillet of my helm
And all indign and base adversities
Make head against my estimation.

[1.3.261–75]

These lines, hardly Othello at his most eloquent, exceed the measure that decorum requires, and do not favor Desdemona. He protests much too much, and hardly betters the case when he urges her off the stage with him:

Come, Desdemona, I have but an hour
Of love, of worldly matter and direction
To spend with thee. We must obey the time.

[1.3.299–301]

If that "hour" is literal, then "love" will be lucky to get twenty minutes of this overbusy general's time. Even with the Turks impending, the state would surely have allowed its chief military officer an extra hour or two for initially embracing his wife. When he arrives on Cyprus, where Desdemona has preceded him, Othello tells us: "Our wars are done, the Turks are drowned." That would seem to provide ample time for the deferred matter of making love to his wife, particularly since public feasting is now decreed. Perhaps it is more proper to wait for evening, and so Othello bids Cassio command the watch, and duly says to Desdemona: "Come, my dear love, / The purchase made, the fruits are to ensue: / That profit's yet to come 'tween me and you," and exits with her. Iago works up a drunken riot, involving Cassio, Roderigo, and Montano, governor of Cyprus, in which Cassio wounds Montano. Othello, aroused by a tolling bell, enters with

Desdemona following soon afterward. We are not told whether there has been time enough for their "rites," but Othello summons her back to bed, while also announcing that he himself will supervise the dressing of Montano's wounds. Which had priority, we do not precisely know, but evidently the general preferred his self-imposed obligation toward the governor to his marital obligation.

Iago's first insinuations of Desdemona's supposed relationship with Cassio would have no effect if Othello knew her to have been a virgin. It is because he does not know that Othello is so vulnerable. "Why did I marry!" he exclaims, and then points to his cuckold's horns when he tells Desdemona: "I have a pain upon my forehead, here," which his poor innocent of a wife attributes to his all-night care of the governor: "Why, that's with watching," and tries to bind it hard with the fatal handkerchief, pushed away by him, and so it falls in Emilia's way. By then, Othello is already Iago's, and is incapable of resolving his doubts through the only sensible course of finally bringing himself to bed Desdemona.

This is a bewildering labyrinth for the audience, and frequently is not overtly addressed by directors of *Othello*, who leave us doubtful of their interpretations, or perhaps they are not even aware of the difficulty that requires interpretation. Shakespeare was capable of carelessness, but not upon so crucial a point, for the entire tragedy turns upon it. Desdemona and Othello, alas, scarcely know each other, and sexually do not know each other at all. Shakespeare's audacious suggestion is that Othello was too frightened or diffident to seize upon the opportunity of the first night in Cyprus, but evaded and delayed the ordeal by devoting himself to the wounded Montano. The further suggestion is that Iago, understanding Othello, fomented the drunken altercation in order to distract his general from consummation, for otherwise Iago's manipulations would have been without consequence. That credits Iago with extraordinary insight into Othello, but no one should be surprised at such an evaluation. We can wonder why Shakespeare did not make all this clearer, except that we need to remember his contemporary audience was far superior to us in comprehending through the ear. They knew how to listen; most of us do not, in our overvisual culture. Shakespeare doubtless would not have agreed with William Blake that what could be made explicit to the idiot was not worth his care, but he had learned from Chaucer, in particular, how to be appropriately sly.

Before turning at last to Iago's triumphalism, I feel obliged to answer my own question: Why did Othello marry when his love for Desdemona was only a secondary response to her primary passion for him? This prelude to tragedy seems plausibly compounded of her ignorance—she is still only a child, rather like Juliet—and his confusion. Othello tells us that he had been nine consecutive months in Venice, away from the battlefield and the camp, and thus he was not himself. Fully engaged in his occupation, he would have been immune to Desdemona's charmed condition and to her generous passion for his living legend. Their shared idealism is also their mutual illusion: the idealism is beautiful, but the illusion would have been dissolved even if Othello had not passed over Iago for promotion and so still had Iago's loving worship, rather than the ancient's vengeful hatred. The fallen Iago will teach Othello that the general's failure to know Desdemona, sexually and otherwise, was because Othello did not want to know. Bradshaw brilliantly observes that Iago's genius "is to persuade others that something they had not thought was something they had not *wanted* to think." Iago, having been thrown into a

comes the Devil-as-matador, and his own best aficionado, since he is nothing if not critical. The only first-rate Iago I have ever seen was Bob Hoskins, who surmounted his director's flaws in Jonathan Miller's BBC television *Othello* of 1981, where Anthony Hopkins as the Moor sank without a trace by being faithful to Miller's Leavisite (or Eliotic) instructions. Hoskins, always best as a gangster, caught many of the accents of Iago's underworld pride in his own preternatural wiliness, and at moments showed what a negative beatification might be, in the pleasure of undoing one's superior at organized violence. Perhaps Hoskins's Iago was a shade more Marlovian than Shakespearean, almost as though Hoskins (or Miller) had *The Jew of Malta* partly in mind, whereas Iago is refined beyond that farcical an intensity.

Triumphalism is Iago's most chilling yet engaging mode; his great soliloquies and asides march to an intellectual music matched in Shakespeare only by aspects of Hamlet, and by a few rare moments when Edmund descends to self-celebration. Iago's inwardness, which sometimes echoes Hamlet's, enhances his repellent fascination for us: how can a sensible emptiness be so labyrinthine? To trace the phases of Iago's entrapment of Othello should answer that question, at least in part. But I pause here to deny that Iago represents something crucial in Othello, an assertion made by many interpreters, the most convincing of whom is Edward Snow. In a reading too reliant upon the Freudian psychic mythology, Snow finds in Iago the overt spirit that is buried in Othello: a universal male horror of female sexuality, and so a hatred of women.

The Age of Freud wanes, and joins itself now, in many, to the Age of Resentment. That all men fear and hate women and sexuality is neither Freudian nor true, though an aversion to otherness is frequent enough, in women as in men. Shakespeare's lovers, men and women alike, are very various; Othello unfortunately is not one of the sanest among them. Stephen Greenblatt suggests that Othello's conversion to Christianity has augmented the Moor's tendency to sexual disgust, a plausible reading of the play's foreground. Iago seems to see this, even as he intuits Othello's reluctance to consummate the marriage, but even that does not mean Iago is an inward component of Othello's psyche, from the start. Nothing can exceed Iago's power of contamination once he truly begins his campaign, and so it is truer to say that Othello comes to represent Iago than to suggest we ought to see Iago as a component of Othello.

Shakespeare's art, as manifested in Iago's ruination of Othello, is in some ways too subtle for criticism to paraphrase. Iago suggests Desdemona's infidelity by at first not suggesting it, hovering near and around it:

Iago   I do beseech you,
   Though I perchance am vicious in my guess –
   As I confess it is my nature's plague
   To spy into abuses, and of my jealousy
   Shape faults that are not – that your wisdom
   From one that so imperfectly conceits
   Would take no notice, nor build yourself a trouble
   Out of his scattering and unsure observance,
   It were not for your quiet nor your good,
   Nor for my manhood, honesty, or wisdom,
   To let you know my thoughts.
Othello   What dost thou mean?
Iago   Good name in man and woman, dear my lord,

Is the immediate jewel of their souls.
Who steals my purse steals trash. 'Tis something, nothing,
'Twas mine, 'tis his, and has been slave to thousands.
But he that filches from me my good name
Robs me of that which not enriches him
And makes me poor indeed.
Othello By heaven, I'll know thy thoughts.
Iago You cannot, if my heart were in your hand;
Nor shall not, whilst 'tis in my custody.
Othello Ha?
Iago O, beware, my lord, of jealousy,
It is the green-eyed monster which doth mock
The meat it feeds on. That cuckold lives in bliss
Who, certain of his fate, loves not his wronger,
But O, what damnèd minutes tells he o'er
Who dotes yet doubts, suspects, yet strongly loves!
Othello O misery!

[3.3.145−72]

This would be outrageous if its interplay between Iago and Othello were not so persuasive. Iago manipulates Othello by exploiting what the Moor shares with the jealous God of the Jews, Christians, and Muslims, a barely repressed vulnerability to betrayal. Yahweh and Othello alike are vulnerable because they have risked extending themselves, Yahweh to the Jews and Othello to Desdemona. Iago, whose motto is "I am not what I am," will triumph by tracking this negativity to Othello, until Othello quite forgets he is a man and becomes jealousy incarnate, a parody of the God of vengeance. We underestimate Iago when we consider him only as a dramatist of the self and a psychologist of genius;

his greatest power is as a negative ontotheologian, a diabolical prophet who has a vocation for destruction. He is not the Christian devil or a parody thereof, but rather a free artist of himself, uniquely equipped, by experience and genius, to entrap spirits greater than his own in a bondage founded upon their inner flaws. In a play that held a genius opposed to his own—a Hamlet or a Falstaff—he would be only a frustrated malcontent. Given a world only of gulls and victims—Othello, Desdemona, Cassio, Roderigo, even Emilia until outrage turns her—Iago scarcely needs to exercise the full range of powers that he keeps discovering. A fire is always raging within him, and the hypocrisy that represses his satirical intensity in his dealings with others evidently costs him considerable suffering.

That must be why he experiences such relief, even ecstasy, in his extraordinary soliloquies and asides, where he applauds his own performance. Though he rhetorically invokes a "divinity of hell," neither he nor we have any reason to believe that any demon is listening to him. Though married, and an esteemed flag officer, with a reputation for "honesty," Iago is as solitary a figure as Edmund, or as Macbeth after Lady Macbeth goes mad. Pleasure, for Iago, is purely sadomasochistic; pleasure, for Othello, consists in the rightful consciousness of command. Othello loves Desdemona, yet primarily as a response to her love for his triumphal consciousness. Passed over, and so nullified, Iago determines to convert his own sadomasochism into a countertriumphalism, one that will commandeer his commander, and then transform the god of his earlier worship into a degradation of godhood. The chaos that Othello rightly feared if he ceased to love Desdemona has been Iago's natural element since Cassio's promotion. From that chaos, Iago rises as a new Demiurge, a master of uncreation.

In proposing an ontotheological Iago, I build upon A. C. Bradley's emphasis on the passed-over ancient's "resentment," and add to Bradley the idea that resentment can become the only mode of freedom for such great negations as Iago's Dostoyevskian disciples, Svidrigailov and Stavrogin. They may seem insane compared with Iago, but they inherited his weird lucidity, and his economics of the will. René Girard, a theoretician of envy and scapegoating, feels compelled to take Iago at his word, and so sees Iago as being sexually jealous of Othello. This is to be yet again entrapped by Iago, and adds an unnecessary irony to Girard's reduction of all Shakespeare to "a theater of envy." Lev Tolstoy, who fiercely resented Shakespeare, complained of Iago, "There are many motives, but they are all vague." To feel betrayed by a god, be he Mars or Yahweh, and to desire restitution for one's wounded self-regard, to me seems the most precise of any villain's motives: return the god to the abyss into which one has been thrown. Tolstoy's odd, rationalist Christianity could not reimagine Iago's negative Christianity.

Iago is one of Shakespeare's most dazzling performers, equal to Edmund and Macbeth and coming only a little short of Rosalind and Cleopatra, Hamlet and Falstaff, superb charismatics. Negative charisma is an odd endowment; Iago represents it uniquely in Shakespeare, and most literary incarnations of it since owe much to Iago. Edmund, in spite of his own nature, has the element of Don Juan in him, the detachment and freedom from hypocrisy that is fatal for those grand hypocrites, Goneril and Regan. Macbeth, whose prophetic imagination has a universal force, excites our sympathies, however bloody his actions. Iago's appeal to us is the power of the negative, which is all of him and only a part of Hamlet. We all have our gods, whom we worship, and by whom we cannot accept rejection. The Sonnets turn upon a painful rejection, of the poet by the young nobleman, a rejection that is more than erotic, and that seems to figure in Falstaff's public disgrace at Hal's coronation. Foregrounding *Othello* requires that we imagine Iago's humiliation at the election of Cassio, so that we hear the full reverberation of

> Though I do hate him as I do hell's pains,
> Yet, for necessity of present life,
> I must show out a flag and sign of love,
> Which is indeed but sign.
>
> [1.1.152–55]

The ensign, or ancient, who would have died faithfully to preserve Othello's colors on the battlefield, expresses his repudiation of his former religion, in lines absolutely central to the play. Love of the war god is now but a sign, even though revenge is as yet more an aspiration than a project. The god of war, grand as Othello may be, is a somewhat less formidable figure than the God of the Jews, Christians, and Muslims, but by a superb ontological instinct, Iago associates the jealousy of one god with that of the other:

> I will in Cassio's lodging lose this napkin,
> And let him find it. Trifles light as air
> Are to the jealous confirmations strong
> As proofs of holy writ. This may do something.
> The Moor already changes with my poison.
> Dangerous conceits are in their natures poisons,
> Which at the first are scarce found to distaste,
> But with a little act upon the blood

Burn like the mines of sulphur. (*seeing Othello approach*) I did
say so.

[3.3.320−29]

The simile works equally well the other way round: proofs of
Holy Writ are, to the jealous God, strong confirmations, but the
airiest trifles can provoke the Yahweh who in Numbers leads the
Israelites through the wilderness. Othello goes mad, and so does
Yahweh in Numbers. Iago's marvelous pride in his "I did say so"
leads on to a critical music new even to Shakespeare, one which
will engender the aestheticism of John Keats and Walter Pater.
The now obsessed Othello stumbles upon the stage, to be greeted
by Iago's most gorgeous outburst of triumphalism:

Look, where he comes. Not poppy, nor mandragora,
Nor all the drowsy syrups of the world,
Shall ever medicine thee to that sweet sleep
Which thou ow'dst yesterday.

[3.3.330−33]

If this were only sadistic exultation, we would not receive so
immortal a wound from it; masochistic nostalgia mingles with the
satisfaction of uncreation, as Iago salutes both his own achievement and the consciousness that Othello never will enjoy again.
Shakespeare's Iago-like subtle art is at its highest, as we come to
understand that Othello *does not know* precisely because he has
not known his wife. Whatever his earlier reluctance to consummate marriage may have been, he now realizes he is incapable of
it, and so cannot attain to the truth about Desdemona and Cassio:

I had been happy if the general camp,
Pioneers and all, had tasted her sweet body,

So I had nothing known. O now, for ever
Farewell the tranquil mind, farewell content,
Farewell the plumèd troops and the big wars,
That makes ambition virtue! O farewell,
Farewell the neighing steed and the shrill trump,
The spirit-stirring drum, th'ear-piercing fife,
The royal banner, and all quality,
Pride, pomp, and circumstance of glorious war!
And O you mortal engines, whose rude throats
The immortal Jove's dread clamours counterfeit,
Farewell. Othello's occupation's gone.

[3.3.345–57]

This Hemingwayesque farewell to the big wars has precisely Ernest Hemingway's blend of masculine posturing and barely concealed fear of impotence. There has been no time since the wedding, whether in Venice or on Cyprus, for Desdemona and Cassio to have made love, but Cassio had been the go-between between Othello and Desdemona in the play's foregrounding. Othello's farewell here essentially is to any possibility of consummation; the lost music of military glory has an undersong in which the martial engines signify more than cannons alone. If Othello's occupation is gone, then so is his manhood, and with it departs also the pride, pomp, and circumstance that compelled Desdemona's passion for him, the "circumstance" being more than pageantry. Chaos comes again, even as Othello's ontological identity vanishes, in Iago's sweetest revenge, marked by the villain's sublime rhetorical question: "Is't possible? my lord?" What follows is the decisive moment of the play, in which Iago realizes, for the first time, that Desdemona must be murdered by Othello:

Othello (*seizing him*) Villain, be sure thou prove my love a whore,
　　Be sure of it. Give me the ocular proof,
　　Or by the worth of mine eternal soul
　　Thou hadst been better have been born a dog
　　Than answer my wakèd wrath!

Iago　　　　　　　　　　　　　Is't come to this?

Othello　Make me to see't, or at the least so prove it
　　That the probation bear no hinge nor loop
　　To hang a doubt on, or woe upon thy life!

Iago　　My noble lord –

Othello　If thou dost slander her, and torture me,
　　Never pray more. Abandon all remorse,
　　On horror's head horrors accumulate,
　　Do deeds to make heaven weep, all earth amazed,
　　For nothing canst thou to damnation add
　　Greater than that.

　　　　　　　　　　　　　[3.3.359–73]

　　Iago's improvisations, until now, had as their purpose the destruction of Othello's identity, fit recompense for Iago's vastation.
Suddenly, Iago confronts a grave threat that is also an opportunity: either he or Desdemona must die, with the consequences of
her death to crown the undoing of Othello. How can Othello's
desire for "the ocular proof" be satisfied?

Iago　　And may. But how? How satisfied, my lord?
　　Would you, the supervisor, grossly gape on?
　　Behold her topped?

Othello　　　　　　　　Death and damnation. O!

Iago　　It were a tedious difficulty, I think,
　　To bring them to that prospect. Damn them then,

If ever mortal eyes do see them bolster
More than their own. What then? How then?
What shall I say? Where's satisfaction?
It is impossible you should see this
Were they as prime as goats, as hot as monkeys,
As salt as wolves in pride, and fools as gross
As ignorance made drunk. But yet, I say,
If imputation and strong circumstances,
Which lead directly to the door of truth,
Will give you satisfaction, you might have't.

[3.3.394–408]

The only ocular proof possible is what Othello will not essay, as Iago well understands, since the Moor will not try his wife's virginity. Shakespeare shows us jealousy in men as centering upon both visual and temporal obsessions, because of the male fear that there will not be enough time and space for him. Iago plays powerfully upon Othello's now monumental aversion from the only door of truth that could give satisfaction, the entrance into Desdemona. Psychological mastery cannot surpass Iago's control of Othello, when the ensign chooses precisely this moment to introduce "a handkerchief, / I am sure it was your wife's, did I today / See Cassio wipe his beard with." Dramatic mastery cannot exceed Iago's exploitation of Othello's stage gesture of kneeling to swear revenge:

Othello Even so my bloody thoughts with violent pace,
    Shall ne'er look back, ne'er ebb to humble love,
    Till that a capable and wide revenge
    Swallow them up. Now, by yond marble heaven,
    In the due reverence of a sacred vow

Othello kneels

I here engage my words.

Iago   Do not rise yet.

Iago kneels

Witness, you ever-burning lights above,
You elements that clip us round about,
Witness that here Iago doth give up
The execution of his wit, hands, heart,
To wronged Othello's service. Let him command,
And to obey shall be in me remorse,
What bloody business ever.

Othello   I greet thy love
Not with vain thanks, but with acceptance bounteous,
And will upon the instant put thee to't.
Within these three days let me hear thee say
That Cassio's not alive.

Iago   My friend is dead.
'Tis done at your request. But let her live.

Othello   Damn her, lewd minx! O damn her! damn her!
Come, go with me apart, I will withdraw
To furnish me with some swift means of death
For the fair devil. Now art thou my lieutenant.

Iago   I am your own for ever.

[3.3.457–79]

It is spectacular theater, with Iago as director: "Do not rise yet."
And it is also a countertheology, transcending any Faustian bargain with the Devil, since the stars and the elements serve as wit-
nesses to a murderous pact, which culminates in the reversal of

the passing over of Iago in the play's foreground. "Now art thou my lieutenant" means something very different from what Othello can understand, while "I am your own for ever" seals Othello's starry and elemental fate. What remains is only the way down and out, for everyone involved.

Shakespeare creates a terrible pathos for us by not showing Desdemona in her full nature and splendor until we know that she is doomed. Dr. Johnson found the death of Cordelia intolerable; the death of Desdemona, in my experience as a reader and theatergoer, is even more unendurable. Shakespeare stages the scene as a sacrifice, as grimly countertheological as are Iago's passed-over nihilism and Othello's "godlike" jealousy. Though Desdemona in her anguish declares she is a Christian, she does not die a martyr to that faith but becomes only another victim of what could be called the religion of Moloch, since she is a sacrifice to the war god whom Iago once worshiped, the Othello he has reduced to incoherence. "Othello's occupation's gone"; the shattered relic of Othello murders in the name of that occupation, for he knows no other, and is the walking ghost of what he was.

Millicent Bell has argued that Othello's is an epistemological tragedy, but only Iago has intellect enough to sustain such a notion, and Iago is not much interested in how he knows what he thinks he knows. *Othello,* as much as *King Lear* and *Macbeth,* is a vision of radical evil; *Hamlet* is Shakespeare's tragedy of an intellectual. Though Shakespeare never would commit himself to specifically Christian terms, he approached a kind of gnostic or heretic tragedy in *Macbeth,* as I will attempt to show. Othello has no transcendental aspect, perhaps because the religion of war does not allow for any. Iago, who makes a new covenant with Othello when they kneel together, had lived and fought in what he took to be an old covenant with his general, until Cassio was preferred to him. A devout adherent to the fire of battle, his sense of merit injured by his god, has degraded that god into "an honorable murderer," Othello's oxymoronic, final vision of his role. Can such degradation allow the dignity required for a tragic protagonist?

A. C. Bradley rated *Othello* below *Hamlet, Lear,* and *Macbeth* primarily because it gives us no sense of universal powers impinging upon the limits of the human. I think those powers hover in *Othello,* but they manifest themselves only in the gap that divides the earlier, foregrounded relationship between Iago and Othello from the process of ruination that we observe between them. Iago is so formidable a figure because he has uncanny abilities, endowments only available to a true believer whose trust has transmuted into nihilism. Cain, rejected by Yahweh in favor of Abel, is as much the father of Iago as Iago is the precursor of Milton's Satan. Iago murders Roderigo and maims Cassio; it is as inconceivable to Iago as to us that Iago seeks to knife Othello. If you have been rejected by your god, then you attack him spiritually or metaphysically, not merely physically. Iago's greatest triumph is that the lapsed Othello sacrifices Desdemona in the name of the war god Othello, the solitary warrior with whom unwisely she has fallen in love. That may be why Desdemona offers no resistance, and makes so relatively unspirited a defense, first of her virtue and then of her life. Her victimization is all the more complete, and our own horror at it thereby is augmented.

Though criticism frequently has blinded itself to this, Shakespeare had no affection for war, or for violence organized or unorganized. His great killing machines come to sorrowful ends: Othello, Macbeth, Antony, Coriolanus. His favorite warrior is Sir John Falstaff, whose motto is: "Give me life!" Othello's motto could be "Give me honor," which sanctions slaughtering a wife he hasn't known, supposedly not "in hate, but all in honour." Dreadfully flawed, even vacuous at the center as Othello is, he still is meant to be the best instance available of a professional mercenary. What Iago once worshiped was real enough, but more vulnerable even than Iago suspected. Shakespeare subtly intimates that Othello's prior nobility and his later incoherent brutality are two faces of the war god, but it remains the same god. Othello's occupation's gone partly because he married at all. Pent-up resentment, and not repressed lust, animates Othello as he avenges his lost autonomy in the name of his honor. Iago's truest triumph comes when Othello loses his sense of war's limits, and joins Iago's incessant campaign against *being*. "I am not what I am," Iago's credo, becomes Othello's implicit cry. The rapidity and totality of Othello's descent seems at once the play's one weakness and its most persuasive strength, as persuasive as Iago.

Desdemona dies so piteously that Shakespeare risks alienating us forever from Othello:

Desdemona (*trying to rise*) O, banish me, my lord, but kill me not!

Othello   Down, strumpet!

Desdemona Kill me tomorrow, let me live tonight!

Othello   Nay, if you strive –

Desdemona But half an hour!

Othello   Being done, there is no pause.

Desdemona But while I say one prayer!

Othello   It is too late.

[5.2.78–83]

Rather operatically, Shakespeare gives Desdemona a dying breath that attempts to exonerate Othello, which would indeed strain credulity if she were not, as Alvin Kernan wonderfully put it, "Shakespeare's word for love." We are made to believe that this was at once the most natural of young women, and also so loyal to her murderer that her exemplary last words sound almost ironic, given Othello's degradation: "Commend me to my kind lord— O, farewell!" It seems too much more for us to bear that Othello should refuse her final act of love: "She's like a liar gone to burning hell: / 'Twas I that killed her." The influential modern assaults upon Othello by T. S. Eliot and F. R. Leavis take their plausibility (such as it is) from Shakespeare's heaping up of Othello's brutality, stupidity, and unmitigated guilt. But Shakespeare allows Othello a great if partial recovery, in an astonishing final speech:

> Soft you, a word or two before you go.
> I have done the state some service, and they know't.
> No more of that. I pray you, in your letters,
> When you shall these unlucky deeds relate,
> Speak of me as I am. Nothing extenuate,
> Nor set down aught in malice. Then must you speak
> Of one that loved not wisely, but too well;
> Of one not easily jealous but, being wrought,
> Perplexed in the extreme. Of one whose hand,
> Like the base Judean, threw a pearl away
> Richer than all his tribe. Of one whose subdued eyes,
> Albeit unusèd to the melting mood,
> Drops tears as fast as the Arabian trees
> Their medicinable gum. Set you down this.
> And say besides, that in Aleppo once,
> Where a malignant and turbaned Turk
> Beat a Venetian and traduced the state,

I took by th' throat the circumcisèd dog
And smote him (*pulls out hidden dagger*) thus.

[5.2.337–55]

This famous and problematic outburst rarely provokes any critic to agree with any other, yet the Eliot–Leavis interpretation, which holds that Othello essentially is "cheering himself up," cannot be right. The Moor remains as divided a character as Shakespeare ever created; we need give no credence to the absurd blindness of "loved not wisely, but too well," or the outrageous self-deception of "one not easily jealous." Yet we are moved by the truth of "perplexed in the extreme," and by the invocation of Herod, "the base Judean" who murdered his Maccabean wife, Mariamme, whom he loved. The association of Othello with Herod the Great is the more shocking for being Othello's own judgment upon himself, and is followed by the Moor's tears, and by his fine image of weeping trees. Nor should a fair critic fail to be impressed by Othello's verdict upon himself: that he has become an enemy of Venice, and as such must be slain. His suicide has nothing Roman in it: Othello passes sentence upon himself, and performs the execution. We need to ask what Venice would have done with Othello, had he allowed himself to survive. I venture that he seeks to forestall what might have been their politic decision: to preserve him until he might be of high use again. Cassio is no Othello; the state has no replacement for the Moor, and might well have used him again, doubtless under some control. All of the rifts in Othello that Iago sensed and exploited are present in this final speech, but so is a final vision of judgment, one in which Othello abandons his nostalgias for glorious war, and pitifully seeks to expiate what cannot be expiated—not, at least, by a farewell to arms.

FURTHER READING

This is not a bibliography but a selective set of starting places.

Texts

McMillin, Scott, ed. *The First Quarto of Othello.* The New Cambridge Shakespeare. Cambridge: Cambridge University Press, 2001.

Shakespeare. *The First Folio of Shakespeare.* 2d ed. Prepared by Charlton Hinman, with a new Introduction by Peter W. M. Blayney. New York: Norton, 1996.

———. *The Complete Works.* Edited by Stanley Wells and Gary Taylor, with Introductions by Stanley Wells. Oxford: Clarendon Press, 1986.

———. *Othello: A New Variorum Edition.* Edited by Horace Howard Furness. New York: Lippincott, 1886. Reprint, New York: Dover Books, 2000.

Language

Houston, John Porter. *The Rhetoric of Poetry in the Renaissance and Seventeenth Century.* Baton Rouge: Louisiana State University Press, 1983.

———. *Shakespearean Sentences: A Study in Style and Syntax.* Baton Rouge: Louisiana State University Press, 1988.

Kermode, Frank. *Shakespeare's Language.* New York: Farrar, Straus and Giroux, 2000.

Kökeritz, Helge. *Shakespeare's Pronunciation.* New Haven: Yale University Press, 1953.

Lanham, Richard A. *The Motives of Eloquence: Literary Rhetoric in the Renaissance.* New Haven and London: Yale University Press, 1976.

Marcus, Leah S. *Unediting the Renaissance: Shakespeare, Marlowe, Milton.* London: Routledge, 1996.

The Oxford English Dictionary: Second Edition on CD-ROM, version 3.0. New York: Oxford University Press, 2002.

Raffel, Burton. *From Stress to Stress: An Autobiography of English Prosody.* Hamden, Conn.: Archon, 1992.

Ronberg, Gert. *A Way with Words: The Language of English Renaissance Literature.* London: Arnold, 1992.

Trousdale, Marion. *Shakespeare and the Rhetoricians.* Chapel Hill: University of North Carolina Press, 1982.

Culture

Anderson, Bonnie S., and Judith P. Zinsser. *A History of Their Own: Women in Europe from Prehistory to the Present.* 2 vols. New York: Harper, 1988.

Barroll, Leeds. *Politics, Plague, and Shakespeare's Theater: The Stuart Years.* Ithaca, N.Y.: Cornell University Press, 1991.

Bascom, William R., and Melville J. Herskovits, eds. *Continuity and Change in African Cultures.* Chicago: University of Chicago Press, 1959.

Bindoff, S.T. *Tudor England.* Baltimore: Penguin, 1950.

Bradbrook, M. C. *Shakespeare: The Poet in His World.* New York: Columbia University Press, 1978.

Brown, Cedric C., ed. *Patronage, Politics, and Literary Tradition in England, 1558–1658.* Detroit, Mich.: Wayne State University Press, 1993.

Buxton, John. *Elizabethan Taste.* London: Harvester, 1963.

Cowan, Alexander. *Urban Europe, 1500–1700.* New York: Oxford University Press, 1998.

Cressy, David. *Birth, Marriage, and Death: Ritual, Religion, and the Life-Cycle in Tudor and Stuart England.* New York: Oxford University Press, 1997.

Englander, David, et al., eds. *Culture and Belief in Europe, 1459–1600: An Anthology of Sources.* Oxford: Blackwell, 1990.

Finucci, Valeria, and Regina Schwartz, eds. *Desire in the Renaissance: Psychoanalysis and Literature.* Princeton, N.J.: Princeton University Press, 1994.

Fumerton, Patricia, and Simon Hunt, eds. *Renaissance Culture and the Everyday.* Philadelphia: University of Pennsylvania Press, 1999.

Halliday, F. E. *Shakespeare in His Age.* South Brunswick, N.J.: Yoseloff, 1965.

Harrison, G. B., ed. *The Elizabethan Journals: Being a Record of Those Things Most Talked of During the Years 1591–1597.* Abridged ed. 2 vols. New York: Doubleday Anchor, 1965.

Harrison, William. *The Description of England: The Classic Contemporary [1577] Account of Tudor Social Life.* Edited by Georges Edelen. Ithaca, N.Y.: Cornell University Press for the Folger Shakespeare Library, 1968. 2d ed., New York: Dover, 1994.

Hufton, Olwen. *The Prospect Before Her: A History of Women in Western Europe, 1500–1800.* New York: Knopf, 1996.

Jardine, Lisa. *Reading Shakespeare Historically.* London: Routledge, 1996.

———. *Worldly Goods: A New History of the Renaissance.* London: Macmillan, 1996.

Jeanneret, Michel. *A Feast of Words: Banquets and Table Talk in the Renaissance.* Translated by Jeremy Whiteley and Emma Hughes. Chicago: University of Chicago Press, 1991.

Lockyer, Roger. *Tudor and Stuart Britain.* London: Longmans, 1964.

Malinowski, Bronislaw. *Magic, Science and Religion, and Other Essays.* Selected and with an Introduction by Robert Redfield. Boston: Beacon Press, 1948.

Rose, Mary Beth, ed. *Renaissance Drama as Cultural History: Essays from Renaissance Drama, 1977–1987.* Evanston, Ill.: Northwestern University Press, 1990.

Sagan, Eli. *At the Dawn of Tyranny: The Origins of Individualism, Political Oppression, and the State.* New York: Knopf, 1985.

Stone, Lawrence. *The Family, Sex and Marriage in England, 1500–1800.* New York: Harper, 1977.

Tillyard, E. M. W. *The Elizabethan World Picture*. London: Chatto and
 Windus, 1943. Reprint, Harmondsworth: Penguin, 1963.

Willey, Basil. *The Seventeenth-Century Background: Studies in the Thought
 of the Age in Relation to Poetry and Religion*. New York: Columbia
 University Press, 1933. Reprint, New York: Doubleday, 1955.

Wilson, F. P. *The Plague in Shakespeare's London*. 2d ed. Oxford: Oxford
 University Press, 1963.

Wilson, John Dover. *Life in Shakespeare's England: A Book of Elizabethan
 Prose*. 2d ed. Cambridge: Cambridge University Press, 1913. Reprint,
 Harmondsworth: Penguin, 1944.

Zimmerman, Susan, and Ronald F. E. Weissman, eds. *Urban Life in the
 Renaissance*. Newark: University of Delaware Press, 1989.

Dramatic Development

Aristotle. *Poetics*. Everyman Library. New York: Dutton, 1934.

Cohen, Walter. *Drama of a Nation: Public Theater in Renaissance England
 and Spain*. Ithaca, N.Y.: Cornell University Press, 1985.

Dessen, Alan C. *Shakespeare and the Late Moral Plays*. Lincoln: University
 of Nebraska Press, 1986.

Fraser, Russell A., and Norman Rabkin, eds. *Drama of the English
 Renaissance*. 2 vols. Upper Saddle River, N.J.: Prentice Hall, 1976.

Happé, Peter, ed. *Tudor Interludes*. Harmondsworth: Penguin, 1972.

Laroque, François. *Shakespeare's Festive World: Elizabethan Seasonal
 Entertainment and the Professional Stage*. Translated by Janet Lloyd.
 Cambridge: Cambridge University Press, 1991.

Norland, Howard B. *Drama in Early Tudor Britain, 1485–1558*. Lincoln:
 University of Nebraska Press, 1995.

Theater and Stage

Doran, Madeleine. *Endeavors of Art: A Study of Form in Elizabethan
 Drama*. Milwaukee: University of Wisconsin Press, 1954.

Gurr, Andrew. *Playgoing in Shakespeare's London*. Cambridge:
 Cambridge University Press, 1987.

———. *The Shakespearian Stage, 1574–1642*. 3d ed. Cambridge:
 Cambridge University Press, 1992.

Harrison, G. B. *Elizabethan Plays and Players*. Ann Arbor: University of Michigan Press, 1956.

Holmes, Martin. *Shakespeare and His Players*. New York: Scribner, 1972.

Ingram, William. *The Business of Playing: The Beginnings of the Adult Professional Theater in Elizabethan London*. Ithaca, N.Y.: Cornell University Press, 1992.

Salgado, Gamini. *Eyewitnesses of Shakespeare: First Hand Accounts of Performances, 1590–1890*. New York: Barnes and Noble, 1975.

Thomson, Peter. *Shakespeare's Professional Career*. Cambridge: Cambridge University Press, 1992.

Weimann, Robert. *Shakespeare and the Popular Tradition in the Theater: Studies in the Social Dimension of the Dramatic Form and Function*. Edited by Robert Schwartz. Baltimore: Johns Hopkins University Press, 1978.

Yachnin, Paul. *Stage-Wrights: Shakespeare, Jonson, Middleton, and the Making of Theatrical Value*. Philadelphia: University of Pennsylvania Press, 1997.

Biography

Halliday, F. E. *The Life of Shakespeare*. Rev. ed. London: Duckworth, 1964.

Honigmann, F. A. J. *Shakespeare: The "Lost Years."* 2d ed. Manchester: Manchester University Press, 1998.

Schoenbaum, Samuel. *Shakespeare's Lives*. New ed. Oxford: Clarendon Press, 1991.

———. *William Shakespeare: A Compact Documentary Life*. Oxford: Oxford University Press, 1977.

General

Bergeron, David M., and Geraldo U. de Sousa. *Shakespeare: A Study and Research Guide*. 3d ed. Lawrence: University of Kansas Press, 1995.

Bradbey, Anne, ed. *Shakespearian Criticism, 1919–35*. London: Oxford University Press, 1936.

Colie, Rosalie L. *Shakespeare's Living Art*. Princeton, N.J.: Princeton University Press, 1974.

Grene, David. *The Actor in History: Studies in Shakespearean Stage Poetry.* University Park: Pennsylvania State University Press, 1988.

Goddard, Harold C. *The Meaning of Shakespeare.* 2 vols. Chicago: University of Chicago Press, 1951.

Kaufmann, Ralph J. *Elizabethan Drama: Modern Essays in Criticism.* New York: Oxford University Press, 1961.

McDonald, Russ. *The Bedford Companion to Shakespeare: An Introduction with Documents.* Boston: Bedford, 1996.

Raffel, Burton. *How to Read a Poem.* New York: Meridian, 1984.

Ricks, Christopher, ed. *English Drama to 1710.* Rev. ed. Harmondsworth: Sphere, 1987.

Siegel, Paul N., ed. *His Infinite Variety: Major Shakespearean Criticism since Johnson.* Philadelphia: Lippincott, 1964.

Sweeting, Elizabeth J. *Early Tudor Criticism: Linguistic and Literary.* Oxford: Blackwell, 1940.

Van Doren, Mark. *Shakespeare.* New York: Holt, 1939.

Weiss, Theodore. *The Breath of Clowns and Kings: Shakespeare's Early Comedies and Histories.* New York: Atheneum, 1971.

Wells, Stanley, ed. *The Cambridge Companion to Shakespeare Studies.* Cambridge: Cambridge University Press, 1986.

FINDING LIST

Repeated unfamiliar words and meanings, alphabetically arranged, with act, scene, and footnote number of first occurrence, in the spelling (form) of that first occurrence

absolute	2.1.195	*brave*	1.3.277
abused	1.1.194	*bring*	1.2.113
accident	1.1.167	*but*	1.1.79
advantage	1.3.282	*by and by*	2.1.282
ancient	Dram. Pers. 3	*camp*	3.3.193
answer	1.1.139	*cast*	2.3.197
apart	2.3.271	*cause*	3.3.2
approve	1.3.13	*certes*	1.1.24
apt	2.1.181	*challenge*	1.3.173
assay	1.3.20	*chances*	1.3.131
beguile	1.3.64	*check*	1.1.174
beseech	1.1.140	*citadel*	2.1.107
bestows	2.1.117	*comfort*	1.3.191
blood	1.1.189	*common*	1.1.147
bold	1.1.150	*complexion*	3.3.123
bosom	1.2.92	*condition*	1.2.37